THE GOATFELL MURDER

FOR DONALD

THE
GOATFELL
MURDER

A Victorian murder mystery

from the Isle of Arran

Calum Smith

First published 2020
by Rymour Books with
Hog's Back Press
45 Needless Road,
PERTH
PH20LE

© Calum Smith 2020

ISBN 978-0-9540704-8-9

Cover design by Ian Spring
Typeset in Garamond
Printed and bound by
Imprint Digital
Seychelles Farm
Upton Pyne
Exeter

The paper used in this book is approved
by the Forest Stewardship Council

CONTENTS

ACKNOWLEDGEMENTS

During my research, the staff of the following organisations were especially helpful: the National Records of Scotland; the Mitchell Library, Glasgow; University of Glasgow Library and Special Collections; University of Strathclyde Library and Special Collections; National Library of Scotland, Glasgow Police Museum, Airdrie Local Studies, Rothesay Museum Archive, the Isle of Arran Heritage Museum (especially Stuart Gough), Brodick Library, Peterhead Prison Museum, North Lanarkshire Archive.

I would especially like to thank Ian Spring for his enthusiasm, as well as his editing, typesetting and design skills, which were all vital to the project. My brother, Donald, also gave welcome support and the book is dedicated to him.

Chapter One

A Very Spruce and Smart Young Man

The Lanarkshire village of Ferniegair was the first station out of Hamilton on the Coalburn branch of the Caledonian Railway. On Tuesday 3 September 1889 a local policeman, James Gordon, based at the nearby village of Rosebank, was waiting for the train home. He was approached by the station-master who told him a man was acting suspiciously and had left the station on seeing a police uniform. He added that he thought he knew who it was. The policeman climbed up the footbridge over the tracks where he could see the individual scurrying off up the Carlisle Road. Constable Gordon began to pursue him at a brisk pace. Noticing he was being followed the man threw away his coat and bolted through a field, then across the railway line to the Lanark road. In hot pursuit the policeman blew his whistle and shouted for assistance as he passed near the Bog Colliery on the outskirts of Larkhall. Several miners at the pit-head joined the chase. By this time the wanted man had disappeared into a small plantation near Merryton farm on the banks of the River Clyde. As Constable Gordon instructed the colliers to surround the wood, a small boy, David Paton, who was employed at the mine and had gone to the wood to fetch water, approached to say that someone was hiding in nearby bushes. When Gordon and one of the miners investigated, they found their quarry with an open razor in his hand after attempting to cut his throat. Young David Paton recalled how the man's collar and tie were covered in blood. When the cornered man was confronted he said: 'I robbed the man but I did not murder him.'

One of the biggest man-hunts in Scottish criminal history was over. The fugitive was John Watson Laurie, wanted for the murder of an English tourist, Edwin Rose, on the mountainside of Goatfell in Arran six weeks earlier. Laurie was arrested and taken to Hamilton police-station. In the following weeks the wood where Laurie was captured would be visited by inquisitive crowds. Constable Gordon was later promoted to Sergeant for his part in Laurie's capture and for the rest of his days would be introduced as 'the man who caught the Goatfell murderer'.

At Hamilton a doctor was called as the two cuts on Laurie's throat required several stitches. The prisoner was described as composed, almost cheerful. He appeared glad of company mentioning that he had not talked to many people in the last few days. He wore dark tweed trousers, a blue serge jacket and waistcoat, and a small grey skullcap. His appearance was pale, emaciated and dirty with two or three days' growth. There was grass in his pockets and it appeared as though he had been sleeping rough. Laurie said he had run out of money two days earlier, and blamed his dirty boots and dishevelled appearance for his arrest. Happy to continue talking, he related how he had wandered around Scotland, even the north of Ireland and had recently been to Aberdeen.

News of Laurie's arrest spread like wildfire and there was soon a large crowd outside the police-station. The evening papers immediately sold out. There was a throng of folk in the streets of his hometown, Coatbridge, where there was great sympathy for his father, a well-respected local figure.

The next morning Laurie was taken to Glasgow where he boarded the steamer *Adela* bound for Rothesay, the county town of Buteshire (Bute, Arran and Cumbraes) in whose jurisdiction the crime occurred, to be formally charged. After being sought throughout Britain for five weeks, Laurie was now a major celebrity. At Rothesay pier there was an enormous crowd waiting for his arrival on the island. The accused, however, was put ashore in a small boat at Craigmore pier a mile to the east. When this diversionary tactic was noticed by the waiting crowd there was a stampede to the courthouse where they all jostled to catch, 'a fleeting glimpse of a bowed figure, clad in a brown suit, being hustled in by the big front door'.

In court, his jacket buttoned at the neck to hide his bandage, Laurie said little. After acknowledging his identity he made the following statement: 'I was last employed as a pattern-maker and my last place of residence was with Mrs King number, I think, 26 North Frederick Street, Glasgow [it was actually 106, but 26 was used throughout his trial]. I am not married. I have nothing to say to the charge in the meantime.' Laurie left Rothesay on the 1.35pm steamer bound for Greenock Prison.

John Watson Laurie was born on 15 March 1861 in Castlecary, near Cumbernauld, where his father James worked as an engineer. John Laurie often gave his birth year as 1864 and his birthplace as Kirkintilloch. He was brought up in a respectable, well-connected family in Coatbridge, about ten miles east of Glasgow, where his father had now set up business as a grain dealer in Academy Street. James Laurie was well known locally, a member of the Old Monkland School Board, a lay preacher who was heavily involved with the United Presbyterian Church in Coatbridge. John Laurie had three brothers: Gavin, James, Matthew, and a sister, Agnes, with whom he was particularly close. Gavin started out as a clerk but went on become a director of the Airdrie Coal Company. After working in the family grain store James emigrated to America. Matthew was a colliery clerk whose whereabouts would later be listed as 'not known'.

Coatbridge, with its abundant coal and ironstone, and cheap immigrant labour from Ireland and the Highlands, was near to the epicentre of Scotland's industrial revolution, an area of Lanarkshire often referred to as the 'Iron Burgh'. The Bairds of Gartsherrie were local ironmasters who would go on to play leading roles in civic matters. Originally tenant farmers, they made a fortune from coal pits on their land and invested this money in ironworks. By 1843 they had 16 furnaces and were the largest single pig-iron producing unit in the world. By Laurie's day their Gartsherrie ironworks employed well over 3,000 workers.

The Bairds developed the town's Dunbeth Hill, laying out Academy Street, Church Street and Baird Street. They feued the land which was then developed with up-market housing, in contrast to the overcrowded and insanitary rows of the miners' and ironworkers' dwellings below. The new housing was described as 'well-mannered bijou stone cottages and villas for the petit bourgeoisie'. The Laurie family home was at 11 Church Street, named after Gartsherrie Church, known locally as Mount Zion and largely built at the Bairds' expense, as was the neighbouring Gartsherrie Academy where John Laurie had his schooling.

At the foot of Church Street was Coatbridge's bustling Main Street which soon brought you to the hub of the town, the complex intersection of Coatbridge Cross with its landmark fountain: 'The cross at Coatbridge ranks among the most unique as one may pass through it by any form of locomotion. One can not only walk, ride or drive past it, but may train over it or sail under it by means of the canal.' The Monkland Canal linked Coatbridge with Glasgow and since the 1770s had carried barges laden with coal for the city. The canal now supplied the furnaces with raw materials and carried away pig iron.

In the space of a few decades Coatbridge had swollen from a village to take in other communities like Langloan, Dundyvan, Gartsherrie and Whifflet and become Scotland's eighth largest town. At this time there were eighty blast furnaces in Scotland; sixty of these congregated in and around Coatbridge. Blast furnaces were simply giant tubes lined with firebricks, into the top of which was loaded coal, ironstone and limestone. The resultant heat removed impurities from the ironstone which became iron in molten form. The slag (a mixture of impurities and coal ash) was separated out and dumped in the bings that became a familiar feature of the Lanarkshire landscape, as one contemporary commentator noted: 'It is a desolate, black district – of smoke, coal and ashes – treeless, sunless, the verdure of Nature's surface scarified and loaded with rubbish heaps'. Murray's Handbook (1894)

Coatbridge's high quality pig iron was processed to produce malleable iron which, with its greater flexibility compared to cast iron, created a host of new possibilities for engineers. It was soon in demand throughout the world in the manufacture and construction of steam locomotives, boilers, bridges, railways and shipping. John Laurie, and many of his contemporaries, would gain employment within this heavy engineering sector.

Late nineteenth century Coatbridge was a grim place. Many descriptions around this time invariably made allusions to hell due to the all-pervasive black smoke, thundering steam hammers, and the demonic roar of the blast furnaces. The town had some of the worst air pollution in the country, perhaps the world, as chimneys spewed out soot, carbon dioxide and sulphur dioxide. It was claimed to be impossible to walk down a Coatbridge street without your shirt changing colour. People covered their mouths with scarves, providing the local joke that everyone looked as though they were going to the dentist. However at night the likes of the Gartsherrie ironworks became 'one of the sights of a lifetime'. One contemporary account said this about the town:

> Though Coatbridge is a most interesting seat of industry, it is anything but beautiful. Dense clouds of smoke roll over it incessantly and impart to the buildings a peculiarly dingy aspect. A coat of black dust overlies everything, and in a few hours the visitor finds his complexion considerably deteriorated by the soot which fills the air, and settles on the face. To appreciate Coatbridge it must be visited at night, when it presents a most extraordinary, and when seen for the first time, startling spectacle... From the steeple of the parish church, which stands on a considerable eminence, the flames of no fewer than fifty blast furnaces can be seen. In the daytime these flames are pale and unimpressive but when night comes on, they appear to burn more frequently, and gradually there is developed in the sky a lurid glow similar to that which hangs over a city when a great conflagration is in progress.

Due to its extensive coal reserves Lanarkshire was one of the first areas of Scotland to have a railway network, with Coatbridge dubbed 'the Crewe of the North' as at one time it had eight railway stations. By 1871 the town was on the North British Glasgow-Edinburgh route. The good communications and prospect of jobs attracted many people from Ireland, especially Donegal. Weekend recreation often took the form of drunken brawls and sectarian clashes between local Orangemen and Irish immigrants. The trains also enabled John Laurie to regularly visit friends and relatives in the area. While on the run from the law he used the network to keep on the move and one ahead of his pursuers.

From his earliest years Laurie is said to have been trouble for his parents. There was a rumour that he had run away as a teenager and was eventually found on one of the Atlantic liners. It was said there was insanity in his family and that he himself had 'shown from infancy decided symptoms of mental aberration'. However some of these traits may well have been exaggerated to provide mitigating circumstances when he is accused of killing Edwin Rose. One of the journalists who reported on Laurie's trial attended school with him and reflected that he was 'the most unlikely boy in the world to be suspected of committing a murder'. Another school friend gave this description of him when he was a pupil at Gartsherrie Academy:

He was steady and regular with his studies, and usually occupied a good position in his classes. Amongst his school fellows he was fairly popular; in disposition he was quiet and sedate, but by no means sullen or morose. While he engaged in most of the boyish pastimes of the playground he did not seem particularly fond of the most athletic sports. Fisticuffs were not amongst his accomplishments and the triumphs of a boyish encounter apparently possessed no charms to his mind. Even in these days his preference for female society was decidedly marked. Not one of his associates at that period could detect the slightest leaning in his temperament or habits towards deeds of violence or acts of larceny, and had they been called upon to express their opinion, it would have been decidedly against his inclination or capability to commit any serious violation of the moral law. Neither was he given to quarrelling nor the use of vile or reprehensible language, and as companions he had the best in the school... He seems to have sustained the esteem in which he was held in those days till very recent times, and usually was placed in positions of prominence and trust in whatever organisations he took part. He was for some time a teacher in the Sabbath School. He led the singing both in the junior and in the senior Bible Classes, and was a prominent member of the Church Choir. During the first few years of the Coatbridge and Airdrie Parliamentary Association he sat on the Conservative benches, and was for some time treasurer to the Coatbridge Junior Conservative Association. In all these positions he seems to have won the good opinions of his associates, and now, strong as the chain of circumstantial evidence is against him, and despite the various divergences from the paths of rectitude that to all appearance have taken place in recent times, nearly all who have been at all intimate or friendly with him find it hard to credit the terrible charge that is now brought against him.

The fact Laurie was treasurer of the Coatbridge Junior Conservative Association (his father was chairman of the local Conservatives) was an obvious embarrassment to the party. In the press this was reported as the more impartial, 'member of a political association'. The reference to being a treasurer was introduced at his trial for the purpose of identifying his handwriting, but in transcripts of the proceedings, for example William Roughead's *Trial of John Watson Laurie*, it was changed to 'member, and treasurer, of an athletic association'.

Laurie was brought up in a deeply religious household which had strong connections with two local churches: Gartsherrie Parish Church at the top of their street and Dunbeth United Presbyterian Church further along the brow of the hill. Laurie himself was heavily involved in church activities: the choir, Sunday school, the Young Mens' Christian Association, the Church Literary Society. When he moved to Glasgow he joined other United Presbyterian congregations, first in Anderston, then Woodlands Road. A fortnight after he is said to have crushed the skull of Edwin Rose with a rock, he was singing hymns at a prayer meeting in Glasgow's West End. A friend who attended the YMCA with him provided this insightful picture of John Watson Laurie:

John was always a very spruce and smart young man; in fact he was a bit of a fop and rather vain of his looks, but a capital fellow for all that, and one who made a large number of friends though he did not always manage to keep them very long. His vanity took a very strange turn sometimes and that led him to try to get introduced to those far above him in situation. When he got a rebuff for this he was not well pleased. He was a young fellow who read a great deal of love stories and got into that state of imagining himself a hero in the eyes of ladies. John was, however, rather fickle in his attachments and it was distinctly with him a case of 'off with the old and on with the new.' There was, however, nothing mean in his nature.

Laurie's obsessive nature emerged in his flirtatious behaviour with women; he had a strong attraction towards the opposite sex. Many people, however, were oblivious to any darker side. One friend of Laurie was astonished when he was linked to the crime, describing him as, 'good-natured, agreeable, sober and well-conducted, a man who was not likely to quarrel with anyone'. People who had known Laurie all of his life were amazed that he could be capable of such a thing. Jeanie Park, a friend from Glasgow, said, 'He was of a quiet disposition, and of pleasant temper.' Her sister Minnie agreed: 'I thought Laurie was an honest truthful lad. He was very quiet in manner and had not much to say.'

We know a lot about Laurie's physical appearance because, as a wanted man, there were regular descriptions, photographs and sketches of him issued through the newspapers. Many notice boards displayed wanted bills of him; there was even one in the signal-box at Ferniegair Station. John Laurie was 5ft 6in, short by today's standards but about average height for late nineteenth-century Scotland. His hair was sometimes described as fair, sometimes brown; similarly his eyes were on occasion recorded as blue, at other times grey. This confusion over his physical characteristics in all probability helped prolong his time on the run. He also had a fresh complexion with a slight moustache and sideburns.

Laurie was memorably pictured in *The Scotsman* as, 'square-shouldered, but slightly built and walks with a rolling gait. His teeth are a conspicuous part of him, and are remarkably white and regular. He is exceedingly fond of dress and was often seen in his knickerbockers.' It was this description which became ingrained in the consciousness of the population and led, like the artist's impression of Bible John in the 1960s, to many innocent people coming under suspicion. Laurie was also said to be, 'Rather good looking, pleasant manner and appears as if he would like to leave a favourable impression.' Other epithets included: 'Generally speaking has a gentlemanly appearance', and 'He is of social disposition.'

Laurie trained as a pattern-maker in the engineering industry. This was a skilled occupation which used engineers' drawings to make moulds used in the casting of metal machinery parts. The pig iron bars produced by the blast furnaces were melted in foundries to produce a wide range of castings. Patterns were used in this process to make a cavity or impression in the mould into which molten metal was pored and left to harden.

In 1882, aged 21, after serving his apprenticeship with Lambertons, a local firm which made heavy machinery for the iron and steel industry, Laurie left home to work in Glasgow. After becoming homesick, he returned to Coatbridge and took up a position with John Gray and Co. in Uddingston where he was involved in the manufacture of winding equipment and steam cranes for Glasgow's new underground railway through Queen Street low-level station.

Laurie's downfall appears to have been triggered by two events. As a young boy he was very affected by the death of his mother, Agnes, after a long illness. His father remarried around 1876 and the next year there was a new addition to the family, David. In his early twenties Laurie's relationship with his stepmother, Jeannie, became very strained and he was effectively ostracised from the family home after some unspecified misconduct. (When asked to give details of his family he would often omit his young stepbrother.) Laurie then moved permanently to Glasgow where he led a somewhat rudderless existence, unable to hold down a job for long and consequently changing his lodgings frequently. In the city he lived beyond his means and started to accumulate debts.

The second event began at a church picnic in the summer of 1887, aged 26, when he started a relationship with a Miss Annie McLean from Rosehall in Coatbridge. Annie was just over 16 and attending Garnethill Public School (the forerunner of Glasgow High School for Girls) with the view to qualifying as a teacher. Her father Peter McLean, a Coatbridge grocer, warned Laurie to stay away from his daughter as she was too young and any relationship would distract her from her studies. Around June 1888 he also asked his daughter not to talk to Laurie, which she complied with. Laurie took offence to this and wrote several 'scurrilous and offensive' letters to Peter McLean and his family. When Annie McLean took up with another man, John Cowan, a teacher then working in Coatbridge, Laurie appeared to be consumed with anger and jealousy and later wrote, 'Since then I have been perfectly careless about what I did, and my one thought was how to punish her enough for the cruel wrong she had done me.' From this time on Laurie's life starts to unravel.

His first brush with the law was in October 1887 when the police were called after he was accused of stealing five pounds from a fellow-lodger in Glasgow's St Vincent Street. Around the time of the relationship break-up he was sacked from his job as a storeman at Bilsland and Co, a bolt and rivet making company in the city's Cranstonhill. A month later, on 27 June 1888, he stole jewellery valued at eighteen pounds from his landlady, Mrs Crawford, in nearby Dover Street and then decamped. The motive for the theft may well have been to fund his annual break, as a few weeks later he visited Rothesay where he knew Annie McLean was holidaying. We also know he visited Lamlash on Arran where he left his lodgings without paying.

Laurie was arrested for the theft of the jewellery on 23 March 1889. He was tried two days later but admonished after his father agreed to reimburse the victim. A photograph taken by police at this time was used for identification purposes in the murder case. By the time of the trial for the theft Laurie had yet another job, with boilermakers Walker, Henderson and Co in Anderston, and was now living at 49 Woodlands Road near Glasgow's Charing Cross.

His landlady there was later interviewed by journalists and gave a revealing insight into Laurie's character. She said he had two distinctive characteristics: meanness and vanity. When he went out he often wore patent leather boots and a satin hat, though on weeknights his favourite headgear was a polo cap. Even going to and from work he dressed in a superior way as he did not want to be taken for a workman. He was also very proud of his teeth.

She went on to say that he often slept in and instead of going to work put on his best clothes to stroll around the city centre. She recalled how one weekend he did not come home as he was in custody over the jewellery theft. He did not smoke and only once was the worse for drink. He never had visitors or went to see his parents but she knew he had an aunt in Moffat with whom he regularly corresponded, as he did with his sister Agnes in Coatbridge. Laurie's landlady ended her character sketch by saying she didn't trust him as he never looked her straight in the eye.

By the end of the nineteenth century Glasgow was the 'Second City of the Empire', synonymous with heavy engineering: producing more than half of Britain's tonnage of shipping and a quarter of all locomotives in the world. It was one of the first cities in Europe to reach a population of over a million. The city's self-confidence was embodied by the International Exhibition of Science, Art and Industry which was held at Kelvingrove over the summer of 1888.

By the spring of 1889 Laurie was working in Springburn in north Glasgow, plying his trade with Sharp, Stewart and Co. This steam locomotive manufacturer had only recently moved from Manchester to the premises of the Clyde Locomotive Company which it renamed the Atlas Works. The firm eventually amalgamated with two others to form the North British Locomotive Company, the largest locomotive manufacturer outside of the USA, capable of building 600 engines a year.

During Laurie's time in Springburn, Sharp, Stewart and Co. would have had a full order book. They were currently supplying established customers from their time in England, as well as the expanding Scottish rail networks and new railway systems throughout the world. There was plentiful overtime, often compulsory, and Laurie would regularly work from 6am till around 8pm. Pattern-maker was one of the higher paid trades. His wages were thirty shillings a week, but with overtime could increase to over two pounds.

The railway workshops were a noisy, dirty and dangerous environment with both overhead cranes and line shafting; the latter transmitting power to machinery by means of belts, pulleys and gears. Health and safety was primitive, even by the standards of the day, with no safety glasses or machinery guards. Fatalities were common and injuries often disabling. Laurie's workbench, lit by gas-light, was in the pattern shop near the foundry. The works were cold draughty places where men would gravitate to the foundry fires to warm themselves. The patterns Laurie and his workmates created were of great benefit to those working on the locomotives as they saved them from having to repeatedly take measurements.

On 8 June Laurie took up residence in Mrs King's at 106 North Frederick Street, a convenient location for catching the train or tram to his work in Springburn. Mrs King was the widow of Charles King, a well-known Glaswegian tragedian and stalwart of Glasgow theatres in the 1870s. He played the title role in *Rob Roy* at the Theatre Royal in 1872 when one reviewer observed: 'It is evident Mr King is not a born Highlander.' Laurie shared a room with Matthew Eaglesome, a letter sorter. Mrs King said that she rarely saw Laurie, who had told her he was a draughtsman, as he left very early for work and was often not back until 10pm. He only took meals at home on Saturday afternoon and Sundays. She described him as, 'temperate, habits regular'.

For his summer holidays of 1889, from 6 to 19 July, Laurie was returning to the popular resort of Rothesay on the Isle of Bute. According to Laurie this was not for the bathing or sea air, but to keep tabs on Miss McLean. About a week before Laurie left for Bute he and Annie McLean, unknown to each other, boarded the same train at Glasgow Central for Coatbridge. When they both alighted at Whifflet she had seen Laurie but tried to avoid him. When Laurie eventually noticed her a chase ensued as she tried to run away from him. Witnesses to the incident said there ensued 'a scene' in which he caught her by the arm and 'made some remarks'.

Laurie himself stated, 'It was to watch her audacious behaviour that I went to Rothesay this and last year'. There is one recorded incident of Laurie confronting Annie McLean and her mother on Bute. However, by the beginning of 1889 he had started another relationship, with Grace Chalmers who worked as a clerk on the *Coatbridge Express*. (During the hunt for Laurie the names of women connected to him were suppressed to protect them from any notoriety by association. Both Annie McLean and Grace Chalmers were cited as witnesses at his trial but not called.)

While on the run from the law Laurie reflected on his new relationship in a letter he wrote: 'I may say that I became acquainted with another young lady whose good qualities I sincerely wish that I had learned to appreciate sooner, as if I had I would be in a very different position today.' As they both attended the same church, she had known Laurie for about three years before they started going out shortly after New Year 1889, as she recalled: 'We walked together about twice a week as a rule. About the end of March or beginning of April last he asked me to marry him but I declined because my father did not approve of him. He repeated the offer of marriage three times but I always put him off. We still continued to keep company.' While on holiday in Rothesay, Laurie would arrange to meet up with his new sweetheart.

Chapter Two

The Madeira of Scotland

Rothesay, 'the Madeira of Scotland', was a quintessential Clyde Coast resort, one of the country's premier holiday destinations, situated on a crescent-shaped bay lined with handsome villas. Competition among steamers and railway companies meant Clyde resorts like Rothesay were now affordable to the less well off. It became a fashionable bathing and watering place that hosted an annual inundation of holiday-makers and day-trippers from Glasgow and the surrounding towns. Around 1890 it was reckoned that during the Glasgow Fair Rothesay's resident population of 9,000 was increased by around 700 families on holiday plus 30-40,000 weekend visitors, an annual exodus known as going 'doon the watter'. Accommodation was obviously at a premium with sometimes up to twenty people sharing a room. Those with nowhere to stay slept out in the woods on the west side of the bay. In the evenings the local police were accustomed to things getting out of hand.

There was a great air of anticipation leading up to the Glasgow Fair, the annual trades holiday, as folk longed to exchange the grime and slums of industrial Glasgow for the fresh air of the seaside. You had a choice of routes from Glasgow to Rothesay including direct steamers from the Broomielaw in the city centre. On Fair Saturday 1883, 16,000 people left Glasgow on twenty steamers before noon.

Many folk, including John Laurie, preferred the combination of train and boat as it was quicker and avoided the foetid sights and smells of the upper Clyde. The river was ostensibly an open sewer, described by one English visitor as 'a continuous stream of reeking filth and noxious vapours'. The nauseating stench permeated as far as Argyle Street. For a more congenial journey you boarded the Glasgow and South Western trains at St Enoch Station to catch the steamer at Prince's Pier, Greenock, or alternatively the Caledonian Railway which connected Glasgow's Central Station with both Wemyss Bay and the recently opened Gourock pier.

Once he had arrived on Bute, Laurie chose to stay in Port Bannatyne, known to locals as 'The Port', a quieter, less fashionable resort two miles north of Rothesay. This was either for economy or because, for his own reasons, he did not want to be near the centre of things. Rothesay and Port Bannatyne were linked by a horse-drawn tram service with open-topped coaches which visitors could utilise when going to and fro. The horses fairly raced along in anticipation of the nosebags at either terminus. Port Bannatyne was originally a small fishing village, but in the 1860s became a planned community with two parallel streets. During the holiday boom of the late nineteenth century city-scale tenements were built in which Glasgow holidaymakers often rented a room for the Fair.

Laurie found accommodation at Iona Place, a two-storey terrace up from the old stone quay. His landlady, Mrs Mary Currie, recalled how he arrived on Saturday 6 July and took a room for a fortnight at one pound a week. (Laurie originally wanted to rent the room for only eight days, suggesting that his original plan was to conclude his holiday on Arran.) Mrs Currie recollected that he had a small brown leather bag, an umbrella, and wore, according to mood and occasion, either a straw boater or brown felt hat. He had introduced himself as 'John Annandale' and she later noticed one of his calling cards with the same name, and an address of 6 Cambridge Street, Glasgow. There was a real John Annandale living at 233 Cambridge Street who had a stationary shop signed with his name at 229, but whether this is linked to Laurie's choice of pseudonym is unknown. For much of his time on Bute and Arran, Laurie calls himself 'John Annandale' but is also socialising with friends who know him as Laurie. [To avoid confusion the author continues to call him Laurie with mention of 'Annandale' where appropriate.]

Jack House, the well-known Glasgow journalist, wrote about the Goatfell murder case, but did not think there was anything sinister about Laurie's new persona. He explained how it was common at holiday times, especially among the working- or lower middle-class, to try and impress young ladies with a more mannered accent, better job, more salubrious address etc. The summer holidays were a prime opportunity to make the acquaintance of the opposite sex through pleasure cruises and excursion trips, and nothing should be left to chance. A second identity was also handy if you were in the habit of leaving your accommodation without paying, one of Laurie's parsimonious foibles.

On Bute, Laurie's behaviour, with one noticeable exception, was typical of any young man enjoying a break from long hours of work; a socially active fortnight that included frequenting some of Rothesay's nineteen public houses, enjoying pleasure trips, dressing up to impress, and flirting with young ladies. The one odd behaviour, on the latter part of his holiday, was that many of the clothes he was wearing to attract attention belonged to a young man he would soon be accused of murdering. The attire was very distinctive and easily recognisable by the many acquaintances of the former owner still on the island.

Rothesay's many attractions included a bowling green, tennis, golf, boat hire and both swimming baths and sea-bathing: 'Beneath the Skeoch Wood, and enclosed by high screens are the Bathing-places for ladies and gentlemen where the art of natation can be practised without fear of waves or of dangerous currents.' Children would stand waist-deep in the sea, in rows holding hands, waiting for the long rollers from the big steamers to wash over them. The town also had tearooms, ice-cream parlours and even a medieval castle with a moat; a music hall, a museum and the Royal Aquarium which incorporated a seal pool and camera obscura.

But Rothesay's holiday heart was its pier and esplanade. In Scotland the latter was the equivalent of a pleasure pier. Rothesay's esplanade was planted with ornamental gardens and dotted with palm trees. At the pier end there was an octagonal bandstand where professional musicians played for several hours every afternoon, and again in the evening. The sea front was used for promenading, a popular way to meet the opposite sex, especially on a Sunday when many other options were closed.

Rothesay pier was an impressive structure where three steamers could berth simultaneously across the front with room for others at either end. In June 1884 new pier buildings were completed that incorporated ticket offices, refreshment rooms, a coffee house and bookstall, all fronted by a glass-covered verandah. Contemporary photographs show the pier and adjacent esplanade swarming with people, all dressed to the nines in their Sunday best. At peak periods folk gathered to watch the arrival and departure of the steamers. Their captains became great heroes to small boys, and many of the fathers. These vessels were the pride of the Clyde and folk took great interest in their relative merits, especially their speed. Steamer racing was encouraged among the companies and provided free entertainment throughout the day with the vessels occasionally leaving while passengers were still on the gangplank.

The excitement at the pier started at 8.15am with the arrival of the newspapers. From 10am onwards the area was thronged with folk out to watch the coming and going of the excursion steamers including the daily dash for the pier between the *Columba* and *Lord of the Isles*. This race often continued through the Kyles of Bute to the village of Colintraive. Then there was the 'twelve o'clock steamers' as the main body of visitors came down the gangways, 'bags and bundles, prams and holdalls, hampers and husbands'. Many returned to see the *Columba* off again at 3.30pm, the *Lord of the Isles* at 5.30pm. Finally there was the 'six o'clock steamers' with men folk returned from work in the city.

Nowadays a holiday in Rothesay does not have the same appeal it once had, but back in the day the steamers offered pleasure cruises of a quality and creativity that today's tourist can only realise through rose-tinted reminiscence. On the promenade deck there was invariably music: a fiddler or piper, or sometimes German students who formed concert parties, playing waltzes and collecting coppers with a large sea-shell. There were also fireworks. On one memorable occasion a London fireworks expert was commissioned to provide a display over the Gareloch; eleven steamers conveyed over 10,000 passengers to the scene from all around the Firth. There were cruises to take in a 'Grand Open-air Concert' with an orchestra and a 150-strong choir performing Handel's *Messiah*. There were romantic evening sailings through the Kyles of Bute where, in the gloaming, you stopped off at one of the islands or in one of the bays for torch-lit dancing to pipers. During the Glasgow International Exhibition in 1901 you might be lucky enough to be entertained on board by the Berlin Philharmonic.

The summer of 1889 is regarded as the start of the golden

age of the Clyde steamer, which lasted up to the First World War, when there was an explosion of investment fuelled by railway expansion. By the summer of 1913 Rothesay had over a hundred steamer calls in a day. The steamer network meant Bute was easy to reach and, once there, you had a choice of scenic cruises among the islands and the other resorts of the Firth of Clyde. One of the finest of these was that by the *Ivanhoe* and it was here the tale of the Goatfell murder, if it was a murder, begins.

In Rothesay Laurie chummed up with James Gillon Aitken from Shawlands in Glasgow who was holidaying with his parents. Aitken, described as a tall, good-looking young man, was a salesman in the family grain company, James Aitken and Sons, based in Glasgow's Hope Street. The two young men had met up the previous summer on Bute but it is highly likely they knew each other for some time through their fathers' connections in the grain trade. This summer they would spend a fair amount of time in each other's company.

On Monday 8 July the pair went for a sail in a small boat together. This was the day Mrs Currie remembered how Laurie arrived back at his lodgings with his clothes dirty, due, he said, to falling off a bicycle. On Tuesday Laurie returned to Glasgow to collect his pay as the works were due to close for the annual trades holiday. Much of the money was soon spent in fashionable city centre outfitters. He stayed the night at North Frederick Street and returned to Port Bannatyne the next morning, arriving at Mrs Currie's wearing 'a stylish brown knickerbocker suit and bright stockings'. That Thursday he went on an excursion to Inveraray and in the evening, wearing his swanky new clothes, again met up with Aitken. Laurie mentioned to his friend that the next day he intended taking the *Ivanhoe* paddle steamer to Arran. Aitken said he might join him if the weather looked promising but the pair made no definite arrangement.

The *Ivanhoe*, a 225-foot twin-funnel saloon steamer, was built by D and W Henderson and Co. in Glasgow in 1880. She was part of a new breed of steamer (the standard was set by David MacBrayne's flagship, the *Columba*) designed along the lines of a private steam yacht, immaculately clean with scrubbed decks and gleaming brasswork; fitted to a high standard with an emphasis on increased comfort and standard of service. The deckhands wore smart uniforms of navy and white while officers sported gold braid and brass buttons. The vessel had all the facilities expected by the discerning tourist, bar one. And that one was a bar.

The *Ivanhoe* was designed to operate on teetotal principles, a riposte to the drunken and rowdy scenes, with concomitant pickpockets and card sharps, that were often prevalent on Clyde steamers, especially on a Sunday when pubs were closed. (However there was something known as an 'Ivanhoe flask'.) At the time the proposal was ridiculed as many companies' profits came largely from the sale of alcohol. Wags predicted the venture would be a 'teetotal failure'.

The *Ivanhoe* amazed the sceptics by proving a great success, appealing not just to non-drinkers but to families and others who appreciated a more sedate and less riotous experience free of 'destitute convivialists'. One advert stated: 'Passengers may rely on having a pleasant sail without the ordinary rabble common on board Clyde steamers during the Glasgow Fair.' The public took to her immediately and she held a special place in the affections of Glaswegians throughout the 1880s.

The newspapers of the day are full of incidents concerning the busy summer traffic on the Firth of Clyde. It was relatively common to see small, often uninsured, craft carrying over a thousand passengers. There were frequent collisions, mechanical failures, the running down of rowing boats and yachts, suicides, and drunken behaviour with reports of riots lasting several hours. The latter were most prevalent on the Sunday steamers and a large battalion of police often awaited the vessel's return to the Broomielaw. Despite its genteel reputation, the *Ivanhoe* was not immune from accidents. In August 1888 near Rothesay pier, but unseen by those on board, a small boat containing two boys was drawn under the vessel's paddle and 'smashed into matchwood'. The occupants were left struggling in the water but were eventually rescued. Due to the rudimentary state of safety regulations, shoddy navigation, frequent overcrowding, and the reckless behaviour of many skippers, it was a miracle that no large-scale disaster ever occurred on the Clyde.

The master of the *Ivanhoe* from her launch in 1880 until 1889 was Captain James Williamson who would later play, as the driving force of the Caledonian Steam Packet Company, a major role in the development of Clyde steamer services. One of Williamson's favourite anecdotes concerned the only time a drink was legally imbibed on the vessel. A passengers on an 1886 excursion was the King of Saxony: 'In the course of a pleasant chat upon the bridge, the King remarked that the sun had passed the meridian, and laughingly suggested that, of course, it was quite out of the question to expect that even a bottle of Rhine wine would be found on a temperance steamer.' A bet was made which the King lost, as Clyde canniness managed to produce a suitable receptacle from the medicine chest.

Another holiday-maker on Bute was Edwin Robert Rose, a congenial young man from London. Rose was 32 years old, 5ft 7in tall with dark hair, mutton-chop sideburns and a luxuriant moustache. He was the middle of seven children, known to his family as 'Ned'. Their father, Benjamin, had taken early retirement from his position as a messenger at the India Office. This was a poorly paid factotum-like post that involved receiving telegrams and other messages; sweeping corridors, putting coal on the fire and escorting visitors. He would receive a paltry pension and in consequence the Rose family, despite their grand-sounding address, Wisset Lodge, were not well off. After Edwin had gone missing on Goatfell they were asked to contribute to the cost of refreshments for the search parties but were unable to do so. There is a sense that the family had fallen on hard times.

The oldest Rose sibling, also named Benjamin, worked as a clerk at the India Office. For a while Edwin worked there too as a temporary clerk, a period when he lodged with Benjamin and his wife Alice. By 1889 Edwin, who was single, had returned to the family home in Upper Tooting, London. His occupation is normally given as a clerk in a Brixton building company but Benjamin describes him as a 'confidential clerk to a retired builder'. Edwin was also a Sunday school teacher, an active member of Balham Congregational Church, and taught the violin in evening classes at Lambeth Polytechnic. He was involved in the temperance movement but on this Scottish holiday would often have a brandy flask in his possession, 'for medicinal reasons'.

On 4 July Rose bought a return to Glasgow for £2 12s 6d and left St Pancras on the 9.15pm overnight train. He was in the habit of taking holidays outside of London and this year had chosen Rothesay largely because his employer's son, the Reverend Gustavus Goodman, whom he had known for several years, would also be there. They were both booked into the up-market Glenburn Hydropathic hotel. Overlooking Rothesay Bay the 'Hydro' was opened in 1843 by the medical entrepreneur Dr William Paterson. It was the first of its kind in Scotland, part of a highly popular movement for spa-like therapies in a hotel setting. The Hydros initially concentrated on services geared towards the recovery of health, the 'cold water cure', but later expanded into providing healthy outdoor pastimes like tennis and golf. The Glenburn had two tennis courts. Edwin Rose was keen on sports and had brought his tennis outfit and racquet with him. These would become crucial pieces of evidence at the trial of John Watson Laurie.

The Glenburn developed into one of the most palatial of all the Firth of Clyde hotels, described as 'more akin to a stately home than a provincial hotel'. The building's architect designed saloons for Clyde passenger liners and this was reflected in the hotel's interior. The Glenburn was situated in a prominent position overlooking Rothesay Bay, reached by steps from Mount Stuart Road. It had been enlarged and refurbished the year before Rose's visit and now boasted electric lighting, smoking rooms, marble floors with Persian carpets and its own golf course. The hotel, which could accommodate 130, was described in one 1888 advert as, 'Delightful Residence, Climate Mild. Protected from east winds. Newly added: an additional drawing room with a southern aspect, overlooking the Flower Garden, with twenty new bedrooms and nursery for children. Large handsome recreation hall, music and billiard room. Baths: Turkish, Salt, Russian, Medicated, Electric and Swimming. Finest in Britain. Dr Philp, Resident Physician.' Andrew Philp, originally from Dunfermline, currently owned both the Glenburn and Dunblane Hydros. He was a close friend of Thomas Cook and likewise a keen supporter of the temperance movement, 'No Intoxicants at Glenburn.' Laurie's church, the United Presbyterians, were long-time supporters of the temperance movement and saw in hydropathy a medical regime in tune with their own aims.

There was a similar establishment on the hill above Laurie's lodgings in Port Bannatyne – the 88-bedroom Kyles of Bute Hydropathic. This was even grander than the Glenburn but, after serving as a Royal Naval shore establishment, HMS *Varbel*, was demolished in the 1970s. The site of the hotel was the scene of a notorious murder in 2018: it was where the body of 6-year-old Alesha MacPhail was discovered after being killed by 16-year-old Aaron Campbell.

Hydros presented themselves as high status and highly respectable establishments with a clientele largely drawn from the professional and middle classes, often with special terms for clergymen. The Glenburn offered a programme of music, charades, mock elections etc. However, if you shared in the values of temperance and, by association, religious commitment, it was possible to mix with a social echelon you would not normally encounter. James Ewing Ritchie, an English travel writer and journalist, wrote about the hotel in the 1880s. On a yacht moored in Rothesay harbour, Ritchie had not anticipated the high volume of steamer traffic and consequently booked into the Glenburn for some peace and quiet:

Here we have good air, pleasant society, lovely scenery, good books, and good living, and what more do you require? Not even a Society journal, with its silly twaddle about Lord Tom Noddy, finds its way here. If you want to read here there is a well-filled library, and the Scotch dailies are at any rate quite as sensible and well written as the London ones. And of an evening there is the handsome recreation room, well-lighted, and always gay with bright young faces. I see in the billiard-room a great many ladies, though I have seen none of them play billiards. Perhaps it is one of the causes of the success of such places as Glenburn that so much of that social equality which is quite out of question in an ordinary hotel prevails there. We are one at meals, amusements, in the whole circle of social life, including morning and evening prayer·

One would expect this level of accommodation to be out of the reach of someone on a clerk's salary. This much-maligned occupation was often prefixed with the word 'lowly' and derogatorily referred to as a 'quill-driver'. Throughout this story there is much conjecture as to Rose's wealth as it was a significant factor in whether the motive for the crime was theft. The consensus appears to be that he was not a man of means, only moderately well-off, but perhaps gave the impression of being more affluent than he actually was. Rose travelled third class on the train to Scotland. His family estimated he had about £15 at the onset of his holiday with only £5 or £6 to hand.

Rose and Laurie were destined to meet on the *Ivanhoe*. If it seemed odd that someone on a relatively low clerk's income could afford to stay for two weeks at a top notch hotel, it was equally curious that a young male employee of a Springburn railway works should choose an excursion on a family-orientated, teetotal steamer. Perhaps Laurie thought there might be some bright-eyed young ladies on board. He was right. Among them would be Miss Cooper and her sisters from Nottingham who were, as Laurie glumly noted, chaperoned by their mother.

The excursion programme for steamers began at the end of May. The *Ivanhoe* was lucky to make the 1889 season as she was almost sold to the United Steamship Company of Copenhagen. When the new Gourock pier was opened on 1 June 1889, the first steamer to call was the *Ivanhoe* with passengers for the 8.30am express to Glasgow. Around this time her regular captain, James Williamson, became overall manager of the Caledonian steamers, based at Gourock, and Captain Allan MacDougall took over on the bridge. For the first half of June she transferred passengers from Gourock before taking up her regular excursion to Arran.

As the 12 July was Glasgow Fair Friday there was a larger crowd than normal gathered on Rothesay pier awaiting the arrival of the *Ivanhoe*. After leaving her base at Craigendoran she picked up passengers at the railway piers of Helensburgh, Greenock and Wemyss Bay to arrive at Rothesay for 11.10am. James Aitken had decided to go on the excursion and met Laurie, resplendent in a straw hat and his new knickerbockers suit, on the pier. Miss Cooper's family was among a group of about twenty from the Hydro forming part of the well-groomed throng. Also in the

Hydro party were Edwin Rose and two new friends he had made at the hotel: Francis Mickel, a wood merchant, and William Thom, a travelling salesman, both from Linlithgow. Rose, nattily dressed in a chocolate and white striped tennis blazer, white flannels and yachting cap, was a gregarious and affable individual, happy to chat to anyone around. The Reverend Goodman was there to see his friend off; he later mentioned that Rose had a flask of brandy with him as 'he was somewhat nervous of the sea'.

Anticipation on the pier mounted as the elegant profile of the *Ivanhoe* steamed gracefully into view, two pennants fluttering from the mast, two yellow funnels, gold ornamentation round both the black hull and paddle-boxes. Up the gangway you were greeted with the comforting aroma of morning kippers; away from the saloons there was the subtler smell of tarry rope. Once on board a quick exploration was in order: to get your bearings and look for familiar faces. The main saloon had a crimson and gold colour scheme and was described as showing 'tasteful luxury'; it also had well-upholstered seats, maple panelling with floral designs, large mirrors, velvet curtains and silver paraffin lamps. Water fountains, with tumblers, were located at various points around the vessel.

The dining saloon, domain of chief steward Mr Latta, was decorated with pictures of scenes from Walter Scott's *Ivanhoe* and had two rows of circular tables laid out in spotless white linen, shaped napkins in precise position, each piece of crockery adorned with the company's crest. Uniquely, the dining saloon had vines planted in pots with branches trailing across the ceiling; these actually produced bunches of grapes which were sometimes presented to special guests. Smoking was only permitted in a designated area which added to the pleasant atmosphere on board.

One of the few downsides to the Clyde steamers were inefficient boilers which failed to completely burn the coal, the funnels billowing out clouds of soot and fragments of hot ash. At Rothesay the worst offenders were the *Ivanhoe*, *Guinevere* and *Lord of the Isles*. Yachtsmen from the Royal Northern and Clyde Yacht Club complained how their sails were soiled by the black smoke. Coastal towns fined vessels for polluting their streets, but at sea the vessels were a law unto themselves. Ladies used parasols to protect themselves and their clothing. Captain Williamson of the *Ivanhoe* addressed the problem by fitting special furnace doors designed to help consume the gases before they formed into the dense black clouds emitted from the funnels.

It was not just the absence of the riff-raff but the vessel's route that made the *Ivanhoe* excursion popular. It was regarded as the finest trip on the Firth of Clyde, passing through the Kyles of Bute, a narrow and picturesque arm of the sea among the Argyllshire hills. It then called at the pretty village of Tighnabruaich before heading for the Arran villages of Corrie, Brodick, Lamlash and Whiting Bay (the last call only on Monday, Wednesday and Friday). One tourist who took the *Ivanhoe* excursion, a few weeks before Laurie and Rose, was Andrew James Symington, a Paisley textile merchant who went on to recount the vessel's route:

From Rothesay Bay the steamer, passing Ardbeg point and Port Bannatyne, proceeds through the Kyles of Bute, the waterway between the island and the mainland. This narrow strait is about seventeen miles long, and presents a great variety of beautiful and picturesque scenery. The atmospheric effects are often very fine. We lately observed that, while the near mountains were green or rocky, the distant vistas of heights beyond rose in pale lilac tints, deep purples, and dark indigo, relieved against dense piled-up cloud masses of snowy white and burnished silver with, here and there, bright sunny openings into the blue sky…Keeping the island of Bute on the left, and on the right passing by Loch Striven and Colintraive, we come to 'the narrows', a point where there is, at low tide, little more than room, between the two rocky sides, for the steamer to get through. A lofty mountain range rises right in front of us, apparently barring the way; Loch Ridden with its rugged grandeur, opens up on the right, extending six mile inland, among the mountains, to Ormidale and Glendaruel. Such magnificent panoramic scenery, viewed morning, noon or night, or at any season of the year, produces many ever-varying and beautiful effects of light, shade and colour, on the near rugged mountain masses or on the distant dreamlike heights.

Once the *Ivanhoe* had set sail from Rothesay, James Aitken bumped into two old friends, Andrew and William Allan, brothers from Glasgow's Langside district, with whom he chatted until the vessel reached the Kyles of Bute. When Laurie made an appearance Aitken introduced him to the Allan brothers. Laurie then went on to relate a strange incident that had just occurred when an English gentleman accosted him in the mistaken impression that Laurie was part of the group from the Hydropathic.

After Edwin Rose approached him, Laurie introduced himself as 'John Annandale' and presented one of his cards. When Rose mentioned he was staying at the prestigious Glenburn hotel, built for the wealthy of Glasgow, Laurie would have been impressed, and inevitably made some assumptions about his new acquaintance. The pair may have appeared chalk and cheese but this was not altogether the case: both were regular church goers active in Sunday schools, both played the violin and had a keen interest in music. Neither fitted the popular notion of murderer and victim.

The *Ivanhoe* was owned by the Frith of Clyde Steam Packet Co. The name was not the result of some corporate spelling error. 'Frith' is the old Scots word for estuary as used by Hugh Macdonald in the title of his book, *Days at the Coast, a Series of Sketches Descriptive of the Frith of Clyde, its Watering-places, its Scenery and its Associations.* William Wordsworth used the term in his poem, 'On the Frith of Clyde in a Steamboat', which begins: 'Arran!; a single-crested Tenerife, / A St Helena next in shape and hue, / Varying her crowded peaks and ridges blue.'

This was the scene Laurie and Rose saw before them as they chatted. The Isle of Arran is the dominant feature of the Firth of Clyde, an area with a world-wide reputation for scenic beauty. The island stretches 19 miles from north to south and ten miles across with its granite peaks grouped together in the north. The early geologists called Arran 'the epitome of the world' and many later visitors would describe it as 'Scotland in miniature'. One regular visitor, the Reverend David Landsborough, said this about the island: 'In few places on this fair earth is there beheld so delightful a mingling of beauty and grandeur.'

Amid the noisy clank of the engines and the constant rush of the paddle-wheels, talk between Laurie and Rose inevitably turned to the prominent cone of Goatfell that dominated the north of the island. We do not know exactly what transpired aboard the vessel though Laurie appears to have mentioned his intention of booking accommodation in Brodick and then returning to explore the hills. In one account of their first meeting Laurie provides Rose with 'a glowing account of the beauties of the mountain scenery of Arran'. It is highly probable Laurie had climbed Goatfell before. Rose would have been impressed, and excited about the possibility of ascending a lofty Scottish peak. On a later occasion John Laurie said this: 'My object in going to Arran was to visit the glens and to ascend Goatfell and I explained to Mr Rose that if he wished my society he would require to accompany me on these excursions.' He would also suggest that Rose somewhat imposed himself upon him.

Goatfell, Arran's highest point at 2866ft (874m), is one of these mountains, like the Cobbler, Ben Lomond and Ben Nevis, that people with no particular interest in hill-walking feel the need to climb. This was as true in 1889 as it is now. Almost everyone who climbed Goatfell felt compelled to describe the famed view from its summit. Here is one example, from many: 'From the summit of its cone, the near view, looking sheer down into the depths of Glen Rosa, and among the precipitous peaks of Cior Mhor, Ben Gnuis, Caisteal Abhael, etc.; is one of the very wildest conceivable; for, although Alpine and other scenes are on a larger scale, this is only a relative term, and is not always essential to the impression or feeling of awe produced on the beholder.'

The glens Laurie refers to are Glen Rosa and Glen Sannox which lie on the west side of Goatfell and are separated from each other by a pass called The Saddle, 1456ft (444m) high. Glen Rosa has been pictured, 'as romantic a glen as any in the Highlands' and was easily accessible from Brodick. Through promotion by earlier writers like John MacCulloch, who described it as 'the sublime of magnitude, and simplicity, and obscurity and silence', Glen Sannox was for many years one of Arran's most renowned tourist draws, often compared to the likes of Glen Coe and Glen Sligachan, and consequently a favourite location for artists.

The afore-mentioned Saddle would feature in the story of Laurie and Rose. It is a place-name that is atypical of the Scottish Highlands where the usual name for a pass is the Gaelic 'bealach'. English place-names in the Scottish mountains are generally evidence of early mountain tourism: there is a Munro called The Saddle in Kintail and a pass with the same name above Loch A'an in the Cairngorms. To many people, including the Arran folk who were witnesses at Laurie's trial, the term 'The Saddle' referred to not just the pass but 'the Saddle route': the ascent or descent of Goatfell by way of The Saddle. This innocuous detail would have a bearing on what became known as 'The Arran Tragedy'.

As the *Ivanhoe* approached Arran, the first village to come into view was Corrie which Laurie and Rose would later visit. In his article Andrew James Symington also described this part of the excursion:

> On approaching the north-east of the island and nearing Corrie, we look right into Glen Sannox, beholding a marvellous spectacle of wild sterile grandeur which reminds one of scenes in the island of Skye. Off the peaceful and pretty little village of Corrie, with its white cottages on the shore road facing the sea, green hills rising immediately behind it and, over them, a range of lofty, bare, reddish, serrated granite peaks, seamed and scarred with torrents foaming down in silver streaks, the scene is absolutely one of the most strikingly picturesque to be seen from the sea anywhere in the British Isles.
>
> The higher regions here are often swathed in white rolling mists from which the mountain tops magically emerge, seeming as if they were severed from earth and standing built in cloudland. At other times the peaks themselves appear to be furiously raking through the mists at a great rate. At Corrie the climate is very mild, many tropical plants being able to thrive well there, and in mild seasons to survive the winter in open air.

Whatever Rose and Laurie agreed, the latter explained that as it was the Glasgow Fair weekend it would not be easy to find somewhere to stay in Brodick. However, if he was able to secure lodgings Rose could share them with him. With this loose arrangement Laurie returned to Aitken's group and mentioned what had occurred. The Allan brothers were staying with family on Arran and Laurie asked their advice on finding accommodation. They replied that enquiring at one of the shops or tearooms was the best bet.

For much of his remaining time on board Laurie roamed the vessel in the hope that his choice of outfit might elicit approbation or catch the eye of some winsome young lady. He has no such luck. One of Laurie's failings was a propensity to ingratiate himself, using pretentious language, into what was then referred to as 'a better class of people'. He often ended up making a fool of himself. Nor had he any success with the rest of Rose's friends from the Hydro. Miss Cooper recalled how Laurie 'attracted attention because of the conspicuous suit of clothes he wore, which elicited quizzing criticism'. Francis Mickel observed how, 'He moved about a great deal and became rather conspicuous'.

As the *Ivanhoe* steamed down Arran's east coast Laurie started to pay less attention to the opposite sex and more to the contours of the island's hills and glens he was keen to explore. Rounding Merkland Point the vessel entered Brodick Bay which was often compared to the Bay of Naples, with Goatfell taking the place of Vesuvius. One of the earliest books to detail the Arran hills was *The Geology of the Island of Arran,* by A C Ramsay, in which he describes the approach to Brodick from the sea:

As the visitor enters Brodick Bay, the scene becomes exceedingly beautiful. The lofty precipices, and gloomy shadows of the rugged ridge of Ben Ghnuis, which often throws a twilight hue over the deep hollow of Glen Rosa, and strongly contrasts with the open and swelling character of the hills around Glen Cloy: the cliffs of Corriegills, the white and sloping beach which rounds the bay, the embattled castle towering above its surrounding woods, the green enclosures, and beyond these, the long expanse of brown heath, from which rises the grey peak of Goatfell. All these form a scene of surpassing beauty, such as cannot be excelled by the most romantic scenery of the far-famed Firth of Clyde.

Chapter Three

Bleak, Bare and Barren

Tourism in Arran developed along different lines from other Clyde resorts like Rothesay. It did not cater for the industrial masses of the Glasgow area but had a more exclusive feel due to the policies of the proprietors, the Dukes of Hamilton, who regarded and protected the island as their personal shooting estate. No feuing of land was permitted nor any developments that might encourage tourism. For many years the only 'official' accommodation in Brodick was the estate-run Old Brodick Inn at Cladach, below Brodick Castle, as well as a small inn at the original village of Brodick near Mossend, about a quarter of a mile to the south of Cladach. The latter had few rooms while the former was often unavailable as it was frequently used for estate business.

Any entrepreneurial effort to exploit the burgeoning tourist industry was frustrated by policies imposed by the estate and policed by the despised factors. With the arrival of the steamers visitors were spilling onto the island with money to spend on accommodation, food, amusement etc but many were unable to find anywhere to stay. Islanders could only look on as the tourists, and their wallets, departed on the first available vessel.

Although there was a tradition of putting up people in villagers' homes, the proprietors even discouraged this. At the start of every season an estate worker was sent round the district reminding households to observe the rules governing the accommodation of tourists. However many disregarded the edicts and eventually there was a formal agreement that estate tenants were permitted to take in visitors, but this came at a price, a commensurate increase in rent. Decades later, tourists would praise the Duke's policies for helping preserve the charm of the island and spare it much of the excesses apparent in the likes of Rothesay and Dunoon.

During the tenure of the 11th Duke (1852-63) the estate implemented many changes in the Brodick area. Many people were moved from the small hamlets near the Castle to new housing in Invercloy such as Alma Terrace and Douglas Place. This phase of development included the building of some large estate-run hotels to exploit the demand for visitor accommodation. Brodick's new Douglas Hotel (named after the heir to the dukedom, the Marquis of Douglas) replaced the Old Inn at Cladach, and was praised to the hilt by most tourist guides, 'a most comfortable and pleasant residence for a few days'. James Beckett's *Tourist Guide to Arran* (1882) described the Douglas as, 'A most spacious and well-conducted hotel, visited by tourists from all quarters of the globe.'

With the ownership of large hotels like the Douglas, which monopolised the market for well-heeled tourists, the estate became more relaxed about islanders taking in paying guests. Due to this, and other unrelated matters, the control of the Hamiltons gradually started to wane.

In the early days of steam, Lamlash was the preferred port on Arran as there was a good quay there, but steamers could only use it at high water. In June 1872 a wrought iron pier was constructed by the estate at Brodick, near the old stone quay below the Douglas Hotel (the iron pier was later replaced by a wooden version as the original began to rust). From this time Brodick, to the abiding chagrin of Lamlash residents, became Arran's main port. For those disembarking from the *Ivanhoe* at Brodick, *Murray's Handbook* provided an introduction to the area:

Brodick, the name of the pier, parish, and post office, but not of the village [which was Invercloy], is undoubtedly the best centre for exploring the island, and the place where most tourists disembark, at an iron pier of peculiar construction with buffer-sides to protect the steamers in rough weather... It must, however, be borne in mind that it is rarely of any use going to Arran without having secured accommodation beforehand, as in summer it is crammed with visitors. At Brodick especially the Duke of Hamilton discourages building and even the smallest cottages are secured months in advance at high rents. There is only one fairly large hotel at the head of the pier. The old inn was near the castle.

At Brodick many people arrived off the steamer to find the

Douglas Hotel full. They asked around locally and usually found a bed in one of a miscellany of properties which, with or without His Grace's blessing, provided basic accommodation, often in small wooden outhouses that were rented out by the week. Those disembarking from the *Ivanhoe* at Brodick pier had about two hours until the vessel's return from its final leg to Lamlash and Whiting Bay. During this time Laurie would try to secure accommodation for the weekend. All being well, they would catch the *Ivanhoe* back to Rothesay then return to Arran the next day (Saturday) after collecting what they needed for climbing Goatfell. On hearing their plans, and seeing the natural beauty of Arran, the rest of the Glenburn party were enthused to also try and stay over at Brodick.

Once disembarked, Laurie sought lodgings in Invercloy while Rose explored the local area. The rear of the *Ivanhoe's* timetable card recommended some walks that could be done in the time available ashore. Rose and his group may well have been tempted by the following one: 'Short walk from Invercloy, near Post-Office, up old Lamlash road. Very beautiful view of Brodick Bay and magnificent surroundings.'

The *Ivanhoe's* timetable card may well have played a critical role in Rose's death. Over the years John Laurie would make at least four confessional statements, all differing in detail, as to what actually happened on Goatfell. In one of these the *Ivanhoe's* innocuous descriptions of walks for visitors would instigate a struggle that left Edwin Rose lying lifeless on the mountainside.

In Brodick the Glenburn party were unable to find lodgings and the idea of staying over was abandoned. Laurie too was having little success, and was about to give up when he decided to have a cup of tea at Wooley's, the seafront tea room, an Arran institution founded by master baker Alexander Wooley, which is still going strong. Laurie asked the waitress if she could help and she suggested Mrs Walker in the lane round the corner. One of Mrs Walker's neighbours, Mrs Shaw, took Laurie the short distance to the house. Esther Walker and her husband William, a shoemaker, were originally from Airdrie, the neighbouring town to Coatbridge. She was the same age as Laurie and would have judged him, as landladies have to do, as a personable young man from a good family.

Mrs Walker said all she could offer was a basic wooden outhouse, 7ft by 14ft, furnished with one bed and a dressing table with wash-basin. Laurie said he would take it for a week. He then enquired if it was alright for a friend to stay with him for a short while. Mrs Walker was agreeable but conceded there was only room for Laurie to have breakfast in the house; his friend would have to go to the tea room. A total charge of one pound for the two was agreed. Laurie then met Rose, as arranged, on Brodick pier to catch the returning steamer. When Laurie informed Rose of the outcome of his enquiries, he seemed pleased with the arrangements and also enthused about what he had seen of the island.

This area around Wooley's would become a hotspot for shed enthusiasts: one outhouse plays a prominent part in a famous Victorian murder mystery while an adjacent building has a scientific pedigree. A few doors along from the tea room, John Thomson, later Lord Kelvin, had a holiday home, Castle View ('S.E.B.' and '1816' are carved above the door) where he continued his scientific work, constructing a makeshift laboratory in a garden shed and a special platform on the roof. The latter created alarm among neighbours when experiments created spectacular sparks. Thomson's experiments also extended to Goatfell where he used a portable electrometer he had devised to try and calculate the electrostatic distortion caused by mountainous topography.

On the passage back to Rothesay, Laurie was playing a dangerous game. On the steamer he chatted with James Aitken who had remained on the vessel for the final leg to Whiting Bay. Laurie told Aitken he had managed to secure lodgings and would be returning to Brodick the next day. He added that Rose appeared keen to join him in an ascent of Goatfell. What was risky was that Aitken knew him as Laurie while he had introduced himself as 'Annandale' to Rose, who in turn had used this name with Mickel and Thom, and the rest of the Hydro group. For the remainder of the excursion Laurie would have to keep these groups apart.

The *Ivanhoe* arrived back in Rothesay at 4.45pm. Edwin Rose invited Laurie to the Glenburn later that evening. But not for drinks as all Hydros were 'dry'. Aitken was asked by Laurie if he wanted to accompany him to the soiree: 'I said certainly not as I had no invitation.' However that evening Aitken is outside the Glenburn (which was near to his holiday accommodation at 10 Battery Place) when he professed to having seen Rose walking near the hotel with a young lady.

Laurie was friendly with two sisters, Jeanie and Minnie Park from Baillieston in Glasgow, whom he had known for several years. Jeanie, who was 20 years old, and her sister, three years younger, were on holiday in Rothesay with their brother. Laurie would call regularly on them at their lodgings in the Rosebank building in Argyle Street. Jeanie later related how he visited that Friday evening, presumably prior to visiting the Glenburn, to tell them about his trip to Arran. They then went for a walk when they bumped into James Aitken. Jeanie recalled, 'I think Laurie told us that he and Aitken had gone to Brodick that day together.' Laurie later asked the sisters if they would see him off to Arran on the pier the next morning. Among island communities, then as now, this was an important social ritual.

Laurie's Port Bannatyne landlady claimed that Laurie left her house that Friday morning saying he was off to Arran for a few days, and that he did not return till Tuesday: 'He left my house again on Friday, the 12th, and said he was going to Arran for a trip. He did not sleep in my house that night.' Mrs Currie was insistent on this point: that Laurie did not stay in Port Bannatyne on the Friday night. The police, however, did not think there was any mystery worth pursuing and came to the conclusion that her memory was at fault.

The next day, Glasgow Fair Saturday, as many as 20,000 people would disembark at Rothesay pier, with steamers arriving every half-hour or so throughout the day. (The width of the passageway at Wemyss Bay Station reflects the scale of passenger numbers.) Many of the holidaymakers already on the island would throng the pier to welcome friends, family and neighbours, or to be part of the general excitement: the Bute Band, the steamer racing, the pipers, the famous pointing porters.

Among the crowd were the Park sisters who had kept their word to see Laurie off. They recalled that he was wearing his tweed knickerbockers and loud stockings, a straw hat, a blue serge jacket, and was carrying a waterproof. Laurie spotted Rose among the crowd and left the sisters for a while to chat with him. When he returned he seemed disgruntled, saying: 'His friend was imposing on his good nature. That he had offered him accommodation for a night but he now said he would stay all the time with him.' When the *Ivanhoe* arrived the sisters waved off Laurie while the Glenburn contingent: Rose, Mickel and Thom, were seen off by a group that included Miss Cooper.

Mickel and Thom intended staying on Arran from Saturday to Monday. In the light of future events they would be keen in their accounts to distance themselves from John Laurie as much as possible. In their testimony at Laurie's trial they credit Rose with most of the communication with Laurie and try to present themselves as bit players, concerned friends in the background, disapproving of Rose's choice of companion. But it is eventually revealed that they do in fact spend a lot of time in the company of both Rose and Laurie over that Fair Weekend on Arran. Mickel and Thom's evidence in court is sometimes both contradictory and disingenuous. They were particularly keen to gloss over the fact that they were in the company of Laurie at the prestigious Glenburn Hotel.

At Laurie's trial Francis Mickel stated this about Rose: 'He said he had met with a man named "Annandale" on board the boat. That was all he told me on the Friday night.' Mickel claims to have met Laurie for the first time the next day, the Saturday, when he was introduced to him by Rose. After being questioned in court Mickel admits to being with Laurie on the Friday evening at the Glenburn.

William Thom also tries to give the impression that the get-together at the Glenburn didn't happen: 'On the Saturday we went again to Arran on the *Ivanhoe*. The deceased had by that time formed the acquaintance of the accused. He [Rose] told me he had met "Annandale" and introduced him to me.' Cross-examined by the Dean of Faculty, Thom answers 'Yes' to the following question, 'Do you remember, on the Friday evening, at the Hydropathic, Rose asking you to show "Annandale" round the place?'

This is spelt out in some detail to show that all is not always 'the truth and the whole truth'. The Edwardians were as capable of connivance, polite perjury and self-interest as any others. The era was probably the apogee of class consciousness and preserving one's place in the order of things could be as important, if not more, than someone's innocence or guilt. To make the chance acquaintance on a steamer of someone accused of murder was admissible, but to introduce him into polite society was an unredeemable faux pas.

When the *Ivanhoe* reached Lamlash, the next call after Brodick, a passenger leaving the steamer noticed that his yellow bag was missing and contacted the police. When the hunt for Laurie was at its height some newspapers were quick to accuse him of the theft. Mrs Currie described the bag he had at Port Bannatyne as being brown yet he arrived at Brodick with a yellow one. There is no mention of him carrying anything save a waterproof when he is seen off at Rothesay.

After disembarking from the *Ivanhoe* at Brodick they dispersed to deposit their luggage. Rose delivered his large black Gladstone bag, a metal-framed portmanteau, to Mrs Walker's while Mickel and Thom left their baggage at a shop. By this time Mickel had formed an unfavourable impression of Laurie, 'He seemed a deep moody young man and seldom spoke. If spoken to he usually replied in a single word'. Mickel made a point of warning Rose about his concerns regarding Laurie. They all then met up for refreshments before taking up an invitation from Thom to visit a friend of his, Andrew Francis Craig Gilmour, a 24-year-old medical student currently on holiday at Corrie. They caught the returning steamer for the village. The increasingly fashionable sea-bathing resort of Corrie, five miles north of Brodick was dominated by the large red sandstone building of the Corrie Hotel, currently run by Mrs Morrison. It too would feature in the mysterious death of Edwin Rose.

At Corrie there was no pier so passengers disembarked on a small tender to the Ferry Rock where a crowd usually gathered to watch proceedings. (One of the ferrymen, Angus Logan, would be among the search party who found Rose's body.) Transferring people this way could be a tricky procedure. A few years earlier a passenger and member of the crew both narrowly missed being drowned; there was a heavy swell at the time which made ferrying folk into the small rowing boat hazardous. As the *Ivanhoe* lurched, a Miss Campbell fell into the water, carrying the ship's mate, Mr Wooley, with her. They were both washed under the steamer but were eventually rescued with the assistance of the purser, Mr Fullarton, a strong swimmer who jumped into the sea to help.

Once they were all safely ashore at Corrie, William Thom led his three companions up the steps to Bluebell Cottage, Gilmour's holiday residence which was situated in an elevated position above the picturesque Corrie Port. Here they all had tea. We know the affable Rose made a good impression as he was invited back.

Robin Campbell wrote an account of the case, 'The Arran Murder of 1889', first published in the *Scottish Mountaineering Club Journal* (2001). In his article Campbell did some detective work to discover that the student Andrew Gilmour was the son of Dr Gilmour the first physician to examine Rose's body. At the start of his lengthy evidence at Laurie's trial, Dr Gilmour introduced himself as a man of substance: 'I have been in general practice as a physician and surgeon for thirty-eight years. I am a licentiate both of the Royal College of Physicians in Edinburgh and of the Faculty of Physicians and Surgeons in Glasgow. I am also a sergeant-major in the auxiliary forces and I have medical charge of the detachment of soldiers stationed at Blackness.' Robin Campbell summed him up: 'Gilmour was Provost and Sheriff of Linlithgow for 19 years, and Master of St Michael's Lodge – in a word, *King* of Linlithgow.'

Despite both Gilmours, father and son, being witnesses at the trial, there is little suggestion during the proceedings that they are connected. Both men would be privy to Mickel and Thom's poor opinion of Laurie, also expressed publicly in court, but a possible 'source of prejudice in the mind of the medical examiner'. Campbell's conclusion here is that everything was done to hide the fact that they 'had entertained a murderer and his victim to tea', public knowledge of which could have serious repercussions for them, socially and politically.

Mickel and Thom had hoped to find accommodation with a friend on Arran, possibly Gilmour, but this was unavailable. The two Linlithgow men were able, fortuitously, to spend the night on board a yacht in Brodick Bay which belonged to another friend, William Horton Smith from Hillhead in Glasgow's West End. During the weekend Smith also spent some time in the company of Rose and Laurie, which included a walk to Lamlash on the Sunday when he recalled: 'They appeared to be on friendly terms.'

Smith was something of an outdoorsman; he had enough experience of the Arran hills to provide Laurie with advice on the best routes, and also managed to acquire some gaiters for Rose. A few years later Smith would focus more on indoor pursuits. He was sent to prison for assaulting his brother-in-law by 'cutting him repeatedly on the face, head and neck with a razor'. Mickel and Thom seem to be continually let down by friends and acquaintances, especially when they resorted to the coarse weaponry of the Gorbals. At Laurie's trial both Mickel and Thom hoped to avoid any mention of Laurie's visit to Corrie. Francis Ord Mickel was also from a prominent Linlithgow family, timber merchants who went on to form the well-known building company Mactaggart and Mickel. Giving evidence in court, he recounted their activities after returning from Corrie: 'After putting our things away, Thom and I went a short walk, came back, had some refreshments and met 'Annandale' and Rose. Rose and the accused each had a bag. I saw them again on the Sunday. We were not a great deal in their company during the day. We walked across to Lamlash and they left us. We saw them at night, as they were returning from Glen Rosa.' Mickel and Thom managed to avoid all mention of the Gilmours until the close of Thom's cross-examination by the defence:

'Had you some friends named Gilmour at Corrie? 'Yes.'
'Did you ask the three gentlemen to visit them?' 'Yes.'
'And you all had tea there?' 'We had.'

On Arran, Laurie's modish garb was, as he had hoped, making him stand out from the crowd. He continued to wear his tweed knickerbocker suit and straw boater while 'a remarkably glaring style of hose attracted the attention of the natives, woven into a strongly pronounced check of brown and grey'.

What happened over the rest of Saturday and Sunday can be difficult to piece together. What information there is comes from courtroom witnesses like Mickel and Thom whom, as we have seen, had reason to be evasive. Other sources, like contemporary newspapers, are at times inconsistent. On Saturday evening some accounts have all four protagonists meeting up for drinks at the Douglas. Another version has Laurie and Rose invited to a party on the yacht with Rose attending and Laurie declining due to toothache.

For many the Glasgow Fair was a temporary release from long hours of often dreary and poorly-paid work. Like New Year it was a time when drunkenness was tolerated, if not accepted as the norm. In an era when pubs were the focal point of many men's lives, the holiday provided an excuse for further excess. However, drinking alcohol was often censored from written accounts. Drinks became refreshments, and bars like that in the Douglas Hotel were referred to as smoking-rooms or refreshment houses.

On the Sunday morning Rose breakfasted at Wooley's. He was not his usual chirpy self, complaining how the previous evening he had 'got among a drinking set'. He then caught up with his correspondence: a letter to the Reverend Goodman at the Glenburn and a postcard home to London:

Dear Frederick [a younger brother],
I shall return to London by train, arriving at St Pancras 8.40 on Thursday. All well. Do not write: time will not permit. This is a charming island.
Ned.

Around 11am Francis Mickel noticed Rose sitting on his own and joined him. Rose took this opportunity to open up to Mickel about some of his concerns. This discussion, among other things, was covered in an report entitled 'How Rose Met Laurie' first published in the London edition of the *New York Herald* and reprinted in several local papers. Rose is reported as saying the following to Mickel:

About 10 o'clock last night (Saturday) I ran along to the Douglas Hotel and got a small flask of brandy, as I don't like to stay in a strange house without having a little brandy at my bed. On arriving at the lodgings I found Laurie suffering from toothache, so I asked him to have a little to soothe his tooth. I handed the bottle to him, and he put the bottle to his mouth and then drank the whole of its contents. I felt very much disgusted at this and thought you were correct in your surmise yesterday.

Rose and Mickel were then joined by Laurie and Thom, along with William Horton Smith and a friend. All six walked over the hill to Lamlash. Rose and Laurie were pressed to stay for dinner, but opted to return to Brodick where they went for a walk up Glen Rosa. They considered continuing over The Saddle to Glen Sannox but decided against it due to lack of time. Some sources have them all together again on Sunday evening socialising with a game or two of billiards at the Douglas Hotel.

On the Monday morning Mickel again found Rose breakfasting at the tea room. Rose mentioned that he and Laurie intended climbing Goatfell that afternoon. Mickel claimed later that he advised Rose, who was dressed in light summer clothes, to change into something warmer as it might be cold on top. Laurie then reappeared and the three of them went for a sail in the bay, visiting Thom on his friend's yacht. They took Thom ashore and all of them, save Laurie, had lunch at Wooley's, Rose's last ever meal. As Mickel and Thom were returning to Rothesay that afternoon, Rose accompanied them to the pier where Laurie again joined them. Mickel was disconcerted by the constant disappearing and reappearing of Laurie. He had previously mentioned this to Rose, who replied: 'You have so often spoken about watching Annandale that I promise to be on my guard, and also not to climb the hill. I was asked to go to Corrie and spend the evening with Mr Gilmour, and would like to go, but Annandale wishes to go with me, and I do not desire his company.'

The source for the article 'How Rose Met Laurie' was presumably Francis Mickel as some of the information is not available elsewhere, and has to be attributable to Mickel as the only person privy to it. However, there is an inconsistency with some of Mickel's role in all this: he expresses misgivings about Laurie and tries to persuade Rose not to climb Goatfell, yet provides Rose with advice about what to wear when doing this. By the time of Mickel's testimony at the High Court any ambiguity has gone: 'I strongly advised the deceased to get rid of him as soon as possible, even if he had to leave his lodgings, and not to go up Goatfell.'

We know a lot about what Rose was wearing for the climb as an inventory was made at his post-mortem: tweed suit and cap, strong nailed boots, merino socks and underpants, linen shirt, knitted vest. Complemented by a waterproof and stout walking stick, this was textbook clothing for the Scottish hills, not some hastily improvised outfit, and proffers the argument that, far from being an enthusiastic novice, Rose already had some experience of hill-walking, and perhaps did not require the advice Mickel claims to have offered. Perhaps it was a shared interest in the hills that helped bring Laurie and Rose together on the *Ivanhoe*.

There were other events that weekend that got village tongues wagging, not an unusual occurrence on a Fair Weekend when drinking featured heavily. One old lady noticed Laurie pacing in the lane outside his room, 'talking to himself and looking very odd'. On its own this appears somewhat sinister, but put into the context of the flask of brandy incident makes more sense.

Over the weekend Mickel's antipathy towards Laurie deepened, describing him as 'very silent and uncommunicative'. He claimed that, despite some prompting, Laurie never provided any personal information and would often head off without explanation: 'On one or two occasions I tried by questions and hints to get Annandale to explain what he did and where he came from but he inevitably seemed to shirk enquiry on these points and he never gave an account of himself in my hearing.' So why did Mickel and Thom continue to tolerate him over the weekend? The answer is presumably loyalty to Rose whom Mickel especially seems to have bonded with.

After being on the run for so long John Laurie became something of a celebrity with newspapers eager to print anything they could discover about him. Interviewees recall him at times to be anxious, quiet, upset, even tearful, but nowhere are there references to him being sullen or anti-social. When he arrived back in Port Bannatyne after the trip to Arran, his landlady said: 'He was as pleasant and chatty and agreeable as before.' Even at his lowest points, for example after his capture and arrest, he was polite and affable. So what is the explanation for his out of character behaviour on Arran? There is an obvious one, that he was suffering from toothache, an ailment most people can identify with. Perhaps he was still miffed at Rose 'imposing on his good nature'. Perhaps he had not taken to Mickel and Thom. Perhaps darker thoughts were intruding.

Waiting until Mickel and Thom departed on the *Ivanhoe*, around 3.15pm, meant Laurie and Rose had a late start for climbing Goatfell. Rose only took some of Mickel's advice. When he set off with Laurie around Brodick Bay for the start of the path at Cladach, he had changed into a tweed tourist suit and matching cap. Around his calves, under the trousers, Rose had strapped 'a leather padding about 6-inches deep'. These were presumably the 'short leggings' or gaiters which William Horton Smith had obtained for him. John Laurie was wearing his favourite Melton overcoat and a tweed cap. Both men carried waterproofs and had sturdy walking sticks.

Arran was unusual in that it was one of few holiday destinations where the ascent of a mountain was promoted as one of the principal attractions. Tourist guidebooks presumed that a priority of any visitor would be an ascent of Goatfell and gave the mountain first billing over the island's other attractions. The Ordnance Survey had carried out their survey of the Arran hills in the 1860s. On their one-inch map the only paths marked in the mountain areas are the tourist route on Goatfell and those in Glen Sannox, and Glen Rosa. These latter paths do not meet in the middle. The longer path is that in Glen Sannox which peters out below the rise to The Saddle. The OS kept a series of Name Books where they recorded name derivations from local people, as well as noting relevant topographical information. Here is what the book had to say about Goatfell:

A mountain whose summit 2875ft above sea level is the highest point of the Island of Arran. Like the hills in its vicinity it is composed of granite, and many cliffs stand out boldly on all sides of it. It is, especially to the south, covered with an enormous quantity of granite boulders. The older people speak the name as near as it can be taken down as Gaotsh- ven, which they consider to be equivalent to Windy Mountain (Gaothach Bheinn). In all probability Goat has been derived from Gaothach; and Fell from the Norse language. Fell, as signifying a high hill, is common on the Cheviot range, as also some other parts of the south of Scotland. Scott when alluding to Goat Fell in the *Lord of the Isles* calls it 'Ben-Ghoil, the mountain of the wind'; this is evidently a contraction from all three words, Beinn Gaothach Fhell. The name is now however universally known as Goat Fell.

One of the most popular guidebook writers of the time was the estimable M J B Baddeley, a classics master whose name became well-known throughout Britain for his series of 'Through Guides'. A keen mountaineer and a founder member of the Climbers' Club, he was one of few guidebook writers to personally check out the information in his guides. Baddeley recommended an excursion that took the visitor up the tourist path on Goatfell then down into Glen Sannox by way of The Saddle. This was most likely the route Laurie and Rose intended to follow. Here is Baddeley's description for the first part of the route: to the summit of Goatfell starting through the castle grounds:

Pass through the gate on the left, and proceed up the drive which leads up to Brodick Castle, the seat of the Duke of Hamilton. This drive shortly enters a shrubbery, and turning sharp to the right crosses the Cnocan Burn beyond which pass through an iron gate on the left, and ascend the broad walk between firs and rhododendrons. Where this walk bends to the right take a rough path to the left which soon emerges on to the open moor. Hence to the top of the eastern ridge of Goat Fell the track cannot be mistaken. It keeps the Cnochan Burn on the left all the way, and in about a mile crosses a smaller burn, which forms a good resting place. At the top of the ridge the path from Corrie is joined, and hence the route to the summit of the mountain is over rough granite boulders, and in places steep, though nowhere difficult. When the boulders appear insuperable in front 'fetch a compass' slightly to the left.

Laurie and Rose reached the start of the path about 4pm

and continued up through the woods of the Castle grounds. Near here they passed Mrs Walker's brother and brother-in-law who were on their way down from Goatfell. The pair were over from Glasgow for the holiday weekend and knew the lodgers by sight. They later commented that Laurie and Rose were going at a fair pace. The path soon rises through woodland, part of a designed landscape created by the 10th Duke around 1820 when he introduced several non-native (to Arran) species including Scots pine, beech and silver fir.

After the pine forest the path continues through more open birch wood. Further on the trees are left behind and the route follows the Cnocan Burn as the view gradually expands to include the tops of Beinn Nuis and Beinn Tarsuinn, and eventually the final cone of Goatfell. Continuing onto the open heather moorland Laurie and Rose caught up with a party of three on holiday in Lamlash: the Reverend Robert Hind, a minister in Paisley, the Reverend Joseph Ritson, a minister in Motherwell and John McCabe, the headmaster of Townhead School in Hamilton. The two clergymen were leading lights in the Primitive Methodist movement which broke away from the main church in order to practise a simpler form of Christianity. They had taken the steamer from Lamlash with the intention of visiting Glen Sannox, but no conveyance was available in Brodick so they opted for an ascent of Goatfell instead.

They all fell in with each other for the next half an hour or so with Rose chatting freely, for example asking if Rothesay could be seen from the summit. Laurie kept aloof, several paces ahead, not contributing to the conversation. Rose informed McCabe that his dour companion was 'his guide'. With the onset of a heavy shower, the Reverend Hind's party sheltered behind some boulders while the other two put on their waterproofs and pressed on. Rose's waterproof was new, often described as 'glazed' or shiny, and was reversible, black on the outside, white inside.

The Reverend Hind also mentions being passed on Goatfell by someone trying to beat the record, 'He was going at a tremendous rate for the top.' The competitive Victorians had reduced the ascent of Goatfell to something of a time-trial, attempting to complete it in under two hours (the 11th Duke reputedly ascended it in 55 minutes).

With the establishment of the Corrie Hotel it also became popular to ascend Goatfell from the historic clachan of High Corrie where a path followed the Corrie Burn, known locally as the 'White Water Glen' due to its many waterfalls. The path continued directly up through Coire Lan to join the summit ridge north of North Goatfell (the latter name was not yet in use). From Coire Lan another path branched off south to gain Goatfell's east shoulder where it met the main path coming up from Brodick. These footpaths could be used in combination to create a circular route.

Laurie and Rose eventually gained the shoulder of Goatfell where a cairn marked the junction with the path coming up the 'White Water Ridge' from Corrie. They were now able to look down into Coire Lan where they could see the other path from Corrie headed directly up to the lowest point of the mainridge. After a brief stop to get their bearings, and admire the fine view back to the Holy Isle, they turned to begin the final pull up to Goatfell's summit. This is the steepest part of the walk where the going is much rougher, between and over granite boulders. Mounting the final rocky rise Laurie and Rose came across Edward Francis, a hatter from London; he had been unable to keep up with his electrician brother Frederick who had forged ahead in his enthusiasm to take some summit photographs. For the last section all three climbed in single file: Rose in the middle, Edward Francis last. These two chatted for a while about photography. Laurie said nothing. They all soon reached the top, described by Baddeley in his guidebook:

> The summit of Goat Fell consists of a confused group of these boulders, whose perpendicular sides enable the climber to find shelter from every wind that blows. The broad belt of sea which surrounds the island gives an extent and variety to the prospect which few mountains in Scotland can boast of. Only on the western side, where the jagged ridges on the other side of Glen Rosa rise to an equal height, is the view curtailed.

The view from the summit of Goatfell was justifiably renowned. On a good day it extended to Cumbria, Northern Ireland and the Isle of Man; the most prominent features were often the Paps of Jura, Ben Cruachan, Ben Lomond, the Cumbraes and Ailsa Craig. Many of the Victorian writers who scaled Goatfell tried to outdo each other with prolix descriptions of the wide-ranging vista. John Laurie would have been aware of the Glasgow journalist Hugh Macdonald, a writer of outdoor articles in local newspapers such as the *Glasgow Citizen*, which were later compiled into bestselling books like *Days at the Coast*. Here is Macdonald's melodramatic take on the prospect from Arran's highest peak:

> In the immediate vicinity of Goatfell there is indeed a terrible congregation of jagged mountain ridges and fantastic peaks with tremendous yawning glens and shadowy corries the vast sides of which are streaked in the strangest manner with a confusion of watercourses and gullies. Everything is bleak, bare and barren in the extreme. On the arid rocks and precipices vegetation has taken but a comparatively slight hold so that one could almost imagine that the volcano and the earthquake had been here at their awful work at a comparatively recent period.

On the summit Frederick Francis was busy trying to capture the scene with his camera when, around 6pm, he noticed his brother arrive along with two others; they all talked for a while, discussing the view and what could be seen. Frederick Francis later recalled: 'One of them looking down the glen back from Brodick remarked it looked like hell. I have an impression Rose asked how long it would take to go down that way but I can't be sure. They were pointing down a little to the right of the glen just spoken of. One of the two seemingly showing the direction. This was in almost a straight line back from Ailsa Craig. I thought the way they were pointing seemed a very dangerous place... Rose and his companion could not be more than 5 or 6 minutes on the top.' His brother Edward recollected, 'I understand from what I heard the first say that he had ascended before and that Rose had not.'

Laurie and Rose did not intend to descend the way they had come, as was the norm, but hoped to take one of the other routes off the mountain. We have no exact record of what they planned to do, but whatever option they chose they would first have to tackle the rocky Stacach ridge between Goatfell and North Goatfell. Standing on one of the large granite boulders, Laurie pointed out to Rose some of the landmarks to the south, then, swivelling round, other places of interest and the way they would now head. Frederick Francis got the impression that the two men were on good terms, happily conversing with each other. Just as Laurie and Rose were about to set off, the Reverend Hind arrived at the summit. He would recall, 'I saw the young men on the farther edge of the summit of the fell from the point where we reached the top.' It was the last sighting of Edwin Rose alive.

Chapter Four

Suspicious Disappearance of English Tourist

Late that Monday evening, between 9pm and 9.30pm, David McKenzie, a shepherd from High Corrie, was near the burial ground in Glen Sannox when he noticed a man come down the glen and take a short cut across a field towards Corrie. He described him as 'awful tired and worn out like, and that he appeared to have had a heavy day's travelling on the hills'. In court McKenzie identified Laurie as the man he had seen. The shepherd had been out for an evening stroll with two young women to whom he mentioned the incident. The women were called as witnesses for the defence and discredited McKenzie's statement by denying having ever heard any such remarks.

By the time Laurie arrived at the Corrie Hotel he thought he might be too late to get a drink as the closing time for the serving of alcohol in rural pubs had recently (1887) been changed to 10pm. He asked a customer getting served at the bar window, James Wilson, a Greenock law clerk whom he presumed to be a guest, to purchase a bottle of beer on his behalf as he had the six miles to walk to Brodick. Wilson duly obliged, and then chatted with Laurie for a short time before going into the smoking-room. He recalled that the man 'did not seem excited or fatigued but cool and composed'.

Laurie drank his beer near the bar window, not entering the smoking-room as was the custom. Before leaving the hotel he bought some spirits to take with him. In his short chat with Wilson, Laurie discovered he was not in fact a hotel resident, but was in a party camping near the Corrie Burn about a mile south of the hotel. Laurie later used this information as part of an alibi when he claimed that he parted from Rose on Goatfell's summit ridge then descended to Corrie where he visited the hotel and met 'several of the gentlemen who were camping out'. (This reveals more of Laurie's knowledge of Goatfell: that he is aware of the alternative route up the mountain from Corrie.) Later that night there was a sighting of a furtive figure near the Brodick Castle woods around midnight. In retrospect many thought this must have been Laurie as the timing fitted his movements.

Laurie intended to be on the first ferry off the island in the morning. He had time for several hours sleep before the *Scotia* sailed for Ardrossan at 7am. In the morning he took Rose's Gladstone bag and most of his things, but left some odds and ends including the tennis racket and his own straw hat. On the way to the pier he was seen carrying two bags, 'one dark, one a sort of yellow'. On the steamer Laurie got a shock. Who was on board but Andrew Gilmour, the medical student he had met at Corrie on the Saturday. Gilmour noticed that Laurie needed a shave: 'He looked as if he had not been in bed the previous night. His dress however was in perfect order. He was very quiet and reserved and said little.' At Ardrossan Harbour he helped Laurie with his luggage and both shared a train compartment to Glasgow where they parted company. (In the trial transcript it is recorded that they leave each other at Greenock but this is most likely a mistake as it was not on the direct route to Glasgow).

In Glasgow Laurie is recorded as visiting 'a gentleman in West Nile Street'. This may be a euphemism as to where he pawned Rose's bag and some of his possessions. The black Gladstone bag was recovered by police from a pawn shop three weeks later. According to a report in the *Glasgow Herald* (13 August) Laurie arrived at his lodgings in North Frederick Street about 11am and stayed about two hours. Mrs King was away 'at the coast' for most of July leaving her elderly domestic help, Jane McLellan, to look after the house. Laurie asked her to wash a tennis suit which was smeared all up the front with mud. He wanted to take it back to Rothesay with him even if it wasn't dry.

So what happened to the tennis suit, and its occupant? The Glasgow Fair 'drinking set'? Any Sherlock Holmes worth their salt would have found this of interest but the detail was never pursued. McLellan claimed in her precognition statement that the same day she saw a gold watch and chain in Laurie's room. If this was Rose's watch it was the only time it was seen in Laurie's possession, important evidence which would help place him at the scene of the crime. There was, however, no reference to this at the trial.

Mrs Currie, the Port Bannatyne landlady, recalled how later the same day Laurie arrived back at Iona Place wearing a grey felt hat, instead of the straw hat he left in, and carrying a small parcel which she later discovered contained a white serge cap and a chocolate-striped tennis jacket: 'In these adornments he arrayed himself during the remainder of his stay.'

Back in Brodick, Mrs Walker had not seen or heard her tenants return from Goatfell. But this was not unusual as their accommodation had its own entrance. (The location of the outhouse was near the rear of the present-day Brodick Bar but was recently demolished). Reckoning they would be tired after their exertions, she let them lie in till 11am before knocking on the door. With no answer she looked in to see an empty room save for a straw hat, a pair of slippers and a tennis racquet (which had Rose's initials on it). For tenants to nip away early without paying the bill was not uncommon, an occupational hazard for all seaside landladies. Mrs Walker didn't even bother reporting it to the police.

The Reverend Gustavus Goodman was still at the Glenburn Hydropathic. On Tuesday, the day Laurie returned to Port Bannatyne, Goodman received the letter Rose had written him from Wooley's in Brodick. It said that he would be back at the Glenburn on Wednesday to collect any mail and to say goodbye. When Rose did not appear the next day the Reverend Goodman was not overly concerned as Rose had already paid his bill and had all his belongings with him. He presumed he had headed directly for London as time was short. (Rose had planned to break his journey south at Leeds to meet a friend, Miss Spencer.)

Edwin Rose was due home in London on Thursday 18 July. This was an inauspicious day when London would be buzzing with news of another Whitechapel murder, Alice McKenzie in Castle Alley, what many regard as Jack the Ripper's last killing. The streets were filled with the hoarse cries of newsboys: 'Murder! Murder! Another murder in Whitechapel! 'Orrible details! One penny!'

Edwin's brother Frederick had arranged to meet him at Wandsworth Common Station. When he did not turn up the family became alarmed and discussed what to do. Was Ned just late or had something more serious occurred? They hoped it was the former but with still no sign of him by Saturday they decided to telegram the Reverend Goodman at the Glenburn but it was too late in the day to do so. They would have to wait till the telegram offices reopened on Monday morning.

As the Rose family were anxiously discussing what to do, John Laurie was gallivanting around Bute wearing Ned's clothes. He had especially taken a fancy to the chocolate and white striped tennis jacket. Many described Laurie as 'a masher', a dandy who paraded in order to attract attention. If we piece together the sightings of Laurie recorded in newspaper articles, as well as testimony in court, he was spotted wearing Rose's clothing on almost every day for the remaining week of his holiday.

On his first evening back at Port Bannatyne he visited Rothesay and called at the Park sisters. They noticed he was wearing a grey felt hat they hadn't seen before, which Laurie claimed he had won in a bet. They all went out for a walk and Jeanie recalled Laurie speaking about his trip to Arran: he had had a good time and climbed Goatfell but his friend was very slow so he had not enjoyed the walk as much as he might have done. Laurie was later spotted by two men from Coatbridge on Rothesay esplanade, 'promenading two young ladies'. The next evening he was observed by the same men 'swaggering along esplanade in tennis suit'. On a couple of days he was recognised in Port Bannatyne wearing the same raffish outfit.

On Wednesday 17 July Laurie had arranged to meet Grace Chalmers in Dunoon. She was accompanied by a friend, Elizabeth Rennie who worked in a Coatbridge bakery. Chalmers related that he arrived dressed in a tennis suit – white flannel trousers and striped jacket: 'Laurie spent the day in our company walking in Dunoon and he saw me off with the boat which leaves Dunoon at 6.50pm.'

Two days later Laurie called at the Park sisters to ask if he could leave his waterproof to save him taking it to Port Bannatyne (he had an ulterior motive for this). He would collect it the next day, the last of his holiday, prior to catching the steamer. Laurie then joined the sisters to see their brother off at the pier. Jeannie would later recall: 'He was then wearing a white yachting cap. I had never seen him with such a cap before that day.' She went on to comment, 'I did not observe any excitement or nervousness about Laurie at any time.' That evening James Aitken spotted Laurie and noticed that the serge yachting cap was very similar to the one he had seen Rose wearing.

To bring attention to yourself in this way, in these circumstances, verges on mental aberration or a desire to be caught. Although Rothesay was an extremely busy place, especially during the Glasgow Fair, it was still a small town. The Reverend Goodman and other friends of Rose from the Glenburn were still around, and would instantly recognise the distinctive apparel as belonging to their friend.

The next day Laurie asked Mrs Currie to have his bill and dinner ready for 1pm as he had to leave sharp. He then went out for a morning stroll and never returned. A still disgruntled Mrs Currie was a witness at the trial: 'I never saw him after he went out in the morning. The amount of his bill was £3 3s. 8d., and it remains unpaid.'

On his way to the pier Laurie called in at the Park sisters to collect his waterproof and say goodbye. He then bumped into the ubiquitous Aitken with whom he had a 15-minute conversation. Aitken would later recall: 'I asked him how he had got on at Arran, he said, 'Very well, that he had met in with a jolly lot of fellows.' So far as I can recollect no mention of Rose's name was made. I did not observe any difference in Laurie's appearance or demeanour during the times I saw him at Rothesay this year. It did occur to me that he was quieter this year and not so jolly as he was.'

Laurie left for Glasgow on the *Caledonia*. We know this because as the vessel was turning in Rothesay Bay it ran down a small boat. There was an appeal for witnesses and one passenger duly stepped forward to give his card, naming him as 'John Annandale' of 106 North Frederick Street. This reveals that Laurie had more than one version of card, as the 'Annandale' card he presented to Mrs Currie in Port Bannatyne had Cambridge Street on it. The *Caledonia* incident only came to light some time later when an official visited North Frederick Street to take a statement.

After arriving back at his lodgings in Glasgow, Laurie unpacked before heading for Coatbridge to visit Grace Chalmers, returning on the 10pm train. The next day, Monday 22 July, he resumed work at Springburn. That same morning, at 8.10am, the now distraught Rose family finally managed to telegram the Reverend Goodman. The message read:

> EDWIN ROSE WROTE FROM ARRAN MONDAY THAT HE WOULD REACH LONDON ON THURSDAY – HAS NOT ARRIVED – SEND ANY INFORMATION OBTAINABLE.
> ROSE WISSET LODGE HENDHAM ROAD

The Reverend Goodman immediately replied that Edwin had planned to leave Rothesay on Wednesday 17 July but had not done so. Alarmed by the news Goodman then left for Brodick on the *Ivanhoe* and made enquires at Wooley's and Mrs Walker's. He discovered that the pair had vanished without paying their bill. Mrs Walker related how they intended to climb Goatfell and she assumed they had arrived back late. She showed Goodman the tennis racquet initialled 'ERR' and the other items that had been left behind. When the Reverend Goodman found out that no-one had seen Rose return from Goatfell, he enquired at the Brodick police station whether they knew anything about his whereabouts. He was advised that the pair were probably 'off on a spree': 'wait and if there is still nothing heard of them, advertise.' He related this back to the Rose family who responded with this telegram:

> THANKS TELEGRAM – DID ROSE LEAVE PORTMANTEAU? NO INFORMATION FEAR SOMETHING SERIOUS HAS OCCURRED – KINDLY SEND BRODICK AND INFORM POLICE – ANXIOUSLY AWAITING – ROSE.

On Tuesday (23 July) the Reverend Goodman had a meeting in Rothesay with John Mackay, the chief constable of Buteshire, to discuss the situation. Mackay suggested a push may have been given and that Rose's body might be lying at the foot of some precipice. Goodman's theory was that Rose may have been drugged, his pockets rifled, and, in coming to, had a fatal fall. He was unwilling to countenance that there had been any deliberate attempt to harm him.

Two days later William Munro, the sergeant at Lamlash, and Arran's most senior police officer, received a telegram from his chief constable alerting him of the missing person and arranging a meeting that day in Brodick. It was decided to organise parties to scour Goatfell starting on Sunday 28 July. This was the most suitable day for large-scale searches as few people were working and the maximum number of volunteers could be mustered.

With a growing realisation that something was seriously wrong, there was a need to find out what everyone knew and get to the bottom of things. Goodman telegrammed Edwin's brother, Benjamin, to inform him of developments, especially the proposed search that Sunday. In the meantime Francis Mickel had also been in touch with Benjamin. The latter then asked Goodman to contact Mickel at his company's offices in Glasgow's Waterloo Street. Later on the Friday, Goodman duly travelled from Rothesay to Glasgow to meet Mickel who told him what he knew and how he had warned Rose that Laurie 'was not a clean potato'. Mickel added that he always felt there was something suspicious about the man he knew as 'Annandale': on the Friday evening at the Glenburn he noticed how all the ladies in the recreation room declined to dance with him.

Mickel went on to tell Goodman how, when he learnt of Edwin's disappearance, he informed Superintendent John Ord of the Glasgow Police of what he knew about the missing person and his suspicions regarding Laurie. In all Mickel spent a week helping the police, making a statement that corroborated much of what was in the article 'How Rose Met Laurie'. However there were some discrepancies: in the police statement he mentions that Rose told him Laurie drank his brandy '*under pretence* of having toothache.' Mickel told police how he warned Rose four times about Laurie, entreated him not to climb Goatfell in his company: 'While changing clothes the mist came down on the hill which had been clear before and when Rose rejoined us I advised him not to attempt the ascent while the mist hung on the hill.'

Benjamin Rose, a tall bearded man, decided to head north to Scotland to see for himself what progress was being made with regard to his missing brother, and to assist with the search of Goatfell. Before he left he telegrammed Goodman to inform him of his travel plans:

MICKEL WRITES FROM BO'NESS – WARNED EDWIN AGAINST ANNANDALE – STEAM MIDLAND EIGHT TWENTY – TONIGHT ROTHESAY – ON ROAD BRODICK THIS SATURDAY – PLEASE MEET ME AT PIER.

Benjamin Rose travelled north on the overnight train from London. After arriving at Glasgow on Saturday morning he went directly to Rothesay where he met Reverend Goodman and heard what Mickel had told him. But Benjamin's main priority was to see the chief constable and establish what progress had been made in finding his missing brother. Once they got together, the pair decided to travel to Brodick that day and talk over the situation with Sergeant Munro. As Benjamin Rose and John Mackay awaited the arrival of their steamer on Rothesay pier, it is possible one of the passengers disembarking was John Laurie who had decided to return to Bute for the day, when he would again meet James Aitken.

Benjamin had brought with him photographs of his brother which were used when making enquiries about Edwin's whereabouts. At Brodick these pictures were placed in shop windows and other locations with a request for any information or sightings. Like any close community there were all sorts of rumours as to what happened to the missing tourist, and where he was.

During the week prior to Benjamin's arrival in Scotland, one of the Davidson brothers from Glen Rosa was on Goatfell with his dogs checking the sheep. At one point the dogs dashed to a large boulder which they started to circle, barking furiously. Davidson, thinking they were chasing a rabbit, whistled them back. Had he investigated more closely, the mystery of Edwin Rose might have been solved sooner.

On the morning of Sunday 21 July, there was a large turnout for the search but it was so wet and misty it was difficult to see more than a few yards. Further small-scale search parties were planned for during the week, including an investigation of the Merkland

Wood, a mile north of the castle. If these were unsuccessful the whole of Goatfell would be combed the following weekend on Sunday 4 August. All this activity was picked up by the press. On Monday 29 July the *Glasgow Evening Citizen* reported:

AN ARRAN MYSTERY
SUSPICIOUS DISAPPEARANCE OF AN ENGLISH TOURIST
AN ACCIDENT OR A CRIME?

What has become of the young man Rose is shrouded in mystery. He has not returned to his friends in England, and there is a growing suspicion that he never left the island. Alarmed at his long absence, a brother reached Arran on Saturday, and has been making an anxious search.

In his first week back at work John Laurie enthused to his workmates about his holiday; he mentioned (black humour alert) that 'he had been up Goatfell on the Monday with his friend, and that he had left him in Arran where he was spending some time'. He told an apprentice that he had obtained the return half of a train ticket to London which he intended to use at the forthcoming New Year's holiday. Once he realised, through the newspapers, that serious efforts were being made to find Rose, Laurie's mood changed. After starting work at 6am there was a stop for breakfast at 9am when newspapers went on sale at the factory gates. That Tuesday there was more about 'Missing English Tourist' and by Wednesday they had linked Rose to the mysterious 'Annandale'. Plans were announced that a large search party was being organised to scour Goatfell. Laurie became increasingly alarmed. Fellow workers noticed how anxious he was to buy a paper and how intently he studied it.

It was on Wednesday 31 July that everything changed. After Laurie started work that morning he surprised a workmate by telling him he was going to leave that day, explaining that he was tired of Springburn and had got a job with another engineering firm. At 9am he called at the office for several days wages due to him, saying he had a new position as a traveller in the grain trade based in Leith. He left soon after but said he would return for his tool-box, which he did about 2pm.

Once Laurie left the employ of Sharp, Stewart and Co, he wandered back into the city centre wondering what to do next. Meanwhile, about 12.30pm, James Aitken was standing outside his office in Hope Street, near the Glasgow Corn Exchange, talking to one of his customers about 'the strange disappearance of Rose'. Who happens to walk by but John Laurie. Aitken proceeded to challenge Laurie about the missing Rose: 'Was not that the name of the man you said you had intended to go to Brodick with?' Aitken also questioned him about the yachting cap he was wearing on the Friday night in Rothesay, and tells Laurie if he does not provide information to the police he will go himself. According to Aitken, Laurie denied any involvement, made his excuses and left.

When Laurie eventually arrived back at his lodgings in North Frederick Street those there reported: 'This was the day when he sat at the window and was observed to be in an extremely depressed condition.' At 4pm a witness placed Laurie with another man in the Saltmarket where he sold his working tools for 25 shillings. He gave his name and address as John Laurie, 268 Bath Street. Back at North Frederick Street he packed his belongings into his black trunk, explaining that he had a new job in Leith, and left hurriedly in a cab at 7pm. The police later tried unsuccessfully to trace the cabman. The next evening, between 11pm and midnight, Laurie returned surreptitiously to his lodgings to collect a letter from Grace Chalmers which he was in the habit of receiving on a Thursday. Two days later Mrs King opened a letter, post-marked Hamilton, to find a message written in pencil on a narrow strip of ruled paper:

> Dear Madam,
> I beg to enclose POO [Post Office Order] for my rent as I can't call for I have to go to Leith. There are some people trying to get me into trouble and I think you should give them no information at all, and I will prove to them how they are mistaken before very long,
> Yours respectfully,
> John Laurie

The Saturday that Ellen King received her unpaid rent, Laurie arranged with Grace Chalmers to have a day out together. After being pestered for several weeks, she finally agreed to accompany him on an excursion to the Falls of Clyde. They met up at Glasgow's Central Station where Laurie would doubtless have greeted her with the requisite box of chocolates or pair of gloves. An incurable romantic, he was undoubtedly in love with Grace but this would be their last recorded time together, Laurie's last day of real freedom, certainly his last taste of happiness.

They would spend the day on a popular excursion run by the Caledonian Railway. With the expansion of their network through the coalfields of Lanarkshire the company were now keen to attract passenger traffic, and in July 1877 inaugurated a tour which could be undertaken from either Glasgow or Edinburgh. It first visited Lanark to see the famous falls before returning to the starting point by way of Craignethan Castle, made famous by Sir Walter Scott. *Black's Guide to Scotland* provided further details:

A circular tour is run daily from both cities by Lanark to the Falls, returning by Crossford, 6 miles. From Lanark, to Tillietudlem Station, the distance from Lanark to Crossford (Inn) being covered by coach, and from Crossford to Tillietudem Station (2 miles) on foot. Half-a-mile short of the latter are the interesting and picturesque ruins of Craignethan Castle above the left bank of the Nethan Water, in the midst of beautiful and romantic scenery (Queen Mary is said to have resided here before the Battle of Langside in 1568).

Laurie's choice of destination was one which had emotional significance. This part of Lanarkshire resonated with him because his father was from farming stock around the nearby village of Stonehouse, an area which held happy memories of carefree childhood holidays. It was near here, to an uncle's farm, that he was sent to convalesce after the trauma of his mother's death.

After meeting in Glasgow, the couple caught the 2.30pm train for Lanark. When Chalmers was later interviewed she related how, not long after the train started, Laurie revealed that this would probably be the last time they would see each other. He also said he had left his job. When she enquired about this he made some excuses and started to cry. Later he composed himself, cheered up, and eventually they both enjoyed their day out. At Lanark they had a meal at the Clydesdale Hotel where they also danced in the ballroom.

The Clydesdale was a historic Georgian coaching inn, 'perhaps the most spacious and elegant country inn in Scotland'. Previous guests of the inn included William and Dorothy Wordsworth, and Charles Dickens. They were also in Lanark to view the nearby Falls of Clyde, one of the first picturesque attractions to be celebrated when Scottish tourism took off in the late eighteenth century. The two waterfalls above New Lanark, Corra Linn and Bonnington Linn, were also visited, and painted, by artists of note including Paul Sandby, Jacob More and J M W Turner.

The Falls of Clyde were the next stop on the Caledonian itinerary but now there were restrictions on access to the waterfalls, 'In consequence of the improper conduct of parties arriving by cheap trains'. You were only permitted to view them at particular points for which a charge was made. The tight-fisted Laurie was pleased to discover that the ticket price was included in the excursion fare.

Once they had viewed the falls the tour party boarded a coach to take them along the Clyde Valley to Crossford. After refreshments at the inn, a scenic walk through the Nethan Gorge (sometimes called Craignethan Glen) brought them to the final attraction, the renowned Craignethan Castle, visited by Walter Scott in 1799 and painted by Turner two years later. A contemporary tourist guidebook provided the following details of the approach to this attraction:

At some parts of the glen through which the Nethan flows, precipitous crags of rugged sandstone tower to a height of hundreds of feet above the stream, while at other places the steeps are clothed with luxuriant foliage. A rustic bridge thrown across the water adds its charm to the way, and then a narrow path overhanging the river has to be taken so thickly studded with overarching boughs that here and there they threaten to intercept further progress. The serpentine windings of the valley combined with the sylvan character of the scenery, prevent (except at certain points) a glimpse of the castle, and not till the openness of the more exalted ground is reached is the eye gratified by a sight of the far-famed Tillietudlem.

Tillietudlem was the name of a fictional castle in Walter Scott's popular novel *Old Mortality*. He set the story in South Lanarkshire, attracting tourists to what was widely regarded as its inspiration, Craignethan Castle, which was consequently often referred to as Tillietudlem. The title gained more authority when, in 1876, the Caledonian Railway added Tillietudlem Station to the nearby Coalburn branch line.

After enjoying the walk through the gorge the young couple had time to explore the remains of the castle before catching their return train. When Laurie learnt the castle was built around 1530 by Sir James Hamilton, illegitimate son of the first Earl of Arran, he would be jolted out of romantic reverie back to the events of the last few weeks. Significantly, they would soon pass through Ferniegair Station.

When they arrived in Coatbridge, Laurie walked Grace to her home in the nearby Caledonian Buildings which they reached about 11pm. He was now too late for the Glasgow train and tells her he is going to stay the night with a friend, Mr Johnston, a spirit merchant who lived in nearby Langloan. Johnston later related how Laurie arrived at his house around midnight in good humour. His visitor had with him a small bottle of brandy and Johnstone remembered how Laurie drank it on Sunday morning. With events unfolding later in the day he would need it. Laurie then thanked his host and left on the 9.30am train for Glasgow. He was spotted on the platform by Grace whose house overlooked the station. While she and Laurie were enjoying their day out in the Clyde Valley the following sign was pinned up outside Brodick police station:

NOTICE: THE MISSING TOURIST

A volunteer search party will assemble at the Kennels, Brodick on Sunday morning at nine o'clock. It is hoped that all who take an interest in this humane work will endeavour to aid the police in their search for Mr Rose.

By order of the police, Brodick 3 August 1889.

Chapter Five

Furiously Wielded by Strong Hands

On Sunday morning over two hundred volunteers answered the call to search Goatfell for the body of Edwin Rose. The plan was to have four large groups starting at different points around the mountain and all converge near the top. One group of fifty, under James Douglas and Alexander Kerr, a local shepherd, set off up Glen Sannox. At the Brodick end over 150 people congregated at 9am near the kennels of Brodick Castle. This group would divide into three parties. The first, led by Sergeant Munro and John Dewar, the Brodick Castle gamekeeper, would sweep both sides of Goatfell's east ridge including Maol Donn. The second party, under James Crawford and Constable Munro of Brodick, would spread out and examine Goatfell's south ridge and the corries on either side. The last group, led by Robert and Peter Davidson, two brothers who lived in Glen Rosa, would search the steep slopes above Glen Shant and Glen Rosa, including the Shant Rocks.

Although the weather looked more promising than the Sunday previous, all parties were initially hampered by morning mist but this gradually cleared. Some of the groups met up with Sergeant Munro's party on the summit. They then moved along to North Goatfell with the intention of examining either side of the ridge descending to The Saddle. With still no trace of Rose many of the searchers congregated on the col to exchange information and have a last look through telescopes before heading home. The Glen Sannox party had searched the north side of the glen and on their way back took in the slopes on the other side. It wasn't long till a shout went up, 'He's here!' Rose's body was found around 2.15pm under a boulder in Coire nam Fuaran, near the head of Glen Sannox at a height of about 1500ft (457m). The 'Arran Mystery' had become the 'Arran Tragedy'.

One of the search party, Francis Logan a Corrie fisherman, had become aware of 'an offensive odour' which he traced to a large boulder above him: 'When I went up, I found there was a dyke built in front of the boulder so as to close up the opening.

Behind this dyke the whole body with the exception of an arm was hidden.' There were also a number of stones on top of the corpse. (For his part in locating the body Logan was later presented by the family with a framed photograph of Rose.)

Further shouts attracted more people. The first policeman to arrive on the scene was Constable Alexander Stewart, closely followed by Sergeant Munro who took control of the situation: he authorised the removal of the stones and sent two local men to alert Dr Gilmour in Corrie. No-one was to move the body until the doctor arrived. After leaving three constables to guard what was now a possible murder scene, Munro himself set off to organise a wooden box for transporting the corpse. By now the clamour had attracted a large crowd. Among them, poignantly, was Benjamin Rose who broke down upon hearing the news. He was eventually able to identify the body as that of his brother.

As they waited for the arrival of the doctor the others looked around to see what else they could find. Alexander Kerr, who was near Logan when the body was discovered, spotted a walking stick in the heather, 'lying head downwards as if dropped', and part of a waterproof in a nearby stream. The upper part of the garment was still on the body. To those at the scene the fact that the waterproof was split in two suggested either there had been a struggle or the body had been dragged along the ground, or possibly both.

A nearby watercourse roughly followed the line of their probable descent route and others searched for evidence higher up the gully. Archibald Young, a Corrie fisherman, came across a knife and a button. Near the knife Angus Logan, a local quarryman, found a pencil. A little higher Logan also discovered one of the most intriguing finds, a tweed cap which had been folded in four and covered with a large stone so that only the peak could be seen. The cap was found at the foot of what became known as the 19-foot drop, one of two short cliffs that would become of keen forensic interest to those examining the 'did he fall or was he pushed?' question. The other rock feature was the 32-foot drop, below and on the other side of the stream, just above where the pencil, knife and button were found. The solemn folding and placement of the cap is suggestive of an act of contrition which supports the argument that Rose died at this spot, the foot of the 19-foot drop.

When Sergeant Munro reached the foot of Glen Sannox, he instructed Alexander McKillop, a local joiner, to quickly construct a suitable receptacle in which to carry the corpse off the hill. Munro then told the news to Dr Gilmour in Corrie, and also made sure that Dr Fullarton, the Lamlash GP, was contacted. It would be 8pm when Dr Gilmour arrived at the scene. With the assistance of one of the constables he lifted the body from under the boulder and laid it down outside. If Gilmour recognised the cadaver as one of the young men who visited his holiday cottage in Corrie three weeks earlier, and had tea with his son, he did not let on.

Gilmour examined Rose's body, making notes on the spot. It had been found face down with the skirt of the jacket drawn carefully over the head. One pocket was turned out. All the pockets were searched but found to be empty. A great deal of the flesh had been eaten by animals. The skull was in eight or nine pieces with the face smashed beyond recognition. In his report Dr Gilmour wrote:'The bones of the left side and top of the head were all fractured and portions of them lying inside the skull or brain cavity, which was empty of brain matter. All it contained was a heap of maggots and pieces of fractured skull bones, which appeared to have been crushed in on the brain.'

From the moment Rose's body was found rumours started to fly: Rose had died in a fall, or if not, was badly injured and Laurie had finished him off and robbed him. Others thought he had been pushed. Benjamin Rose later stated: 'The opinion I formed from seeing the remains is that my brother was first drugged near the place where he was found and then carried into the cavity.' William Munro: 'My opinion is the deed was committed higher up the hill than the boulder, about 100yds or so, where the cap was found; from that place the body was carried or dragged or probably both to the cavity.'

Around 9pm the mortal remains of Edwin Rose were placed in the deal box that had been sent up, and then carried down to Corrie by eight volunteers taking shifts. This task was completed in four hours, a fast time considering the rough terrain, and that much of it was undertaken in darkness. The body was left in the hotel coach-house overnight. The next day at 1pm a post-mortem was carried out in the same location by Gilmour and Fullarton: 'The body was in an advanced state of decomposition and was covered with maggots which swarmed all over it and the box in which it lay.' Also in the box were the tweed cap and a stained linen handkerchief.

The body was dressed in a tweed suit similar to the cloth of the cap and there was a portion of a black glazed waterproof coat covering the upper part of the trunk and head. The clothing was otherwise intact save for holes at the left hip and left shoulder. These corresponded to cavities in the flesh below which were presumed to have been made by rats or other small animals. Gilmour and Fullarton's conclusion was that the injuries to Rose's head, and his subsequent death, were 'caused by repeated blows on the left side of the head, and these blows were inflicted by some heavy instrument, probably a stone'. The last three words were omitted from the final version read out at Laurie's trial.

Once the post-mortem was over, a service was conducted at the coach-house by the Reverend Mr McDougall of Sannox. In the late afternoon Rose's remains were taken in a plain black coffin back along the shore road and buried in the small secluded graveyard at the foot of Glen Sannox. At the graveside another short service was led by the Reverend Mr Thomson, pastor of the United Presbyterian Church in Greenock. Those attending included Benjamin Rose and a large turn-out of local people. Benjamin had contacted the rest of his family to inform them of Edwin's death. They tried to keep the news from their mother who was in 'very enfeebled health'. (The last census entry at the Rose family home for Edwin's mother, Rebecca, was in 1871. Sometime after this she may have been admitted to a hospital or nursing home which might explain her husband's early retirement, and consequently the family's financial situation.

There was one last twist in the story of Edwin Rose. Prior to the funeral his nailed boots were removed and buried by one of the constables below the low water mark at the nearby beach. Local superstition held that murder victims would haunt the local area, and tradition advocated the disposal of any footwear to prevent the dead man's spirit from 'walking'. The burial of the boots would cause the police a major embarrassment at Laurie's trial, as the condition of the nails was seen as an important factor in whether Rose's injuries were caused by an accidental slip. In short, they had disposed of important evidence. In the police's defence, murders were almost unknown on Arran; the island's officers were more used to dealing with the occasional unruly tourist, or a lost wedding ring on Brodick beach.

But why did Laurie and Rose descend the mountain the way they did, an unusual choice of route? Most people returned to Brodick the way they had come, by the tourist path. However, once at the summit, the more adventurous had a choice of options that included the path to Corrie by way of Coire Lan, or the descent to The Saddle. For both these routes you would first have to traverse the narrow ridge, known as Stacach, which linked Goatfell's summit with North Goatfell (this latter name was not yet in use), where the descent to The Saddle started. Here's M J B Baddeley's description of this route, from the top of Goatfell to The Saddle:

> At first the ridge goes northwards, having on the right the depression which gives to Corrie its name, and which opens out on to the sea about a mile south of that hamlet. Beyond this depression the arm of the mountain stretching in a north-easterly direction must be avoided, and a rapid descent made along the top of the ridge in a north-westerly direction to the col which is plainly visible below, backed by the precipitous crags of Cir Mhor.

The granite pinnacles of the Stacach ridge could be either scrambled over or avoided completely. The hardest of the three tors was the most northerly which, taken directly, offered rock scrambling of a moderate standard: the most sporting variations were marked by scratches from umpteen boot nails. However, there was also the option of flanking tracks that avoided any difficulty. These paths were not as well worn as they are today, but were distinct enough to easily follow; they were most obvious on the eastern, Corrie side which also involved less loss of height. The first Scottish Mountaineering Club guide to Arran (1908) summed up what the route entailed: 'The route to North Goatfell along the ridge called Stacach affords good scrambling if the castellated tors be conscientiously taken, but sheep tracks lead along both sides of these. To reach The Saddle, one should go right over North Goatfell and then follow down the narrow wind-swept ridge towards Cir Mhor.'

From The Saddle, you had a choice of returning to Brodick by way of Glen Rosa or by following Glen Sannox to Corrie. Coire nam Fuaran ('Corrie of the Springs'), where Rose's body was found, lay on the Glen Sannox side of the north-west ridge. Two questions arise here. From the top of Goatfell, why did they head for Glen Sannox when the descent down Coire Lan to Corrie was simpler, on a better path, and quicker (their late start made this an important consideration); and why Coire nam Fuaran?

The answer to the first question is simpler. Nowadays it is difficult to comprehend how inflated Glen Sannox's scenic reputation once was, but at the time it was one of the most prestigious tourist attractions in Scotland due to endorsements by many famous writers and artists. Laurie and Rose had already seen Glen Rosa, and now they had climbed Goatfell. It only remained to tick off the much-vaunted Glen Sannox and they would have completed the set, all three of Arran's essential scenic showcases. Edwin Rose had travelled a long distance to Scotland, another reason for wanting to visit all the major attractions.

The choice of Coire nam Fuaran is more complex. It was not an established descent route but was regarded by some as a useful short cut into Glen Sannox. At John Laurie's trial Constable Munro stated, 'I should imagine that down by the boulder is the way that is travelled by people who, being on the top of Goatfell, want to get down by Glen Sannox.' The Coire nam Fuaran route also had the advantage of avoiding the descent from The Saddle into Glen Sannox which at the time still had a reputation for difficulty.

Today the route over The Saddle between Glen Rosa and Glen Sannox is regarded as a popular family walk, albeit one that requires care. There is a short section of easy scrambling on the Glen Sannox side of the pass. A direct descent of the Sannox side, however, from the lowest point of the col, leads towards a line of cliffs and over the years this has been the scene of many accidents, including some fatalities. F S (Frank) Goggs, writing in 1904, explained how the difficulties were not well documented:

The guidebooks apparently consider that there is now a highroad between the glens, as only one I have seen hints at there being any difficulty in the passage. The ordinary tourist coming up Glen Rosa will, I think, be very disagreeably surprised when he reaches the Saddle and sees what a precipitous descent it is into Glen Sannox. A member of the Geological Survey in *The Geology of North Arran* describes the descent as "precipitous and difficult". The exact route down is not at all obvious to the inexperienced eye.

Goggs also informs readers that the trick was to walk about 150 yards towards Cir Mhor where a small cairn indicated the start of the easiest descent, much of it down a rocky gully, known as 'the whin dyke', which eventually leads to easier ground. The correct route, however, could be hard to locate in mist. Here's the advice Goggs provides:

> After descending some fifty feet, you will see on your left a wall of rock, at the base of which runs a dyke with the usual stair-like rock steps. Go down this dyke, and then the bed of a burn and the path intertwine and change into each other amid heather and rock, till the main burn in Glen Sannox is reached.

However, in the summer of 1889 there was as yet no connecting path over The Saddle and no clear description as to what the difficulties entailed, or how best to negotiate them. The pass, with some justification, developed a reputation as being potentially hazardous, though its difficulty was often exaggerated. Around this time one writer warned, 'It is said that the practicality of passing from Rosa into Sannox was not known, except by a few shepherds who had occasionally tried it.' All this speculation made some walkers doubt their ability to undertake the excursion, and they often opted for a more transparent alternative. If Laurie and Rose made a deliberate decision to go by way of Coire nam Fuaran, it may well have been to bypass any problems at The Saddle.

There was also the possibility that Laurie and Rose intended to take the recognised route to The Saddle, but made a navigational error. Maps show North Goatfell as a sharply defined peak with three narrow ridges radiating from its top, including the north-west ridge. However, in reality navigation hereabouts was more complex than the maps suggested; the summit cairn was in a small depression between competing high points of blocky granite which, in misty conditions, made it difficult to locate the correct point from which to begin the descent to The Saddle.

The weather is therefore an important consideration in assessing whether Laurie and Rose lost their way. We know they were caught by some heavy showers on the way up. We know that conditions on the summit of Goatfell were clear as they were able to enjoy the view. However the Reverend Ritson later said this: 'The mist was on the very summit, and on the west and south-west.' Another heavy shower may well have resulted in the mist quickly closing in. When Rose died he was wearing his waterproof (the upper part of the garment was still on his body when it was found). The weather forecast in that morning's *Glasgow Herald* read: 'Shallow depressions are likely to pass across our islands in the course of ensuing 24 hours. Showery weather will probably continue to prevail. Westerly winds light, changeable, some showers.'

In Victorian times few hill-goers carried a map or compass. Ordnance Survey maps of the Arran hills were published 1868-69 but were not initially intended for use by the public; they were not readily available in shops but had to be ordered specially. If walkers on Arran did carry a map it would most likely be a small scale version of the whole island like those included in tourist vade-mecums. Compasses like the prismatic only became available around 1885 and, like OS maps, would have been very costly. (The Silva version was not available until 1932.) In poor visibility parties planning to return by the same route built small cairns, called stone-men, or placed stones on prominent boulders to show the way back, while popular routes like Goatfell's well-trodden tourist path were marked by larger, more permanent cairns and fingerposts.

As mentioned, an increasing number of walkers, Laurie and Rose included, were not content with returning the way they had come but sought more challenging excursions that used a different descent route to create a more satisfying round trip. But in the mist, without map or compass, any deviation from the way-marked routes could be a risky proposition. Regardless, many felt the urge to press on from the summit of Goatfell along the turreted ridge to North Goatfell and then descend either left to The Saddle, or right down Coire Lan to Corrie. For the latter route a large cairn identified the point where you cut off from the summit ridge. Coincidentally this also marked the descent to Coire nam Fuaran, down the opposite side of the ridge. In poor visibility Laurie and Rose may even have assumed that such a prominent cairn pointed out the start of the descent to The Saddle. On the OS map this point (Grid Reference 991425) was indicated by a spot height of 2472ft, the lowest part of the summit ridge between Goatfell and Mullach Buidhe.

The weather would also be a contributory factor in the accident theory, that Rose slipped and was fatally injured in a fall. Arran granite erodes into small gravel-like stones which can produce a slippery ball-bearing type effect. One of the earliest accounts of negotiating Coire nam Fuaran was in 1840 by the Reverend Thomas Grierson who found the terrain there difficult: 'Returning by a somewhat different route, I descended at great hazard into the upper part of Glen Sannox.' Witnesses at Laurie's trial stated that on this route there were short walls and slabs of granite though all these difficulties were avoidable. The incident occurred at what was the most likely place on the whole route to have an accident, especially in wet conditions. There were many other prior, and better, opportunities for pushing someone over a cliff.

On Monday 5 August the main headline in the morning's newspapers read: 'The Dervish Advance upon Egypt Effectively Checked'. Further on John Laurie was startled to find: 'The Arran Mystery: the Body Found, and Supposed Murder of Tourist.' He went on to read that the body of Edwin Rose had been located, hidden under a boulder on the slopes of Goatfell. It was highly likely he had been murdered and suspicion was said to rest with Rose's companion and lodger, 'John Annandale', which was known to be a pseudonym.

After reading the newspaper article, Laurie phoned Grace

Chalmers from a call office in Sauchiehall Street and arranged to meet her that evening at 6pm near Dundyvan School in Coatbridge. He doesn't turn up. According to *The Scotsman* the police had been keeping tabs on Laurie and were there waiting for him. From this point on Laurie takes flight.

It was Robert Mickel who first put the police on the scent of Laurie but there were others who suspected him, like his lodger in North Frederick Street, Matthew Eaglesome, and a colleague at work, both of whom recognised a connection between his holiday stories and the missing tourist on Arran. When James Aitken read the article in the newspaper he also decided to go to the police. During the interview he discovered that the police already knew that 'Annandale' and Laurie were the same person. They had visited Laurie's father in Coatbridge and his lodgings in North Frederick Street where Mrs King had showed them the letter she had received from Laurie and articles he had left in his room. A photograph of 'Annandale' was taken to the Atlas Works in Springburn where it was identified by workmates as Laurie. However, as soon as the newspaper article was published the trail was lost.

On Tuesday 6 August the *North British Daily Mail*, the precursor of the *Daily Record*, published a comprehensive and informative article about the discovery of Rose's body and the probable cause of death: 'An examination of the skull showed also that the injuries were such as could not have been caused by a fall... No other conclusion seemed to be possible from the appearance it presented than that Mr Rose had been brutally hammered on the head with a weighty stone furiously wielded by strong hands. It is clear that he was murdered. The story appears to be that of a man without money reduced to desperate circumstances, seeking the acquaintance of a gentleman who seemed to be well off, inducing him to go in his company to a distant and lonely place, and there deliberately and of set purpose murdering him for his money.'

Realising the police knew his identity and were on his trail, Laurie fled Scotland, probably on the Monday, and arrived in Liverpool on Tuesday 6 August. Coincidentally, this is the very place and very day that one of the year's sensational murder cases came to a conclusion. Mrs Florence Maybrick was convicted and sentenced to death, later commuted to life imprisonment, for murdering her husband James, a Liverpool cotton merchant, by poisoning him with arsenic. (In 1992 a document purporting to be James Maybrick's diary surfaced which led to him becoming a prime suspect for Jack the Ripper.)

Like most metropolitan stations, Liverpool's Lime Street had a wide range of nearby accommodation, decreasing in price and quality with distance from the main entrance. Towards its rear, at 10 Greek Street, Laurie noticed a sign in the window advertising, 'Apartments'. He told the landlady, Mrs Elizabeth Ennitt, that he was a commercial traveller in the cotton trade. After giving the impression of staying a long time, a paid a week's rent in advance.

On Thursday 8 August many newspapers, including the *Liverpool Courier*, picked up on the story of what was now referred to as 'The Arran Murder' and recounted events so far. They confirmed Annandale's true identity as John Watson Laurie and told how he had fled his job and his lodgings in Glasgow. The papers also berated the police over their continued failure to apprehend him. In Laurie's home town many were shocked that the suspect was a local man: 'The news spread like wildfire in Coatbridge where Laurie is pretty well known and respectably connected.' The same day Laurie surprised Mrs Ennitt by saying he had a new job in Manchester and would be departing in a few hours. He asked if he could leave his trunk. Laurie later said: 'After destroying my papers, I left my box, with no intention of ever calling for it again, as it was an encumbrance to me.'

<hr />

Back in Scotland the story of the Goatfell tragedy was big news. Descriptions of Laurie, along with his picture, were prominently placed in most newspapers. The police were inundated with sightings of the fugitive despite a rumour going round he had already been detained by Glasgow's Marine Division. Men in Edinburgh and Paisley were arrested as Laurie. There were further 'sightings' in Leith, Govan and several in the Coatbridge area: at Summerlee on 6 August and two days later at Sunnyside railway station, 'looking downcast'.

By now many, especially in his home area, thought Laurie had committed suicide and an old pit shaft at Mossend, three miles south of Coatbridge, was searched for this possibility. Apparently he had previously tried to poison himself. The day Laurie left Mrs Ennitt's a body was pulled out of Loch Lomond at Luss but eventually identified as someone else. There was debate as to whether the Monkland Canal, the scene of many drownings, should be dragged.

There were two sightings the police took very seriously. One witness, a medical student, recalled how he had taken the overnight Greenock to Liverpool steamer, the *Owl*, on the night of 5 August. He went on to say that one of his fellow passengers looked very similar to Laurie: he often broke into song on the voyage and was inebriated by the time the vessel docked at Liverpool's Clarence Docks. Two days later a railway guard at Liverpool's Lime Street Station was convinced that someone he had spoken to was the wanted man.

Laurie, who by now had shaved off his moustache to alter his appearance, was following the story in the newspapers. Frustrated by the many inaccuracies and his poor public image, he decided to write to them to put the record straight. A letter, with Liverpool postmark, dated 10 August, appeared that Monday (12 August) in the *Glasgow Mail*. (See Appendix I for full text.) In the letter Laurie says that he intends to commit suicide. He blames his problems to being rejected by his then sweetheart who had transferred her affections to another. He went on to claim that Rose had joined him in Arran uninvited. At the top of Goatfell he had left Rose in the company of two men who had come from Lochranza and intended descending to Brodick. He concludes:

I went down to Corrie and met some friends, and we afterwards visited the hotel, where we met several of the gentlemen who were camping out, and I left for Brodick about ten. I can easily prove what I say is true, but I decline to bring the names of my friends into this disgraceful affair, so will content myself by wishing them a last adieu.
    Yours truly,
    John W Laurie.

It was regarded by some newspapers as a forgery but the handwriting was verified by the police. The letter is the last that iis heard of John Laurie for over two weeks. It is highly likely he sailed from Liverpool to Ireland where the press, and police, would have less interest in him.

Chapter Six

I Robbed the Man, I Did Not Murder Him

The same day that Laurie's letter appeared in the *Glasgow Mail*, Benjamin Rose wrote from London to thank the people of Arran for all their help and kindness during these difficult times. When Benjamin left Brodick on 7 August he was interviewed on board the Scotia by a reporter from the *Ardrossan and Saltcoats Herald*. This was the local newspaper for Arran at the time which had been commissioned by the London edition of the *New York Herald* to cover the story and forward details of the investigation. Benjamin later wrote to the Ayrshire paper:

> Dear Sir,
> I found it quite impossible before leaving Arran last Wednesday to personally thank but very few of those who so kindly aided me in the search for my poor brother, Mr Edwin Rose. I have, on behalf of my parents, myself, and the rest of our family to ask you to be so good as to allow us through the medium of your valuable paper to return our most sincere and grateful thanks to the people of Arran for their hearty sympathy and most willing and valuable assistance. And I would more especially beg to express my deep gratitude to all those who, at great personal risk, helped me, from morning to night, for over a week, in the long and arduous search of Goatfell and its glens, and in the ultimate recovery of my poor brother's remains. The memory of the disinterested and truly Christian kindness displayed by every one in Arran will ever be one of the great consolations to us in our dreadful loss.
> Thanking you in anticipation for the insertion of this letter, which gives but a most inadequate expression of our gratitude.
> I remain, Sir, yours sincerely,
> Benjamin J Rose

The first Sunday after the burial large numbers visited Edwin Rose's grave, a raised mound covered with wreaths, as well as bouquets of flowers and heather. Throughout the following weeks scores of people continued to come to the grave 'out of curiosity or sympathy', leaving flowers, ribbons and visiting cards. After being witnesses at Laurie's trial in Edinburgh, Benjamin Rose and his two sisters travelled to Arran to lay a wreath on their brother's grave, and also to again thank islanders for the many messages of support and sympathy they had received throughout their ordeal.

On the first anniversary of Rose's death 'with better intention than taste' a large granite boulder was brought down from Glen Sannox and placed on the grave. On it was carved the inscription, 'In loving memory of Edwin R Rose, who died on Goatfell, 15 July, 1889.' The grave became a place of pilgrimage. The nature of the crime, an amiable English tourist seemingly murdered while enjoying a walk on a Scottish mountain-side, touched many people. For almost 25 years, up to the First World War, Rose's death remained a cause celebre; the floral tributes continued, as did visits to the boulder in Glen Sannox.

On Monday 12 August there was another development on Arran. Near the boulder where Rose's body was found, a visitor discovered a small glass bottle which smelled strongly of laudanum. Perhaps Rose was drugged before he was killed? Did the bottle belong to Laurie who was known to suffer from neuralgia? In truth it could have been left by any of countless visitors eager to see for themselves the location of the crime.

Murder tourism was a prominent phenomenon throughout the Victorian era. The merchandising for particularly notorious crimes included waxwork models, broadsheet ballads and Staffordshire figurines of the dramatis personae. Guided tours of the scene of the crime were popular and there are records of some where the corpse was still in situ, left for examination by the jury. Regarding recent events on Goatfell, postcards were soon produced of the infamous Coire nam Fuaran boulder (some of which showed a large cross that had recently been carved on the rock).

On the top of the boulder a cairn was erected as a crude memorial, but the spot soon became a ghoulish tourist attraction for the hordes of sight-seers keen to visit the scene of Rose's bloody end. A bamboo cane with a white flag was later added to the cairn of stones, 'so that other pilgrims may have no difficulty in finding this tragic spot in the wild and lonely valley under the shadow of Goatfell'. The cairn is still there. Typical of these tourists were two young men staying at the Corrie Hotel who set out to repeat Rose and Laurie's route and see for themselves the infamous chamber where the body was hidden:

> The two became separated and there was much excitement and alarm when one failed to return to the inn. A search was made, and on the Monday morning the missing gentleman was found at the bottom of a cliff where he had become fixed in a crevasse. He was in an exhausted condition, having been thus wedged in all night, and was only extracted after considerable difficulty.

The same day as Laurie's Liverpool letter appeared in the *Glasgow Mail*, other newspapers printed the warrant for his arrest along with a further description of the wanted man and his trunk: 'Laurie, between 9 and 10 stone, high cheekbones, plays the violin. An American box about 3ft 6in long covered with black leather studded with brass nails. Now much worn.' After Laurie's hurried departure Mrs Ennitt became suspicious. Perhaps it was the newspaper description of the trunk that finally made her contact the police.

On Wednesday 14 August a Glasgow policeman travelled south to Liverpool to examine the trunk and its contents as possible evidence. He was 24-year-old Detective John Pyper of the Western Division, Glasgow Police, who was originally from Aberdeenshire. In 1909, Pyper, then detective inspector, sailed from Glasgow to New York to arrest Oscar Slater, the victim of a notorious miscarriage of justice. Pyper was later implicated in the conspiracy to convict Slater of murder after perjuring himself at the trial. Coincidentally, John Laurie may well have known the murder victim, Marion Gilchrist, as they were once both members of the congregation at Woodlands United Presbyterian Church just along from his lodgings.

Pyper knew Laurie well. It was he who apprehended him over the theft of the jewellery, and also, eighteen months earlier, the charge of stealing from a fellow-lodger. Many years later there was a newspaper series, 'Famous Scottish Detectives', which featured Detective Pyper who related the following anecdote about Laurie:

> Two years previously Laurie had been implicated in a robbery, which his friends had endeavoured to clear up by offering to pay the financial loss involved. Shortly after this exploit, Laurie, who was a plausible sort of fellow, wrote quite a touching letter to a colleague of Mr Pyper's in the detective department of the Western District. Laurie knew this officer very well, and, having heard that the detective had recently lost a child, he expressed his deep sympathy with the father in his bereavement.

He referred to the robbery for which he was 'wanted'. He mentioned the efforts of his friends to settle the claims, hoped no further proceedings would be taken, and concluded by asking the detective to meet him at a certain spot at a certain time. This officer and Mr Pyper did meet him and, as a matter of fact, took him into custody. He was tried before the sheriff, but, in view of the fact that his friends had paid up the claims he was dismissed with an admonition.

Detective Pyper arrived at Mrs Ennitt's along with James Ferguson, a detective sergeant from the Liverpool police. The trunk was locked but Ferguson had a key which managed to open it. Inside they found shirts, collars, gloves, trousers, slippers, a toilet bag, brushes and a box containing a name stamp. The white linen shirts were impressed with the name 'John W Laurie'. (This is not a sign of Laurie's renowned vanity. Prior to household washing machines people used laundry firms or public wash-houses which meant some form of identification on clothes was necessary.)

On the first day of John Laurie's trial, the last witness to be called was Alice Barnes who worked for a London laundry firm. What she had to say would elicit a collective gasp from the packed courtroom, waking those who had earlier succumbed to the complex medical testimony: 'We do the washing of the Rose family. [Shown label No 18] I recognise the washing mark '48T' on this shirt shown to me. It belonged to the deceased Mr Rose. I put it there to distinguish the Rose family. I also see a stamped impression "John W Laurie". That was not on it when I washed the shirt.'

Detective Pyper remained in Liverpool for a week in case Laurie returned for his trunk. Meanwhile, back in Scotland, the debate over the extent of Laurie's guilt continued. Public sympathy was initially for Rose's family but there was also much commiseration when Laurie's 59-year-old father was taken seriously ill through the stress caused by his son's actions. The following letter appeared in the *Airdrie Advertiser* on 17 August, nine days after Laurie's disappearance from Mrs Ennitt's in Liverpool:

Glasgow, August 15, 1889

Sir, All who can dispassionately consider the aspects of the Maybrick trial and the disappearance of the young man Laurie must agree with your recent articles on both topics. In the one case there was an inducement to commit the murder; in the other there is a total absence of any inducement. On the contrary, the inducement would be to make the most of the new-found friendship of Mr Rose. Laurie has shown himself to be vain and foolish and impulsive, and probably timid. I have from the first had the same idea as that thrown out as a possibility by yourself, that Rose having been accidentally killed, Laurie, seized with sudden fear of being accused, tried to hide the body.

It is quite possible the medical men may be right in holding that the wounds on the head could not have been caused by a fall, but it is equally possible they were caused after death by the stones pitched in frantic excitement and in hot haste to cover the body. People who have lived as long as I have, must have noted similar, though minor cases, where innocent persons struck with panic have acted as foolishly as Laurie. I think, in fairness to the relatives of the unfortunate fugitive, that this view of his actions should be more considered than it appears to be,

I am etc,

Three Score and Ten.

The letter provoked the following response the next week:

The wonder here is if any of these correspondents can have read the account given of the finding of the body. Beneath a huge boulder, from the front of which the earth had been carried away by the rain, so that a pretty large cavity had been formed, quite suitable for a place of sepulchre, the body was carefully laid, face downwards; then between 40 and 50 stones, I think, were carefully selected and built in dry-stone fashion in a very tradesman-like style, with here and there tufts of grass and heather, placed in the crevices to give the wall the appearance of age; and it was the stench alone from the decomposing body that attracted attention, not the rude workmanship of the hidden grave. Surely there were no signs here of either 'hot haste' or 'frantic excitement'.

By now there were daily reports in the newspapers of the attempts to trace and capture Laurie. The headline 'The Arran Mystery' would often adjoin a neighbouring column with the title 'Whitechapel Murders'. The hunt for Laurie was creating intense excitement and there were frequent 'sightings' of him: at Hungryside Bridge near Torrance, asking for food at a house near Shotts, in a pub in Kilmarnock, in Longniddry. 'Laurie in London.' A stevedore thought he saw Laurie boarding the steamer *Toward* for Cork. On 23 August he was spotted in Cardiff. 'Police are keeping a close watch on all recruiting stations.'

A man who had worked alongside him in Springburn swore he saw him in Glasgow's Stockwell Street, opposite the Scotia Music Hall. He was seen on a train by another old workmate who reported this to the police, telling them that Laurie got off at Uddingston West. They surmised that he might try to walk the four miles cross-country to Coatbridge and consequently the town and its approaches were swamped by uniformed and plain-clothed officers.

There was another sighting in the Northern Bar, a pub in George Street in Aberdeen. Around noon the publican, Alexander Cowie, noticed a young man in the snug. He stayed about two hours drinking alternate brandy and beer. He spent the time mostly writing letters, asking at the bar to borrow some blotting paper. Cowie was convinced he fitted the description of Laurie, but before he could alert a policeman some customers arrived and diverted his attention. By the time Cowie finished serving them the man had vanished.

When Laurie left the pub he posted one of the letters to the *Glasgow Herald*, maintaining his innocence and telling his side of the story: 'I read so many absurd and mad things in the daily papers, that I feel it is my duty to correct some of them.' (See Appendix I for full text.) There was also a private letter to the editor, withheld from publication, which made further scurrilous remarks about the character of Annie McLean and John Cowan. The newspaper published the main letter on Thursday 29 August which precipitated a rash of Laurie 'sightings' in North-East Scotland.

Alexander Cowie, described by reporters as 'a genial, good-natured Aberdonian', went on to receive a postcard from 'Laurie' as well as a parcel containing a Bowie knife. The publican later positively identified a photograph of Laurie as the man drinking in his pub. Cowie remembered that the suspect pronounced 'yes' as 'yaas'. (Due to this peculiarity 'Yaas' became Laurie's nickname in Coatbridge.) The police recovered the blotting paper on which an impression of some writing could be made out which fitted part of Laurie's letter to the *Glasgow Herald*.

After spending the night at Aberdeen's Waverley Hotel, Laurie caught the steamer *St Magnus* to Leith. In the last week prior to his capture there are various reports or sightings of Laurie. He spent a little time in Edinburgh, and it was near here he later claimed to have attempted suicide by poisoning himself. He then headed for Stirling where he set off on foot for the Vale of Leven. By now he was running out of money.

When Laurie arrived at Jamestown near Balloch he asked whether there was any nearby accommodation. He was directed toward Mrs Gunn who had a small confectioner's shop and also took in lodgers. Laurie introduced himself as 'John Edmund' from Irvine and said he had a new job as ticket checker at Jamestown Station. Mrs Gunn later told a reporter that though he looked tired he was very communicative; he was sunburnt, his feet were blistered and 'he was dirty looking, aye, he looked right travelled stained'. The next day he left for Balloch Station to collect his luggage, saying he would be back at 12pm for a cup of tea. It was the last she would see of Laurie who, in characteristic fashion, was already heading rapidly towards Glasgow.

According to Laurie he then went to Lanark from where he walked to Hamilton. His intention in returning to Lanarkshire was to see Grace Chalmers. Newspapers later commented, 'Had it not been for a desire to see the girl he loves, he says, he would not have been apprehended where he was.' He managed to slip a letter under the door of her workplace but, according to both parties, they never met up. Laurie himself claimed he didn't get into Coatbridge as it was too closely watched. However many of his statements, especially while on the run from the law, should be taken with a pitch of salt.

In times of adversity people often return to places imbued with happier memories. Laurie, besotted by his sweetheart but denied physical contact, would have been drawn, consciously or unconsciously, to where he could make an emotional connection, for example their last time together, their last kiss, the romantic day out canoodling at Tillietudlem. Prior to his capture it was thought by some that Laurie was sleeping rough in an old adit mine in the Nethan Gorge below Craignethan Castle, the same area he had visited with Grace Chalmers a month earlier.

The *Airdrie Advertiser* gave credence to this theory: 'The truth is that whilst Laurie did go through Lanark on the Monday of 2nd September, he passed the night in an 'in-gannee' mine, a quarter of a mile down the glen from Tillietudlem Castle, that is, an old pit, entrance to which was obtained from the side of a hill. Laurie in his boyhood knew a great deal about the old castle, and it is quite possible that he slept in the dungeons one or more nights after his disappearance.'

That same Monday Laurie was recognised on the Lanark-Hamilton road near Crossford by a Mrs Hannah. In the evening an elderly man saw him filling a glass flask at the River Nethan. Early the next morning, the day of his capture, Laurie was spotted in the same area by two groups of miners on their way to work, and again by Mrs Hannah a couple of hours later as he headed off towards Hamilton. Later that morning Thomas Barr, a hedger on the Duke of Hamilton's estate, passed a man he thought looked like Laurie near the Avon Bridge on the outskirts of Hamilton. Barr later chatted to a postman who mentioned that there had been several sightings of Laurie in the area that morning.

(In retrospect, it was estimated that while Laurie was a fugitive there were over a hundred genuine sightings of him, especially in Lanarkshire, by people who either knew or recognised him but did not report him to the authorities. This was largely due to a general distaste for the death sentence which, if found guilty, he would most likely face.)

Throughout Laurie's time on the run the Hamilton-Larkhall district appears to be an area with some significance to him. It is to Hamilton he first heads for when he flees Glasgow. It is the same town he visits prior to his arrest. Sometime before his capture it was rumoured he passed through the village of Stonehouse on a brewer's cart. The stationmaster at Ferniegair related how Laurie had stated his intention of buying a ticket to Larkhall but had not done so. It is highly likely friends or relatives in this part of south Lanarkshire gave him assistance.

In Laurie's account of his capture he claims that earlier in the day he had visited friends in Hamilton, where he also bought a newspaper to see what was being said about him. He then left the town by way of the Carlisle Road, stopping off around 2pm for a drink at the Ferniegair Inn. Some in the pub later claimed they recognised him but he left unchallenged. He then walked along the road towards Larkhall. As this was busy with miners returning home at the end of their shift, he diverted into the nearby Ferniegair Station but noticed there was a policeman on the platform.

Also awaiting a train was a Mr Russell, the cashier at the nearby Allanton Colliery, who thought he recognised the man as Laurie. When Russell asked the stationmaster his opinion, he in turn recalled the man as someone he had seen at the station during the Hamilton races and whom at the time he had suspected of being Laurie. His doubts were due to Laurie having shaved off his moustache. This time he was more certain and approached Constable Gordon. The next day's headlines in the North British *Daily Mail* (4 September) were:

ARREST OF LAURIE
RECOGNISED AT LARKHALL
FLIGHT AND PURSUIT

CAPTURED IN A WOOD
HE ATTEMPTS SUICIDE

After his arrest Laurie related to the police how he had been to Liverpool, York and Leeds. He became apprehensive in England about being recognised due to his distinctive Scottish accent. He also spent some time in Belfast and Dublin before returning to Scotland. He later mentioned he had been to Birmingham and had passed a day or two in Ayr prior to Aberdeen.

After his court appearance in Rothesay, Laurie was taken by the steamer *Caledonia* to Gourock and then by train to Greenock West Station. From here he was marched, through an inquisitive crowd to Greenock Prison which was then located in Nelson Street adjacent to the Sheriff Court building. On his arrival at the jail Laurie revealed to the doctor that he had taken poison several times with the intent of committing suicide. He was consequently put on a 24-hour watch by warders, as well as a special diet due to his weakened state. His particulars were recorded:

Hair: dark brown.
Build: slight.
Weight: 133lbs.
Class of Life: Very vain and tends to pass himself as a man of position and means, and said not to be over scrupulous in settling any little claim against him.
Mode and habits of life: Fond of company and associating with those above him in life.

In the prison Laurie was allowed to wear his own clothes. He was provided with books, newspapers and writing material though all letters were vetted. His demeanour and behaviour were reported daily in the *Glasgow Herald*. The newspaper appeared to have a source inside the jail, presumably a warder, who provided them with information about his state of mind and daily routine: 'It is said that he is disposed to read but that his taste in this respect is not fastidious.'

Laurie spoke openly to the warders about being on the run and his travels throughout Britain. He was reluctant to mention the crime he was accused of and appeared to show little compassion for Rose's fate, speaking obdurately of him as a vain person who boasted how wealthy he was. (Rose left a modest estate of £198.) On account of the crowds he was attracting, Laurie quipped that the best thing the warders could do was take him to the St Andrew's Halls in Glasgow and exhibit him for a week, charging sixpence for admission. That way he would be able to afford the best legal defence in the country.

On his first Sunday in prison he declined to go to the chapel service as he did not want to be stared at by other inmates. On 11 September 1889, a week after his capture, Laurie was examined before Sheriff Orr at Greenock. He was described as looking very pale and emaciated with a haggard, hunted look. He admitted his identity. On being shown the cap, waterproof and other articles belonging to Rose, which had been found near the boulder, he declared, 'I wish to say nothing about any of these articles.'

After Laurie's arrest there was an opinion expressed in one of the newspapers that if he was seen by witnesses on the summit of Goatfell at 6.15pm and later at the Corrie Hotel at 9.30pm, he did not have time to commit the alleged murder and conceal Rose's corpse. This is a valid point as the body would have to be dragged a considerable way, almost 200m over rough ground to the boulder. Building the concealing wall, carefully constructed from over forty stones, would also have taken some time. There was no path between the boulder and the Glen Sannox path, and much of the route to gain the path was through deep heather –energy-sapping and time-consuming terrain. Unless you had knowledge of the best line, using occasional sheep and deer tracks, this could be slow and exasperating ground to cover. However, Laurie would have the advantage of an almost full moon.

On Saturday 14 September, Dr Fullarton, Sergeant Munro and Constables Munro and Coll retraced the route taken by Laurie and Rose. From the top of Goatfell to the boulder took them half an hour; the boulder to Corrie Hotel was covered in 1 hour 44 minutes. This was just under two and a quarter hours for a total distance of nearly six miles, almost all downhill. They concluded: 'It could be done in less time at a smarter pace.' However timings like this should be treated with some caution. The three decades prior to the First World War were imbued with a very competitive ethos. Accounts of days out on the Scottish hills were often recorded in an understated style that belied the often hell-for-leather nature of their execution.

When Sergeant Munro's party made a comparison of the relative times little allowance was made for the Arran party's local knowledge, for example when traversing the Stacach ridge, nor for Laurie and Rose's caution and prevarication as the path became less evident and their decision-making more hesitant. Laurie also claimed he was slowed down by Rose's lack of fitness.

With their black sheep in Greenock Prison charged with murder, Laurie's family did what they could to assist him. His older brother Gavin, currently store manager at the Gartsherrie ironworks, and George Garrett, who was married to Laurie's cousin, decided to conduct their own test. They also followed the Coire nam Fuaran route to check the accuracy of Sergeant Munro's party's findings. Garrett, originally from Wales, was a prominent engineer who had previously been engaged by the Russian government to erect an ironworks in St Petersburg. In Coatbridge he founded the Waverley Iron and Steel Works, and was also manager of Dunbeth Church for 25 years.

On 25 September, accompanied by Cossimo Latona, 'a guide from Brodick', Garrett and Gavin Laurie repeated the route 'at a smart pace': 'The guide pointed out the spot where Mr Rose's body was found. At many parts of the descent a false step meant being precipitated down the cliffs and death.' They took a walking time of 2 hours 55 minutes from the summit of Goatfell to Corrie which would have left only 20 minutes for Laurie to commit the murder and conceal the body. However Laurie's actual time of arrival at Corrie was nearer 10pm (closing time) which would have given him nearer 50 minutes.

On 31 October and 2 November George Garrett returned to Goatfell along with two Glasgow engineers to complete a survey of the descent. He concluded: 'From the nature of the ground I am of the opinion that in many places a tourist might readily slip and fall and if he did so his life would be lost.' The engineers involved, Robert Strathern and Robert Simpson, were cited as witnesses for the defence at Laurie's trial but not asked to give evidence.

However, Cossimo Latona was called as a witness for the defence. He was a 22 year-old fisherman, originally from Sicily.

After being shipwrecked on Arran three years earlier he decided to settle on the island, marrying a Perthshire woman in 1894. In his early days on Arran he bought a derelict smack called the *Wemyss Castle* which he towed up the Rosa Burn and used as a houseboat. An entrepreneurial character, he ran a coal delivery company as well as a boat-hiring business. With the latter he had a very public feud with the Brodick Free Church minister over operating on a Sunday.

Latona was referred to throughout the trial, and in the press, as a (mountain) 'guide'. Through his preliminary examination it was evident that he actually had very little knowledge or experience of the Arran hills. This, and his title of 'guide' created a discrepancy that could only further weaken Laurie's case. This is the statement Latona made at his precognition:

> I have been several times up Goatfell but only once acted as a guide to two gentlemen over the hill. This was some time after the date of the murder about the month of September. I was, however, twice over the hill and down Glen Sannox in company with Constable Munro and Mr Macdonald when the latter was taking photographs of the various parts of the hill. [These photographs were used to assist the jury at Laurie's trial] I was not acting as their guide but went with them to assist in carrying the photographic apparatus.
>
> I have never before completed the circuit over the hill down Coire nam Fuaran through Glen Sannox to Corrie, previous to my accompanying them. I had gone over the top of Goatfell and down The Saddle to where the body was found on the day when the search party discovered the body. I never went down the face of Coire nam Fuaran before the time above mentioned. On the day I was with the two gentlemen over Goatfell I think we took about an hour from Goatfell to the boulder. On that day we made numerous stops while I pointed out the various places to them. [...] I never went down Glen Sannox before the time I was there with the constable. I never took note of the time. I have no idea of the distance.
>
> During July last I was not on Goatfell until the Sunday that the first search party was engaged searching the hill and I never was in Glen Sannox till I went there with Constable Munro

and was not at Corrie this year until I was there with Constable Munro. I know nothing of the distance on the hills from point to point.

Laurie's defence appeared to have nothing to gain from Latona's testimony, and a lot of credibility to lose, yet he was one of only four non-medical witnesses called. If his purpose was as an expert witness on the Arran hills, using his local knowledge to show that Laurie did not have the time to commit the murder, they would be disappointed. At the trial Latona stated: 'For the last three years I have been acting as a guide at Brodick. As a guide I know the tracks tourists usually take for the purpose of reaching the points of view and seeing the scenery.

Cross-examined by Mr Graham Murray:

Murray: 'How many times have you guided people over the hills in Arran?
Latona: 'I did not guide any people at all before Rose's body was found.'
Murray: 'Had you ever been in Glen Sannox at all before Rose's body was found?'
Latona: 'No.'

On 27 September Edwin Rose's body was exhumed so that the internal organs, missed on the first post-mortem, could be examined. The second post-mortem was carried out by Dr Fullarton, the Lamlash GP, and Dr (later Sir) Henry Littlejohn. Dr Neil Fullarton began his Arran practice in 1878. As a keen ornithologist he knew the Arran hills well. In 1891 he treated Helen Asquith, wife of HH Asquith, MP for East Fife and later Prime Minister. After contracting typhoid while on holiday on Arran with her children, she died on 11 September 1891 and is buried in Lamlash cemetery.

Henry Littlejohn was a surgeon, forensic scientist, and public health pioneer who did much to eradicate cholera and typhus from the city of Edinburgh. His enormous contribution to medicine is still being evaluated. A police surgeon, he taught Arthur Conan Doyle forensic medicine and was cited, along with Joseph Bell, as an inspiration for Sherlock Holmes. The physicians were also accompanied by Mr Maddever, the Rothesay Procurator Fiscal, and the Sheriff, Mr Campbell. This sensitive task was kept as low key as possible with Sergeant Munro guarding the cemetery gate to prevent anyone entering. Both Littlejohn and Fullarton concurred that Edwin Rose's death had been sustained by repeated blows to the left side of the head, inflicted with a heavy, blunt instrument.

But by whom, and why?

Chapter Seven

I am Condemned to Die

On 29 October, Laurie had to plead at Greenock Sheriff Court to the charge of murder, a preliminary to his trial at the High Court in Edinburgh. He was brought to the court along the subterranean passage connecting it to the prison. When he climbed the stairs into the crowded courtroom there was a flutter of excitement from those anxious to get a glimpse of him. One reporter commented: 'When seated in the dock with his back to the spectators, he raised his head and it was then seen that his features were good-looking and pleasant.'

By now Laurie looked dramatically different from the somewhat pathetic figure captured near Larkhall. The wound to his neck appeared to have healed; the bandage he previously wore was replaced by a clean collar and silk tie. He had shaved, save for a thin moustache, looked much healthier and 'was dressed with scrupulous care and neatness, the well-known overcoat tidy looking and squarely set upon his shoulders, and his hair brushed smoothly and parted at one side'. It was the same light-brown overcoat he had thrown away at his arrest and which featured in 'wanted' descriptions of him in the press. Laurie appeared calm but some noticed his hands were trembling.

As the Crier of Court called out, 'The Crown against John Watson Laurie', the prisoner stood up and faced the bench with a firm eye. For a brief period two famous names from the roster of Scottish mountaineering came face to face: John Watson Laurie, the only person to be accused of a murder on the Scottish mountains, and Sheriff Alexander Nicolson who had made the first ascent of two Munros in Skye: Sgurr Dubh Mor and Sgurr Alasdair. The latter, the highest mountain on the island, is named after him (Alasdair is Gaelic for Alexander). Sheriff Nicolson began to read the indictment: 'John Watson Laurie, the charge against you is that, on 15th July, 1889, at Corr-na-Fourin, near the head of Glen Sannox, in the island of Arran, Buteshire, you did assault Edwin Robert Rose, Wisset Lodge, Hendham Road, Trinity Road, Upper Tooting, London, and did throw him down, beat him and murder him.' Thereafter followed the plea:

Sheriff Nicolson (to accused): 'Are you guilty or not guilty?'
Accused responded in a clear, loud voice, 'Not Guilty, my Lord.'
Sheriff Nicolson: 'The you are remitted to trial at the High Court of Justiciary, Edinburgh on 8 November.'

The High Court in Parliament Square near St Giles Cathedral was Scotland's supreme criminal court which had exclusive jurisdiction over serious crimes. Prior to the trial Laurie was visited in Greenock Prison by many of the witnesses who had been asked to make a formal identification of him. About a week before the trial he was moved to Edinburgh's Calton Prison, below Calton Hill.

On the morning of the first day of the trial, a Friday, the High Court was besieged by a crowd estimated to be around two thousand and the doors had to be opened an hour early. Policemen guarding the entrance refused entry to anyone who did not have a ticket, including many members of the legal profession. Many friends and acquaintances of Laurie, who had travelled from Lanarkshire, were frustrated to find themselves denied admission. Throughout the trial the doors of the court were besieged by those hoping to gain a seat vacated by someone leaving early.

The presiding judge was the politically Conservative John Hay Athole Macdonald (Lord Kingsburgh) who was Lord Justice-Clerk, the second most senior judge in Scotland (Lord President of the Court of Session was the highest ranking position). He took the title 'Kingsburgh' from the village on the Isle of Skye where his ancestors, who included Flora Macdonald, came from. When Macdonald was a pupil at Edinburgh Academy his father chose as his tutor, a friend of the family (and distant cousin), the afore-mentioned Alexander Nicolson, then a law student. A legal directory listed Lord Kingsburgh's hobbies as: golf, tennis, driving and electricity. He was also a keen inventor.

Leading the prosecution was the Solicitor-General, M T Stormonth Darling, who was assisted by Andrew Graham Murray and Dugald McKechnie. Darling was currently the Conservative

MP for Edinburgh and St Andrews Universities. During the precognition of witnesses he had assessed their efficacy using his own rough grading system which he marked with a pencil in the margin of their transcript, for example: 'useless', 'absolutely useless', 'worse than useless'.

However, it would be Andrew Graham Murray, 'one of the most promising young advocates at the Bar', who would do most of the prosecution examination of witnesses. Murray studied law at Edinburgh University and was friendly with Robert Louis Stevenson who is said to have consulted him for advice when writing *Weir of Hermiston* whose title character was Lord Justice Clerk. Another writer, Rebecca West, described Murray as a talented sportsman and elegant dancer, a regular on the Highland ball circuit where he was 'master of the new American ballroom dances such as the two-step'. Both Murray's parents belonged to families with great influence in legal circles where he made rapid progress.

The defence team was led by Dean of Faculty, J B Balfour, 'the prince of cross-examining counsel in Scotland', assisted by C Scott Dickson. Balfour was currently the Liberal MP for Clackmannan and Kinross, while Dickson would later become a Unionist MP in Glasgow.

As this was a high-profile murder case, both legal teams comprised the cream of their profession. Dickson, Balfour and Murray all, at various times, held the post of Lord Advocate, Scotland's leading law officer, and all three would eventually be appointed Lord Justice-Clerk. Stormonth Darling was currently Solicitor-General, the Lord Advocate's deputy. In 1882-84, when Balfour was Lord Advocate, he was responsible for the deployment of troops and Glasgow policemen to Skye to arrest the ring-leaders of the land agitation.

At 9.50am the Clerk of Court, Mr Charles Scott, called the roll of jurymen who all answered to their names. The productions for the case were then brought into the court: a walking-stick, several buttons, studs and links; a coat, a felt hat, a tennis racquet, a trunk and various other articles of clothing. At 9.58am the trap door was raised and the macer rang the bell several times. After a short delay the object of everyone's interest, the defendant (know in Scotland as the pannel) John Watson Laurie, entered the court.

The lawyer and criminologist William Roughead (pronounced Rockheed) was one of those present at the trial. He was a prolific author of the true crime genre, very successful in the United States where Franklin D Roosevelt was a big admirer. Roughead wrote a full account of the case, *Trial of John Watson Laurie* (1932), in which he described Laurie's initial appearance in court: 'At a few minutes before ten o'clock, on Friday 8 November, 1889, the trapdoor in front of the dock was raised and the prisoner, in charge of two constables, came up into Court from the cells below. The appearance of the man was surprising; he looked so unlike one's conception of the murderer. Well dressed and groomed, commonplace, calm, and respectable, could this be the brutal ruffian of Coire-na-fuhren?'

The *Glasgow Herald* added more detail to this dramatic moment:

When Laurie stepped into the dock from the stairs leading from the cells, the audience, which included a large proportion of ladies, were hoping to catch a glimpse of the man whose strange, eventful career has recently engrossed public attention. In this they were not successful. Laurie kept his head bowed and between the stalwart policemen, by whom he was proceeded and followed, his diminutive figure was almost entirely concealed from the spectators.

On the stroke of ten the Lord Justice-Clerk took his seat upon the bench. The Clerk of Court intimated the plea of Not Guilty which Laurie had tendered to Sheriff Nicolson at Greenock on 29 October. The Lord Justice-Clerk asked: 'Do you adhere to your plea of Not Guilty?' The accused answered: 'Yes, my Lord.'

It only remained for the jury to be balloted and empanelled; they numbered fifteen and were all male. Had Laurie been a landowner he would have been entitled to a majority of his peers on the jury; otherwise 'five special jurors and ten common jurors' were chosen. Those selected were all from the Edinburgh area and, with the exception of an engineer and missionary, were working class: traders, farmers, shopkeepers etc. The charge was read out to the jury who were then sworn in. The trial commenced.

The first day of the trial comprised two contrasting parts. Firstly there were largely consentient witnesses from Arran. This was followed by the more complex evidence of the prosecution medical team. Initially, the prosecution aimed to prove Rose met his death by murder and then to connect the prisoner to the crime. They also tried to prove that Rose was murdered by being struck by a rock on the left side of the head, delivered from above and behind. His face was then battered to prevent recognition. Rose's shoulder was injured by a blow that missed the head. Laurie then rifled Rose's clothes before hiding the body beneath a boulder. The defence countered that Rose died after a fall.

Poignantly, among the last witnesses on the first day were Edwin's sisters, Mary and Louise, 'young ladies who appeared dressed in deep mourning'; they were asked to identify some of their brother's clothing and possessions.

When proceedings stopped at 7pm the Judge announced it was imperative the trial be concluded the following day and not carried over to Sunday: 'He wished it to be distinctly understood and he was sure the jury would agree with him, that he intended to finish the case tomorrow night.' The jury, some of whom responded with a 'hear, hear', stayed overnight in the Waterloo Hotel. This announcement would later be the focus of some controversy. A trial of such importance would be expected to last a fortnight. And surely proceedings should have started on a Monday rather than a Friday.

The second day of the trial started at 10am. As Laurie stepped into the dock he looked less confident than the previous day, though his appearance was as immaculate as ever. The prosecution now sought to prove the prisoner's connection with the crime. They began by establishing that Laurie had stolen from Rose: Laurie had taken Rose's belongings from Mrs Walker's in Brodick; Rose's shirts and other items were found in Liverpool. They then tried to counter the fall theory. Had Laurie claimed Rose died in a fall and then admitted he'd robbed him, as advised by his counsel, the prosecution would have had their work cut out. Laurie, however, refused to do this, maintaining what he wrote in his letter to the *Glasgow Mail*, that he parted from Rose near the summit of Goatfell and never set eyes on him again. Another option was the defence of insanity or 'alienation of reason', where the accused admits the criminal act but asserts that his mental state at the time of the offence was such as to relieve him of liability. This option does not appear to have been considered.

The motive is one of the most fascinating aspects of the case. The prosecution admitted that the motive of robbery appeared incommensurate to the nature of the crime. They also argued that Rose was not involved in a fall because witnesses said there were no unavoidable difficulties on the descent, nor was there a locality in the vicinity which had all the features necessary for producing the particular injuries incurred. There were no tears to Rose's clothing which would be expected by a fall onto rough granite.

Laurie was initially very attentive to what was being said, but began to look a trifle bored as the day wore on. He rarely looked around at the crowded public gallery. If proceedings came to critical point his right hand went up to stroke his moustache, but he displayed few traces of nervousness. Francis Ord Mickel's forceful evidence exuded an emphatic dislike for Laurie, 'which caused the prisoner to make an uncomfortable attempt of a smile'. One of the final witnesses for the prosecution was Laurie's friend James Aitken. His evidence made a deep impression on the court, especially his dramatic encounter with the accused on Hope Street. A reporter for the *Coatbridge Express* was more discerning:

> All forenoon the Dean of Faculty had allowed witness after witness to pass without endeavouring to put them through any cross-examination. When the Solicitor-General was done with questioning Mr Aitken, Mr Balfour took him in hand. Contrary, however, to expectation he limited himself to one or two queries, none of which seemed of much consequence.

The prosecution examination finished at 2pm and for the next three hours the defence put forward their case. They initially challenged any notion of premeditation: Laurie was calling himself 'Annandale' prior to encountering Rose, whom he did not know he was going to meet. It is Rose that takes the initiative when they first chanced upon each other on the *Ivanhoe*. Laurie is not hounding Rose.

Laurie's later actions, going willingly back to Rothesay where people had seen him leave with Rose, were not those of a murderer. The defence claimed that wearing Rose's clothes on Bute was the behaviour of a thief not a murderer, but hastily added that neither was robbery a motive as 'he being only a clerk near the end of his holidays, it could not have been much'. They were at pains to point out that this was not an admission that Laurie robbed the body. They continued, rather cheekily: 'We admit nothing of the kind. It may be that somebody did it. Very likely, at these Fair Holidays, there would be plenty of people on the island who would do that.' It was only after Laurie met James Aitken in Hope Street and realised he might be treated as a suspect, that he panicked and fled Glasgow.

More convincingly, they argued that the prosecution had failed to prove Rose died of 'wilful murder'; the evidence was all circumstantial: there were no witnesses, no murder weapon, no blood on Laurie's clothing. Laurie was not placed at the scene of crime; nothing Rose had on him on Goatfell was ever traced to Laurie. There was no evidence to dispute that Laurie left Rose on the summit of Goatfell [with Laurie then descending the path to Corrie where witnesses placed him in the evening]. Other points made by the defence were that the position of the cap, knife and pencil were more consistent with a fall than a murder. The Crown failed to explain why, if a murder, Laurie took great care to conceal the body but left considerable evidence, including part of Rose's waterproof, with its conspicuous white lining, scattered about the hill-side.

However, it was the medical evidence that was the real battleground of the trial. The prosecution medical team was led by Henry Littlejohn, assisted by Andrew Gilmour and Neil Fullarton. Littlejohn was a seasoned campaigner in such cases. The judge Lord Young once said of him: 'There are four classes of witnesses: liars, damned liars, expert witnesses, and Sir Henry Littlejohn.' He had appeared as an expert witness in more than a hundred capital charges including the famous murder trials of Dr Pritchard (Glasgow, 1865), Eugene Marie Chantrelle (Edinburgh, 1878) and the sensational trial of Arthur Monson for the shooting of his aristocratic pupil, Cecil Hamborough (1893). (In the latter case, known as the Ardlamont murder, Lord Kingsburgh was also the judge and claimed the complexities of the trial caused him sleepless nights and unprecedented emotional strain.)

The medical witnesses for the prosecution concurred that Rose's death was the result of direct violence by blows to the head; they maintained that the injuries received by him would require 'continual and repeated concussions'. Littlejohn claimed that a fall would have resulted in broken limbs and/or damage to the internal organs which the second post-mortem confirmed did not occur. Rose's upper jaw bone had become detached. Dr Littlejohn commented that this was unlikely in the event of a fall, but more likely if there were repeated blows. As the jawbone attachment was one of the strongest in the body, its dislodgement was highly unusual, so much so that Littlejohn retained it for examination by students at Edinburgh University's Department of Forensic Medicine.

The defence medical team was led by the distinguished Dr (later Sir) Patrick Heron Watson, an old rival of Littlejohn. Watson served as a surgeon during the Crimean War where he got to know Florence Nightingale, 'a very dowdy old maid'. In the Laurie case Watson was assisted by Dr Charles Macgillivray, and Dr Henry Alexis Thomson who later became professor of surgery at Edinburgh University.

None of the defence medical team had been able to examine Rose's body though Macgillivray and Thomson had visited the crime scene. In the gully above the boulder they identified two locations where a fall might have occurred. They countered the prosecution by presenting impressive arguments that the injuries were consistent with a fall, and inconsistent with repeated blows. Watson thought death was instantaneous as there was so little bleeding. Had the skull been repeatedly smashed Laurie could not have moved Rose's body any distance without getting himself covered in blood. One of the key factors against the fall theory was that there were no wounds to the hands which you would instinctively use to protect yourself. The defence countered this by claiming that if the fall was backwards it would not result in this type of injury.

Despite impressive presentations on either side, neither were able to absolutely negate the other's theory. Much of the medical evidence was highly technical with some harrowing descriptions. It was a relief for many in the court when proceedings eventually returned to more mundane territory: 'Some diversion was caused by the advent of a good-natured damsel who favoured the counsel so copiously with smiles, as to move even their judicial countenances to a responsive grin.'

With the conclusion of the evidence for the defence there was a short adjournment for tea. On returning, a large-scale map of Arran and the photographs taken by Alexander Macdonald were shown to the jury, and the various localities mentioned pointed out. At 5.30pm Stormonth Darling began the summing up for the prosecution:

Gentlemen of the jury, you have been investigating during these past two days a tragedy the circumstances of which lie far out of the ordinary track of crime. The recent acquaintance of these two young men, Laurie and Rose, the holiday character of their expedition, the solitude and grandeur of the scene in which the crime took place, all incline to invest it with an interest altogether exceptional... The salient facts of the case are these: two young men went up a hill and only one came down. The other was found, after an interval of weeks, with his body horribly mutilated, hidden away among the rocks of the hillside, and with all his portable property removed. The one who came down was seen within a few hours of the time when the death of his friend must have taken place. He returned from the excursion on which they both started, and gave no sign or hint that anything had happened to his friend, or that he had not returned with him. The next morning he left Arran, and resumed his ordinary occupation until the hue and cry began. Then, when it did begin, he took to flight; and, finally, when he was about to be arrested, he attempted to cut his throat.

The Dean of Faculty, J B Balfour, then summed up for the defence. He spoke for an hour and a half. He claimed that no murder had been committed; there was no murder weapon or evidence of a struggle. Rose's injuries and the way his possessions were scattered about were consistent with a fall. Laurie's behaviour in openly wearing Rose's clothes were not those of a murderer. When arrested he had said: 'I robbed the man, I did not murder him.' Balfour clarified that this confession was not in regard to rifling Rose's body but to taking his possessions from Mrs Walker's. In conclusion he maintained that the Crown had failed to prove that there was any murder, and, if there had been, that Laurie was the murderer.

Following the Dean of Faculty's speech there was another interval. In the waiting-room below the court, Laurie talked freely about the possible verdict. He was of the opinion that the evidence against him was not strong enough; the prosecution had brought out few strong points against him, and after such a fine summing up by Balfour he felt that any doubts the jury may have had would have been removed. Throughout this interval, and other breaks, Laurie's appetite remained good. He was, as usual, very attentive to his personal appearance, frequently washing his hands, smoothing his hair, and paying particular attention to the tidiness of his collar, tie and cuffs.

The Judge began his summing up at 8.40pm. It lasted exactly one hour. He described the case 'as one of the most remarkable that had ever come before a Court of Justice'. At 9.45pm the jury retired. No one was allowed access to the jury room while they deliberated, save, for example, a doctor in a medical emergency. In Scots law there are three possible verdicts: one of conviction, 'guilty'; and two of acquittal, 'not guilty' and 'not proven'. The latter, unique to Scots law, is used where there is insufficient evidence to establish guilt or innocence. The jury did not need to be unanimous, a majority would suffice.

If the jury found the accused guilty in a capital case, the court had no discretion but to pronounce the sentence of death, though it could give a recommendation for mercy due to mitigating circumstances such as youth, good character or 'weak intellect'. At this time there was no court of appeal in Scotland so Laurie could be sentenced to death without any opportunity to challenge the decision. (It was not until 1907 that you had the right of appeal against the conviction of murder, but not against the death sentence. Another change in the Scottish legal system, in 1898, was that defendants could be examined as witnesses.) The mounting tension in the courtroom was recorded by a reporter from the Dundee *Evening Telegraph*:

As the minutes passed and it became evident that there was some delay, Laurie, who had been sitting still with bent head, was again removed, and the hum of talk went freely on. The public and advocates in the body of the Court chatted unrestrainedly, as if the life of a fellow-creature were not trembling in the balance. The pros and cons of the case were eagerly discussed, and eatables and drinkables were produced from mysterious receptacles and openly enjoyed. Within the bar all was animation, and the counsel on both sides joined in the general conversation. Even the Lord Justice-Clerk, in his white and scarlet robes, and seemingly unwearied by the twelve hours, for it was now wearing on to ten o'clock at night, that he had sat on the bench, sauntered at and about his platform, shook hands with acquaintances, and, sinking his dignity, chatted cheerily with the medical experts for the defence. Slowly the minutes passed. A quarter, half, three-quarters of an hour were gone, and still no jury. After that terrible summing up, could it be that Laurie had still a chance? Suddenly from far below the bell sounded faintly, and the cry of 'Hush! Seats please' went around... Eager necks were stretched forward to catch a glimpse of Laurie as he ascended for the last time to listen to the verdict that was to acquit or condemn him. Pale, emotionless, but with strained, set features, he emerged through the trap-door and sat down erect in the dock between the policemen. The Lord Justice-Clerk sat still in his chair of justice, and waited. The noisy chatter died away, and sandwiches and flasks were furtively stowed out of sight...

The reason for the delay in the jury room only became evident later. After 40 minutes of deliberation each member of the jury recorded their verdict on the ballot paper. One juryman noted a colleague writing 'gilty' while someone else voted 'guilty not proven'. The ballot was rerun to remove any doubt and it would be 10.30pm before they had completed their deliberation.

'Hush! They are coming.' The side door swung noiselessly open, and through it silently, solemnly, with on some faces a desperate endeavour to look indifferent, the jurymen came trooping back to their seats. As one by one they took their places, Laurie raised his head, and with a quick rub of his glossy hair, glanced nervously from the jury-box to the Judge. 'What is your verdict, gentlemen?' said the clear voice of the Clerk of Court. There was a deep silence for a moment. Then from a corner of the jury seat, concealed from public view, there came in subdued accents the dread word 'Guilty'... Atrocious as was the crime of which he had been proved guilty, and appalling as was his position, he took it calmly. Not so the audience, through whom a sudden and perceptible shudder passed, followed by the deepest silence. Then a long and awkward pause, during which the stillness of the Court was broken only by the scratching of a pen as the Clerk wrote out the sentence, and by the muffled footsteps of the Judge's messenger as he fetched what appeared to be the black cap. It seemed impossible that that quiet, well-behaved, well-dressed young man in front, who sat looking steadily before him, could in another minute or two be going to be sentenced to death.

There was an expectant silence when the foreman, Archibald Jamieson, a fishmonger in Castle Street, announced: 'The verdict is guilty,' and after a short pause, 'by a majority'. Although not disclosed at the time, the majority was a single vote: eight guilty, seven not proven. William Roughead gave his take of the dramatic denouement in *Twelve Scots Trials*:

No one who witnessed the closing act of this famous trial can forget the impressive character of the scene. Without, in the black November night, a great crowd silently awaited the issue of life or death. The lofty, dimly-lighted Court-room, the candles glimmering in the shadows of the Bench, the imposing presence of the Justice-Clerk in his robes of scarlet and white, the tiers of tense, expectant faces, and in the dock the cause and object of it all: that calm, commonplace, respectable figure, the callous and brutal murderer whom Justice had tardily unmasked.

Laurie's reaction to the verdict was observed by the press reporters sitting directly behind him: 'Laurie gave a heavy sigh and became pale, but beyond a slightly nervous twitching of the mouth, he maintained the same cool demeanour that he had shown throughout the trial. A painful stillness prevailed in Court while the verdict was being recorded. Laurie glanced round once or twice at the jury-box, stroked his moustache and compressed his lips, but otherwise showed no sign of emotion.'[33]

After the Clerk of Court read out the verdict, Mr Graham Murray moved for sentence. There was now a dramatic six-minute pause before the prisoner was asked to stand up and the Lord Justice-Clerk, now wearing the black cap, began: 'John Watson Laurie, you have been convicted by the jury of one of the most terrible crimes that our country has ever known... The sentence of the Court upon you is that you be removed to the prison of Edinburgh, and thence transferred to the prison of Greenock, in the precincts of which prison you will be hanged by the neck between the hours of eight and ten in the forenoon of 30 November.' The *Glasgow Herald* recorded Laurie's reaction:

When he stood up to receive his sentence he drew himself erect and looked determinedly at the judge, who, on the contrary, was visibly affected, and uttered with a break in his voice the solemn words in which he besought Laurie to repent and turn to the God whom he had offended. But no sooner had his Lordship pronounced the closing prayer, 'May the Lord have mercy on your soul,' than the prisoner turned himself about and faced the hushed audience. He glanced all round hurriedly, and then said in a clear, firm tone, but with a look of tears in his eyes: 'Ladies and gentlemen, I am innocent of the charge.'

Lord Kingsburgh interrupted Laurie, saying that the prisoner could not be allowed to make a speech. Several years earlier the Judge had written a book, *A Practical Treatise on the Criminal Law of Scotland*, in which he stated: 'Sentence having been moved for, the accused is entitled to be heard, if he has any grounds to oppose judgement.' The book, for lack of anything better, was for years the standard reference work on the subject. In it Kingsburgh, then plain John Macdonald, also pointed out a quirk of the Scottish legal system: if south of the River Forth the death sentence had to be carried out between 15 and 21 days after the judgement, while north of the river you might have an extra week to live, the required period being between 21 and 27 days.

Throughout the Saturday, Parliament Square was thronged with people discussing the trial. When it appeared that the verdict was imminent the crowd swelled to fill both the square and the adjoining High Street. The verdict was received with a slight cheer mingled with some booing, but the overall reaction was largely one of surprise. In Coatbridge arrangements had been made for the result to be phoned to Mr Pettigrew's stationary shop in Main Street where a large crowd had assembled to hear the news. At 10.40pm a bill was posted in the shop window which simply said 'guilty'. The crowd dispersed in silence. In Glasgow, news vendors were besieged; a special late edition of the *Evening Times* was rushed out at 11pm and dispatched throughout the city. A verdict of not proven had been expected.

On Laurie's return to Calton Jail a raucous crowd followed the prison van, some cheering, some booing. He would spend the rest of the weekend in the jail. After the Sunday service Laurie was allowed time for exercise when the prison chaplain, the Reverend Mr Fleming, took the opportunity to talk with the condemned man. He advised him not to set great store on a reprieve but to 'immediately prepare for the next world'. Laurie's priorities, though, were finding out if the jury were unanimous and whether they had made any recommendation for mercy. In this, the chaplain was unable to help.

On Monday morning Laurie was taken by train from Edinburgh's Haymarket Station to Greenock where he attempted to make a speech to the waiting crowd. As a condemned man Laurie was now a commodity, like a parcel, that had to be signed for at every destination. As the resident Greenock Sheriff, Alexander Nicolson was required to be present at the execution. On 11 November Laurie was handed over to the jurisdiction of Greenock where Sheriff Nicolson issued a receipt for his delivery:

Received from John Mackenzie, Sheriff Officer Edinburgh, Certified Copy Death Warrant against John Watson Laurie sentenced to death on 9 November current in the High Court of Justiciary Edinburgh and to be executed at Greenock on the thirtieth November, and also the person of the said John Watson Laurie.

(Signed) Alex Nicolson

With Laurie's love of music it was apt that, as was the custom, broadsheets were soon on sale with a newly composed ballad covering recent events:

My name is John Watson Laurie
In prison here I lie
For the dreadful crime of murder
I am condemned to die

Mr Rose an English tourist
Took me his guide to be
He was a nice young gentleman
And was very kind to me

In the year of 1889
On the twelfth day of July
We started in the morning
For to climb the mountains high

Mr Rose fell o'er a precipice
Upon that fateful day
And now they say I murdered him
And took his life away

They say I took his travelling bag,
Containing all his clothes
A watch and chain, and diamond ring
Belonging to Mr Rose

I know I'd be suspected
So I quickly took my flight
But my troubled mind no rest could find
By day or yet by night

When they found poor Rose's body
'Twas covered up with stones
His head was sorely battered

THE GOATFELL MURDER

And broken was his bones

I roamed about from place to place
But rest I could not find
For thinking of that awful crime
Distressed my wretched mind

I have a sweetheart in Coatbridge
I will not tell her name
For this pretty fair maid
I feel a burning shame

At the High Court in Edinburgh
My trial I did stand
Like Job awaiting patiently
To hear the high command

Before the judge and jurymen
Found guilty for to be
So now I fear I'm doomed to die
Upon the gallow's tree

The judge in passing sentence
A few words to me did say
For the sure thing that you have
To look to God to pray

And ask the Lord to be your guard
From sin he'll set you free
On the third day of November
You shall die on the gallow's tree

And my own aged father
Thy mercy now I crave
I'm afraid this dreadful conduct
Bring your grey hairs to the grave

From this dark and dreary prison cell
I wish that I were free

CALUM SMITH

Come all you young and thoughtless youths
A warning take by me

And ask the Lord to be your guide
And soon he will set you free
But mind John Watson Laurie
Who's to hang on the gallows tree

Chapter Eight

Prepare for Thy Doom

When Laurie arrived back in Greenock Prison there were nineteen days left until his execution on Saturday 30 November. He was now in the condemned cell, the largest and most comfortable in the prison, often with the luxury of a fireplace. The Governor, medical officer and chief warder would visit him twice a day. The chaplain had free access. Laurie was not allowed to be left alone and warders, working 8-hour shifts, were with him around the clock. Those entrusted with these deathwatch duties often had a difficult, sometimes stressful time as they had to divert the prisoner's attention, comfort him and prevent him from committing suicide. The warders would occupy the time with games like chess, cards and dominoes. It was also their duty to record everything Laurie said, in case a confession, partial admission of guilt or some new piece of evidence came to light which would help the police close outstanding files on other crimes.

Laurie was described as remarkably calm and composed. One explanation for this was that he had now learnt how narrow the verdict had been and was convinced that, in these circumstances, the authorities would not hang someone. On other occasions it was noted that his composure lapsed and he broke down. Later, when he was asked what it was like to receive the death sentence, he recalled how he had a curious sense of detachment; he felt it was someone else who was being referred to, a sensation that lasted several days.

When Laurie was informed by the warders that he was a star attraction at the waxworks in Glasgow's Argyle Street, he regretted not knowing earlier as he would have been intrigued to see his likeness. According to some accounts he tried to persuade the prison staff to let him visit. Had he gone Laurie might not have been so upbeat. There were not just wax models but all sorts of bizarre exhibits and novelties. After public executions were outlawed in 1868 any ghoulish curiosity could be satisfied by viewing working models of hangings, a popular feature of such establishments.

The Glasgow waxworks included a menagerie, a coin-operated barrel organ and other automata, a fortune-teller and freak show. To find himself, Laurie would have had to climb the stairs past the World's Ugliest Woman, the Human Blister and the Lion-Faced Lady to the top floor, for many the highlight of their visit, the Murderers' Gallery, sometimes referred to as the 'Chamber of Horrors'. This incorporated a tableau of any forthcoming execution. Whenever a murderer was due to be hanged, the clothes of the dummy on the gallows were changed appropriately, in Laurie's case presumably to gaudy knickerbocker suit, yachting cap and his by now famous brown overcoat.

At Greenock Prison Laurie's visitors were strictly controlled, with permits only issued to those who could persuade the authorities that the meeting was of due relevance and importance. He had an average of four or five visitors a day: 'He listens attentively but on occasions he has very little to say in return.' He had no shortage of support from the church. The prison chaplain, the Reverend Archibald Fullarton, saw him frequently. He was also visited regularly by the Reverend Robert Somers of Gartsherrie Parish Church and the Reverend William Millar, the interim minister at Dunbeth United Presbyterian Church. The presbytery of the latter church also appointed the Rev J B Smith to look after his spiritual needs.

On Sunday 17 November Laurie was mentioned in many ministers' prayers and sermons. The *Glasgow Herald* continued to report on his emotional state:

> His behaviour in prison is a perfect enigma to those whose duty it is to look after his physical and spiritual welfare. While his demeanour towards the ministers of the gospel exhibits the utmost respect they have not yet detected that perturbation of manner which is expected to be shown by persons under sentence of death. Towards his prison officials he bears himself with something akin to dignity and continues remarkably fastidious as to his food and person.

With the gallows hanging over him, many people canvassed on Laurie's behalf, either because they believed in his innocence or they were against the death sentence. Had the case been tried in England where the jury had to be unanimous, there would have been no conviction. Had one majority juror voted a different way Laurie would have been freed. It was felt by many that the narrowness of the verdict, one vote, did not sit well with capital punishment. The *Coatbridge Express* summed up this vexed question: 'It may be a defect in the law that no verdict was possible save that which either condemned or liberated Laurie, but it is horrible beyond expression to think that for this man the difference between absolute freedom and a criminal's death was determined by the vote of a single fagged-out juryman. Surely in a case so surrounded with difficulties, and when the deliberations of the jury so nearly came to the point of breaking down, the right, the reasonable, and the humane course is to take the side of leniency.'

The respect in which Laurie's father was held, and the general wave of sympathy for his family, meant that John Watson Laurie had a relatively powerful and influential body of backers, perhaps not in respect of his innocence but certainly to save him from the gallows. The local community's response to Laurie's predicament would also demonstrate how deeply entrenched both the iron industry and the church were in the life of late Victorian Coatbridge. On the evening of Thursday 14 November there was a meeting in the Municipal Chambers that was attended by many local politicians, ministers, members of the medical profession, and representatives of the steel works and foundries. It was unanimously decided that steps should be taken to try and overturn the death sentence passed on Laurie. Committees were appointed for each ward of the town to obtain signatures for a petition. The *Coatbridge Express*, Grace Chalmer's workplace, became the hub of the campaign where petition sheets were printed and distributed.

In the three weeks till the date of execution a vigorous debate ensued in the correspondence pages of the newspapers as to the fairness of the sentence. One of the first letters was in the *Glasgow Herald* on the Monday immediately after the trial. It was by Dr Campbell Black, later professor of physiology at the Anderson Medical School in Glasgow. He began: 'Sir, One of the most painful cases occurring during the past years in the range of criminal jurisprudence, and almost amid unparalleled public excitement in the west of Scotland, terminated late on Saturday; and as I consider that the conclusions arrived at by the jury were not warranted, by the medical evidence at least, I shall feel obliged, by your permission, briefly to state, through your columns, the grounds on which this opinion is based.'

In his letter Dr Black continued to outline his objections to the prosecution's conclusions. He felt so strongly about this he published a 13-page pamphlet entitled: *The Laurie Case: The Medical Evidence Dissected*, 'Dedicated (without permission) to "Medical Experts".' As the title suggests, Black lacerates both the evidence and reputation of the defence medical team of Dr Gilmour, Dr Fullarton and Dr Littlejohn. 'It is not sufficient to discover *a* cause of death; it is *the* cause of death that is desiderated.' His most excoriating criticism is for Gilmour: 'Hazy on decomposition, doubtful in surgery, illogical in argument, strong in assumption, consistent alone in the theory of the defence.' Black's conclusions are as follows:

1. That it has *not* been proved that Rose was murdered at all.
2. That death was instantaneous, thus accounting for the absence of much or any haemorrhage.
3. That Rose fell on the vertex of the skull, falling backwards, and that all the fractures thereof occurred then and thereby.
4. That the injury to the spinal column was probably the cause of instant death, and that it *could only* be produced in this manner.

Dr James Adams, who really did live in Cambridge Street, read Black's letter and responded in the *Glasgow Herald* (18 November). He supported Black's conclusions and was also convinced that Rose's death was instantaneous, most likely the result of a tumble headlong from a height, not from repeated blows. He also pointed out the possibility of a fall caused by sudden illness. The next day the *Scottish Leader* included a long article in favour of a reprieve. It concluded, 'If murder were done, then within Laurie's nature there is enclosed a psychological enigma which the general human experience is powerless to explain.'

Despite this support, there was a growing realisation among

Laurie's family that his defence appeared weak. George Garrett and the Reverend Miller visited Laurie in Greenock Prison on Thursday 14 November when they informed him that his father was very ill. Garrett, according to prison sources, said something along the lines of: 'John, your father, brother and all your relatives believe you murdered Rose and you better make a clean breast of it and be done with it.' Laurie replied to the effect that if they had visited to try and make him give a confession they had made a great mistake. The next day Laurie was expecting letters of sympathy from his friends, especially Grace Chalmers, but none arrived. On the Saturday he asked the prison governor, William Napier, to contact his law agent, John McIntyre, and ask him to visit. In the presence of Napier and McIntyre, Laurie made the following statement:

I, John Watson Laurie declare that on the 15th day of July 1889 I went in company with Rose to the top of Goatfell to the ridge overlooking Glen Sannox and descended on the right side of the burn. I was some distance behind Rose when he slipped and fell head foremost and alighted on his head and the fleshy part of one of his ears was severed. When I got down to where he was I found him groaning and dying. I spoke to him but he gave me no answer; his eyes were closed and he died in that spot in my presence. He bled very copiously from the mouth and nose, so much so that I think no blood was left in his body. I tried to carry him down but could not. I then took his waterproof off and threw it a distance from me. I also threw his stick down the hill. His knife and pencil must have dropped from his pocket when I was dragging him down the hill. I went partly by the burn and then on the left side of the burn to the stone, his head and shoulder must have received injury in dragging him.

I rifled his pockets and took out his watch and chain and thirty shillings in silver money, also some letters and papers. He had no pocket money on his person but I found it in his bag. I found the railway ticket in the pocket book. I placed the body under the boulder and concealed it with stones, plenty of which were lying about. My object in doing so was not to have the body exposed. It took me about an hour to do so. I then ascended the hill and came down Corrie Glen. I met no one on the road. I arrived at Corrie Hotel about 10pm and went in and had a drink. I afterwards went to Brodick and went to bed. I did not raise the alarm for fear I would be blamed for killing him and for that same reason I hid the body. I threw the watch and chain away near the spot where he died. I never lifted a hand to Rose nor a stone, nor did I push him over.

All truth

Signed John W Laurie

The same day that Laurie wrote the above statement, Alexander Nicolson opened a letter postmarked Dysart in Fife, and simply addressed 'Sheriff Nicolson, Greenock'. It appeared to be a crank letter saying the writer was responsible for Rose's death. (The 'Dear Boss' and 'From Hell' letters in the Jack the Ripper case were still strong in the public consciousness.) Nevertheless, Nicolson forwarded it to Stormonth Darling with an accompanying letter: 'My Dear Darling, I got the enclosed this morning, and think it right to send it to you, though it does not seem to me of importance. I haven't the least idea who the writer is, probably an old acquaintance of Laurie's desirous to do him a good turn.' The letter read:

Dear Sir,

Could be taken up and tried now for the Rose Murder. After you have tried Laurie for the same, he saw me hit Rose and knock him down…I'll tell you how the doctors could not see the way his face was smashed. The way was this. He began to groan as I felt his pockets and I tumbled him over the place. I next burgled him where he was got. I made short stay and I saw the shepherd, the same shepherd as says it was Laurie. It was me. I was in the court at your trial. I could easily chased him but self first. It was a wonder he did not cope me with his eye when he turned round to speak. That was the only time I was feared.

I live in a lodging house but I wont tell you where. No No till I here how things can be profitable. I have very little conscience as you have none for me. I wants to let you know you croak an innocent man if you croak Laurie. I wont write no more as

have no paper but I know a thing or two and you should know
me as I have had to do with you before now
David Cameron
Alias other names

Another letter, this time in capital letters, was addressed to
the 'Lord Advocate, Council Chambers, Edinburgh', postmarked
Glasgow 14 November. Although having all the characteristics
of another crank letter, the writer appears very well informed
as to some of the people involved. For example the Reverend
Hind and the Reverend Goodman had indeed, for several years,
stayed near each other in the Newcastle area: Hind in Gateshead,
Goodman at Walker-on-Tyne. This information had not been
published anywhere, and was not common knowledge:

MAN FOUND DEAD AT ARRAN IS THE CARIER
THAT TOOK ROSE'S BODY FROM WALKER'S HUT.
NOW THEY HAVE DRUGED HIM. MRS SHAW HAS
KNOWN POOR FOOLISH LAURIE FOR YEARS. THE
GILMOURS, MICKIL, THOM, GOODMAN ALL KNOW
LAURIE AS LAURIE. HIND DID NOT NEED TO ASK
ROSE, FOR GOODMAN AND HIM ARE KNOWN FOR
TWO BLACGUARDS IN NEWCASTLE. MRS CURRIE
WAS WELL KNOWN TO THE GILMOURS, THOM,
MICKIL AND GOODMAN AND THEY ALL KNEW
LAURIE WAS STAYING WITH HER. SHE HAS KNOWN
HIM FOR YEARS.
THE MAN WAS DEAD LONG BEFORE HE WAS
SMASHED AND HIS BODY WAS NOT TAKEN TO THE
HOLE ON MONDAY NIGHT. ASK MICKLE. WHAT
HE WANTED THE SMITHS YACHT FOR. YOU MUST
SEARCH INTO THIS FOR GOD WILL HOLD YOU
RESPONSIBLE. SUCH A YOUNG SOUL MUST NOT
SUFFER ALONE FOR SO MANY. AITKEN KNOWES
ALL THIS AND KNOWS ALL NAMED HERE. SO DID
POOR YOUNG LYE THAT WAS MURDERED AND HIS
MURDERS WALKING THE STREET. LAURIES FATHER
MUST BE TOLD ALL THIS, ALSO THE MAIL FOR THE
PUBLIC MUST KNOW ALL

In the press more conventional letters filled the correspondence pages. On 14 November there was a letter from 'A Scotchman': 'Sir, In the name of common sense, what is coming over us all that this hysterical howl for a reprieve is raised every time a person is convicted of murder nowadays?' (Reprieves were very rare in cases involving shooting or poisoning.) Four days later further views were published in the *Evening Citizen*: 'If circumstantial evidence is to go for anything, there could scarcely be a clearer case of guilt than Laurie's'. There was also: 'I can only say that I hope the Home Secretary will not accede to public clamour, but will deal out justice without fear or favour'. The *Saturday Review* stated, 'Except that the victim was an Englishman, while the prisoner is a Scotchman, we can suggest no reason why Laurie should not be hanged.'

The mystery remained, however, as to why Laurie and Rose took the descent route they did. After leaving the summit of Goatfell, they had to first descend a couple of hundred feet over rocky ground to the start of the Stacach ridge. Due to large boulders the correct way here was not initially obvious. In misty conditions it was important to strike the ridge at the correct point and not veer too far left, where walkers could eventually find themselves on treacherous granite slabs above Glen Rosa.

As well as the path to Corrie and The Saddle route, guidebook writer M J B Baddeley mentioned another descent option – the trackless route directly down from Goatfell's summit into Glen Rosa. He himself had ascended Goatfell this way, but thought it unsatisfactory: 'The writer will only say that he found it, in ascending, too steep and fatiguing to justify his recommending it for a descent.' Nevertheless, for a time this become a popular short cut for those wanting to visit Glen Rosa on their way back to Brodick.

This Glen Rosa side of Goatfell was very similar in character to the Glen Sannox flank of the mountain that Laurie and Rose eventually descended. Both these slopes have extensive areas of potentially hazardous granite slabs, features that may have some bearing on what happened to Rose. In ascent these are easy to avoid but going down, especially in poor visibility, can prove fraught with danger. There are records of people getting into difficulties hereabouts with at least one fatality (in 1857). The accident statistics also included a Victorian celebrity, Sir William Smith, a classics scholar familiar to many students at the time through his popular textbooks. After becoming separated from his party, Smith became cragfast on the rocks, unable to move up or down, and was eventually benighted.

When Laurie's recent acquaintance, Sheriff Nicolson, the man who would eventually sign his death warrant, was geologising on Arran in April 1872 with his friend Archibald Geikie, he heard about this episode which had occurred a few years earlier. Nicolson later wrote about Smith's misfortune, which he regarded as a direct result of climbing the hills on the Sabbath: 'There stood, with his back against the rock, during all the long hours of an August night, with nothing to console him but his cigar case... With the first blink of dawn a searching party from the Douglas Hotel came and found him, still perched in his unpleasant fastness and waving on the top of his stick a sheet of the *Times!*' By the time rescuers reached Smith he had been stuck for 18 hours: 'By the aid of ropes he was got out of his perilous position, and by the help of a little mountain dew his speech was restored.'

After Laurie and Rose negotiated the Stacach ridge, they would reach the foot of North Goatfell where a well-defined path bypasses the 200ft climb to the summit by contouring the peak's east flank. Since the path traverses the Corrie side, any view down to The Saddle is obscured. This may be a significant factor in what happened to Laurie and Rose. Even in ideal conditions it is not difficult to saunter past North Goatfell and miss the correct turn off for The Saddle, arriving eventually at a dip in the ridge where a cairn marked the descent to Corrie on one side and Coire nam Fuaran on the other.

Two theories have already been tendered as to why Laurie and Rose descended by way of Coire nam Fuaran: the first is that they felt this route was quicker and safer than The Saddle route, the second is that they intended to go by The Saddle but made a navigational error. However, there is a third possible scenario: that Laurie and Rose 'got lost' because they followed an inaccurate description in a tourist guidebook. Many of these books were full of errors and following their directions could lead you, not to The Saddle, but down the fateful gully to Coire nam Fuaran.

This confusion was exacerbated by the interpretation placed on the term 'The Saddle'. Nowadays it refers to the mountain pass between Glen Rosa and Glen Sannox, but the Victorians regarded it, conversely, as the lowest point of the ridge between Cir Mhor and North Goatfell. The normally reliable Baddeley guide states: 'The descent to the col between Glen Rosa and Glen Sannox is by a narrow ridge called The Saddle.' As late as 1928 Tom S Hall portrayed The Saddle as 'a high ridge dipping down from Cir Mhor to rise again to the Goatfell range.' This otherwise inconsequential distinction would impact on how the route was described in early guidebooks.

At this time route descriptions for the Arran mountains, Goatfell's tourist path aside, were often compiled by people with little or no first-hand knowledge of the ground covered; they were often created using information rehashed from other publications. (In fairness some did recommend a guide for any less-frequented itineraries.) As previously outlined, the established route from Goatfell's summit to Glen Sannox had two sections where walkers needed to take care: the way off the Goatfell ridge down to The Saddle, and the descent from The Saddle itself into Glen Sannox. Some tourist guidebooks, however, got these two areas mixed up, leaving a topographical muddle for walkers to figure out as best they could. *Oliver and Boyd's Scottish Tourist* provides one example of this ambiguous and misleading advice:

Should the tourist have active limbs and enjoy perfect freedom from giddiness which is sometimes produced by looking from a height, we recommend him, instead of returning by the same route, to proceed from the summit of Goatfell in a direction nearly north, by scrambling along the ridge called 'The Saddle', which separates the head of Glen Rosa (the valley which passes in a curve round the west and north west of the mountain) from Glen Sannox (the glen which opens to the eastward). Let him proceed almost to the farther extremity of this ridge, and he will there find, at its lowest point, a place where he can descend into Glen Sannox.

The above description has been paraphrased from a rival guidebook, and because of the changes made to avoid charges of plagiarism, any accuracy, or indeed sense, has been lost. Some of the instruction for descending from The Saddle into Glen Sannox has been mistakenly transposed to describe the descent off North Goatfell with the reader being informed that the summit ridge of Goatfell is known as 'The Saddle'. Many of the walkers trying to follow these directions would now assume that the correct descent was from the lowest point on *this* ridge (the summit ridge) – which would lead you down into Coire nam Fuaran.

Consequently, when Laurie and Rose reached the afore-mentioned cairn they may have presumed that this marked the descent to The Saddle. When they walked towards the Glen Sannox side and peered gingerly down, they could see that initially the going looked relatively straightforward. As they descended, the gully widened with a watercourse on the left (looking down) where the stream bed consisting of water-worn granite, much of it wet. On the right side of the burn there was an ominous rocky prow, the 'projecting rock' mentioned at the trial by Sergeant William Munro and others. The '19-foot drop' was directly below this.

The fact there was no longer a well-defined path, combined with the unfriendliness of the terrain, would have created a growing realisation in both Laurie and Rose that they had come the wrong way. Tempers may have frayed. Mounting tension and pent-up frustration, aggravated by tiredness, may well have precipitated the events that led to Rose's demise. However, there was nothing particularly difficult-looking about the ground below. But that was the problem. Granite slabs are notorious for appearing innocuously easy, an opinion quickly altered once you set foot on them. To the far left and far right there were easier options that circumvented any potential difficulties. The right side of the stream, below the rocky prow, seemed the obvious, most direct line to take. But could they safely descend this way?

In Greenock Prison, as the date of his execution drew ever nearer, Laurie became increasingly uneasy. On 19 November his brother Gavin and his aunt Bella from Moffat visited. It is highly probable they repeated the family's wishes that he tell the truth about what happened on Goatfell. With the reality sinking in that he may only have ten days left to live, Laurie decided to expand on his earlier statement and sent the following letter to Lord Lothian, the Scottish Secretary:

My Lord,
Permit me to make the following statement which I am ashamed and sorry to say I did not make to the agent who acted on my behalf at the trial, the issue of which has resulted so unfortunately for me.

The only excuse I can offer for this is that I had begun my defence in the foolish letters which I sent to the newspapers, and which contained what I vainly thought was my best defence I could have, and which defence, My Lord, nearly set me at liberty without having to acquaint the public with the story of my madness and the terrible manner in which I had failed to do my duty.

From the evidence it was apparent that I had not sought Mr Rose's company, indeed the manner he assumed in informing me that he would stay with me a few days at Arran astonished me so much I could not avoid talking about it to my friends. My object in going to Arran was to visit the glens and to ascend Goatfell and I explained to Mr Rose that if he wished my society he would require to accompany me on these excursions.

On the afternoon of Sunday 14 July Rose and I walked up Glen Rosa and on that occasion he behaved himself more like a boy than a tourist by delighting himself in perching on rocks rather than admiring the grand scenery with which we were surrounded. On the forenoon of July 15 we were all together in the Brodick hotel and Rose and I talked about ascending Goatfell and returning to Brodick by way of Glen Sannox. Mr Smith, one of the witnesses of the Crown but who was not called to give evidence explained to us that he had made the journey, and directed me by way of The Saddle to Glen

Sannox. About three o'clock Rose and I left Brodick pier
for Goatfell, and when on the top we decided to go to Glen
Sannox by way of the ridge which we mistook for The Saddle
and I may say here that I hardly believe that the foot of man
ever crossed that ground before. We soon saw our mistake
but kept on not willing to retrace our steps. After we got over
the ridge and began to descend into Glen Sannox the ground
became so dangerous that I suggested to Rose that we should
go back by way of Corrie Glen and visit Corrie instead, but he
preferred to proceed on the way we had come.

We were at this time descending on the right hand side of
a deep gully, when it occurred to me that the descent might
be safer on the left hand side so I crossed the gully with the
intention of seeing if it would be, and deciding that it would,
I turned to call Rose who had gone on ahead, and near to
the edge of a high cliff, where he either got giddy or slipped.
I can't say which, but he went straight over and was killed. I
became horrified and scrambled down after him, and found
him breathing heavily and dying. I tried to raise him, but my
strength had left me and all that I could do was to look on
and see him die. His face was terribly bruised and the blood
streamed from his mouth and nose, in fact he lost so much
blood that I think there could scarcely be a drop left in his
body.

I am afraid my Lord that I can offer no satisfactory excuse for
my conduct after this, but I am of a very nervous temperament
and I must have gone off my head with fear and dread lest it
should be said that I had killed him or was with him when it
happened at all. I madly decided to carry the poor fellow off
the rocks and bury him and fly the place. This proved to be no
easy task as I slipped and fell with him more than once, and
that may account for the knife and things which fell from his
pockets. His macintosh was torn so I took it off and threw it
away. I then caught hold of his jacket and dragged him to the
crevice of a boulder which I saw and which presented itself as
a suitable place to lay the body.

I was going away then, but I returned and took from his pocket
a pocket book which contained some papers, a sovereign and
some odd silver. I took his watch from his pocket and threw

it away among the heather. It was an old silver Geneva watch with a brass chain attached. I then covered up the body with stones, hundreds of which were lying close at hand. I then left for Corrie where I met the witness Mr Wilson. I went back to my lodgings at Brodick where I went to bed and in the morning I left taking Rose's bag as well as my own as I wanted it to be thought that we had left the island together, and that accounts for me having had his things in my possession, and which things I did not take the least pains to put out of the way, but left them to be part of a chain of evidence in a case of murder which was never anything of the kind. I believed that poor Rose would never be thought of or sought after, but I went back to my work in a very unhappy state of mind.

A few days after I saw that Mr Rose's brother was making enquiries for him, and it was well known that Rose and I had been together, I knew that before long I would be asked to account for him. I acted madly again by giving up my work and everything else with the intention of committing suicide which I actually tried to do more than once. All this trouble has come to me because I tried to hide the fact that Rose met with an accident while in my company.

I swear by Almighty God as I will be brought before him in the great day of judgement that I did not stone Rose. I did not throw him down and I did not murder him.

The first thing that goes against the Doctors' evidence is the fact that they said that the body presented no signs of bleeding, when the truth is that poor Rose bled to death, and if I had murdered him by stoning him, I don't think it consistent with common sense that I would have dislocated his shoulder bone or broke his ribs.

I will just say before I close this document, which I regret I have had to write rather hurriedly, that the question of me being a murderer is opposed by the whole of my previous life.

I hope my Lord that under these circumstances the death sentence will not be carried out.

I am my Lord
Your obedient servant
John W Laurie

Laurie's pleas were in vain as his request was refused. In reply he wrote: 'I have read your letter which was handed me today, and I take from it that the confession which I made to you will have no effect in changing the sentence which has been pronounced to me. As I did not stone Mr Rose and as he was dead before I touched him with my hands, I have no other confession to make, so I suppose that the matter must remain as it is and that I may also prepare for my doom'.

John Watson Laurie

Edwin Robert Rose

The *Ivanhoe* leaves Brodick pier, with Goatfell behind.

The Glenburn Hydropathic where Rose stayed during his holiday in Rothesay.

Rothesay from Chapel Hill around 1890.

A view of Brodick Bay showing the tourist path up Goatfell.

Looking from Goatfell to Cir Mhor and Caisteal Abhail. The Saddle is above the couple on the left.

Looking from Caisteal Abhail towards Goatfell, with the north-west ridge leading down to The Saddle. The **X** marks where Laurie and Rose started their descent; **A** marks the location of Rose's fall, and **B** the boulder where his body was hidden.

Brodick in 1889. The arrow indicates the hut occupied by Laurie and Rose.

Looking from the summit of Goatfell along the Stacach ridge to North Goatfell. The **X** marks where Laurie and Rose started their descent into Coire nam Fuaran.

Rose's grave in Glen Sannox.

The location of Rose's fall.

The capture of John Laurie near Larkhall (*Illustrated Police News*).

Rose's body was discovered in the cavity under the large boulder—the remains of the cairn can be seen on its top.

James Muirhead, alias 'Scotch Jamie', one of Laurie's fellow inmates at Peterhead Prison.

John Laurie on reception at Perth Prison in 1889.

One of the cell blocks at Peterhead Prison.

A cell at Peterhead Prison similar to that occupied by Laurie.

The granite quarries near Peterhead Prison. The convicts were transported between the prison and the quarries on specially designed trains.

Chapter Nine

A Brain of Putty

Arrangements for Laurie's execution were officially the responsibility of the prison Visiting Committee, the Sheriff-Substitute and the Procurator Fiscal. In practice, however, it was the Greenock magistrates who did much of the organising. They decided the press would be admitted to the prison where they would be provided with information but would not be asked to witness the hanging. By Act of Parliament the governor, chaplain and medical officer had to attend.

The site of the execution, behind the County Courthouse, was totally enclosed in case anyone climbed onto the roofs of the surrounding houses, the only feasible viewpoint. Once this screening was completed the scaffold arrived on a lorry and was placed in position. The flagstaff was then erected for hoisting the black flag. It only remained to contact the hangman, James Berry, who arranged to arrive on Friday, the day before the execution, to inspect the scaffold and give any instructions he thought necessary. Berry had already made two trips to Scotland that year for a couple of high-profile clients: Jessie King, the Edinburgh baby farmer, hanged in March for infanticide, and William Henry Bury, executed the next month for the murder of his wife. Bury had recently moved from Whitechapel to Dundee where the press, and Berry, suspected that he may have been Jack the Ripper.

Berry was an ex-policeman from Bradford who carried out 130 hangings between 1884 and 1891. An archetypal Yorkshire-man, he was one of 1400 applicants for the post. His business card read: 'James Berry, Executioner'. Some hangmen, including Berry, had a reputation for holding court in local pubs after executions, entertaining locals with tales of their gruesome trade, sometimes selling the used rope. This led to questions being asked in Parliament, and in 1885 the Home Office decreed that hangmen should be required to lodge within the prison on the night before the execution. The prisoner's clothes, however, remained the hangman's property and were often purchased by waxworks or cut into small pieces for sale as souvenirs.

Berry used his own rope, 13ft (4m) long, three-quarters of an inch (2cm) thick, made of the finest Italian hemp. There was a brass ring at one end through which the other end was passed to create a noose. The ring was placed just behind the left ear. The most important part of the hangman's job was calculating the 'drop', the exact length of rope required. If this was correct death would be immediate through severance of the spinal cord, if wrong there was either strangulation or decapitation. As yet there was no official guide for calculating the correct length and Berry devised his own table, testing it using bags of sand equivalent to the victim's weight. Laurie was 133lb (60kg) and would require a drop of 9ft 6in (2.9m).

Laurie would be hoping there would be a repeat of one of Berry's clients four years earlier, a prisoner named John 'Babbacombe' Lee. Twenty-year-old Lee was convicted of the murder of his elderly employer Emma Keyse for whom he worked as a footman. When Berry pulled the lever for the trap-door nothing happened despite several warders proceeding to stamp on it. Lee was taken to his cell and the lever was tested, but worked perfectly. The process was repeated and the same thing happened. After a third unsuccessful attempt the governor stayed the execution while he consulted the Home Office. Lee was later reprieved and became known as 'The man they couldn't hang'. He inspired the Fairport Convention album *Babbacombe Lee*.

Berry regarded himself as good at his job. However hangmen received no formal training and botched executions were common. In the few years prior to Laurie's conviction, Berry was having serious problems getting things right. The same year as 'Babbacombe' Lee, he decapitated two prisoners. To counter this he shortened his rope but his next three executions led to death from asphyxia. On one of these the doctor descended into the pit to find the pulse of the victim, Edward Hewitt, 'racing at 80 to the minute with the victim struggling to free his hands and arms': 'On removing the white cap about one and a half minutes after the fall I found the eyes staring from the sockets and the tongue protruded the face exhibiting unmistakeable evidence of intense agony.'

For Laurie's last weeks his welfare was looked after by specially chosen warders. The chaplain would be at his side for his last few hours. From the time Berry entered his cell Laurie would have three minutes to live. The hangman would immediately pinion his arms with a broad leather body-belt; his wrists were then strapped to the belt, an opportunity for a last confession. As the procession moved towards the scaffold the chaplain would start to read the service for the funeral of the dead. The condemned man was positioned under the beam, his legs secured by a leather strap; a white hood placed over his head, the noose adjusted, the lever pulled and the heavy oak trap door would open.

The black flag was then hoisted to inform those at the prison gates that the execution was completed. The body was left for an hour, hanging above a pit to catch excrement and bodily fluids. It was then lowered into a simple coffin, made in the prison, and carried to the mortuary for an inquest. At this point, if the deceased was well-known, a death mask was often made. It was common practice to bury the victim in an unmarked grave within the prison grounds.

Over the weekend of 16-17 November and through the next week the petition campaign gained momentum as the collection of signatures went on apace. In Coatbridge folk queued to sign near the Whitelaw Fountain at the Cross; tables were placed in all the churches with clerks in charge. In Glasgow there were copies of the petition in churches, banks, pubs, shops and public institutions; in Edinburgh you could sign at tables in the street, and there was also a door-to-door canvas. At Greenock there were sheets in all the banks and public buildings.

From his shop in Coatbridge's Main Street, Alexander Pettigrew organised the distribution of petition sheets throughout Central Scotland and as far afield as Inverness and Aberdeen. There were even signatures coming in from England and Ireland. On Friday 22 November, eight days before the execution, the number of signatures totalled 138,140. That evening the petition, weighing over 150kg, was dispatched on the 10pm night mail to London for the attention of Lord Lothian, the Scottish Secretary.

The petition argued that the evidence did not sufficiently

establish the guilt of the accused; much of this was circumstantial, and the medical evidence was inconclusive. There were examples of other fatalities with similar injuries to Rose that had been caused by a fall. Laurie was a first offender. There was a history of insanity in the prisoner's family. Pressure had also been put on the jury to conclude the trial within a specific time. The recent commutation of the death sentence pronounced on Mrs Maybrick was popularly held to justify Laurie getting the benefit of the doubt.

Robert R Laurie (no relation) wrote to the press to complain about the means by which some of the petition signatures had been obtained: the same people signing many different sheets or on the same sheet with different names, 'school-children marched in hundreds to sign it'. 'W' wrote from Kilmacolm about the same issue:

It would be very interesting to know what percentage of that number are ratepayers and entitled to a vote at either municipal or Parliamentary elections, for I consider that people who are not eligible to vote at these elections have no right or business, and should not be allowed to sign petitions trying to alter the laws of our country. I question very much if 90 per cent of those who have signed are not apprentices, office and message boys, servant girls, and mill workers.

The petition polarised popular opinion as to Laurie's sentence, and the spate of correspondence in the newspapers continued. Mrs L M Dunbar of Rutherglen, a stalwart supporter of Laurie, started a letter-writing campaign. She was convinced Rose's death was as a result of a fall due to giddiness, as her husband had suffered in a similar manner during an ascent of Goatfell in 1878. She even wrote Queen Victoria:

To our Royal Lady, The Queen
For a brief space I crave audience of thee, in that I intrude my importunate petition privately before the notice of my revered and beloved Queen. I pray thee to grant a free pardon, or at least commute the sentence of death to one of thy subjects, a young man of 25 years, John Watson Laurie by name.

One of Laurie's neighbours in North Frederick Street was of the opposite opinion to Mrs Dunbar. He wrote to Lord Lothian: 'The Defender has turned out what I always thought he would, seeing he was one of the Devil's Own. We were all glad when the land shark was caught and think surely that your Lordship will not allow him to break the net in any way, and then he will do for some other. The cat-o'-nine tails stopped the garrotters about twenty years ago and any man who sends another below the ground should be carried himself above the ground with rope around his neck.'

The garrotters were the cause of a moral panic in the early 1860s when several wealthy people were strangled and robbed in London. It led to the Garrotters Act of 1863 which introduced flogging as a punishment for similar crimes.

On the same day as the petition was sent to the Scottish Office there was an unusual turn of events. A common element in Victorian melodramas was a shady band of gypsies lurking in the narrative wings. The Laurie case was no exception. A 'red-headed tinker' named Mrs McCallum boasted of her involvement in Rose's murder. This was overheard by two other women named Brodie and McGinlay who contacted the police. The Procurator Fiscal in Dumbarton, W Bartie, thought this unlikely but decided to investigate more fully due to 'the excited state of public opinion regarding Laurie'. He traced the travellers to Balloch at the foot of Loch Lomond where McCallum admitted she had told the story, but that it was untrue as she had been under the influence of drink at the time. She also stated that she had not been to Arran for nine years, a fact confirmed by her husband. Bartie made further enquiries and discovered the McCallums were released from Glasgow Prison on Saturday 13 July and on the day of Rose's murder were probably camped in a quarry near Duntocher. He thought it unlikely they had the money to go to Arran.

With time running out it was becoming apparent to Laurie's supporters that the best chance to save his life was on the grounds that he was insane. This would require some prying into the mental health of many of Laurie's relatives. The Reverend Alexander Ramsay, who had been minister at Dunbeth Church until he left for another position in Highgate, London, would petition with regard to insanity in the Laurie family. He knew them extremely well and related how Laurie's sister, Agnes, had previously written to him complaining that he was making defamatory remarks about her personal appearance in both his sermons and prayers. Many of her letters were incoherent. The Reverend Ramsay's opinion was that John Laurie was similarly insane: 'He was a vain, frivolous youth, very fond of dress, simple-headed and foppish.' He reckoned that Laurie's actions came from a fit of insanity similar to that which his sister was prone to: 'Everyone who knew him saw that he was empty-headed and likely to be of very little use in the world.' The Reverend Ramsay revealed that Laurie had once emigrated to America but returned after a few months.

A special commission was appointed by the Secretary for Scotland to investigate the mental condition of John Watson Laurie. It comprised Sir Arthur Mitchell, a Commissioner in Lunacy who was a pioneer of psychiatric epidemiology as well as a professor of ancient history, W T (William) Gairdner, professor of medicine at Glasgow University, and Dr David Yellowlees, the medical superintendent of Glasgow Royal Asylum (Gartnavel).

The moves for Laurie's reprieve would bring his case centre stage in the long-running crime and insanity debate where alienists saw exculpation in madness whereas the law regarded much of this as a convenient excuse. Alienists were physicians who dealt with alienated minds (today's psychiatrists). Many of them, like Yellowlees, superintended lunatic asylums and were active in campaigning against the execution of the insane.

The popular legal and medical definition of insanity was someone who was defective in intellect and reasoning, usually accompanied by delusions and hallucinations. Alienists tried to extend pleas to those in whom feelings or emotions were disordered; those who offended repeatedly without remorse (known to us as psychopaths). They particularly promoted the plea of moral insanity, the degradation of morals without a concomitant loss of reason: a state of mind, not a set of behaviours.

The commission examined Laurie from Saturday 23 until Monday 25 November. They interviewed him for over an hour on the Saturday, all of Sunday and also for some time on Monday. Many of Laurie's friends and family were aware that this was the last chance to save his life. They used all the influence they could muster to obtain the cooperation of some of the most influential figures in the Coatbridge area. On 25 November, six days prior to the hanging, the Medical Commission presented their report:

We examined the Governor and Medical Officer of the prison, and carefully considered various letters and statements written by the prisoner since his trial. We then had a long interview with the prisoner himself. Subsequently we examined the following gentlemen from Coatbridge who gave us information from personal knowledge as to Laurie's history and conduct:

1. Reverend Robert Somers, minister of Gartsherrie Parish Church.
2. Mr Peter McLean, grocer, Coatbridge.
3. W Alex Pettigrew, merchant, Coatbridge.
4. S Farquharson, Coatbridge.
5. Baillie Thomas Gilchrist, Coatbridge.
6. W Andrew Lamberton, Coatbridge.

The Reverend Somers, originally from Perthshire, was a graduate of St Andrews University. Alexander Pettigrew was a popular figure in the Coatbridge area who was the session clerk at Dunbeth Church for over forty years. It was at his printing business and stationery shop that the result of Laurie's trial was announced. Thomas Gilchrist was a prominent public figure, the first Senior Baillie of Coatbridge. Andrew Lamberton was a notable industrial innovator who started his own engineering works in the town. A personal friend of Andrew Carnegie, Lamberton's name is writ large on his old factory above Coatbridge Sunnyside Station. The medical report on Laurie continued:

All gentlemen appear to be truthful and unbiased, and what they told us was of great value.

We were informed that Laurie has been called 'daft' when he was at school. That while he was an apprentice with Messrs Lamberton and Co, engineers, he made no real endeavour to acquire his trade and was regarded as incapable of acquiring it; and that at the end of a five years' apprenticeship he was kept on at his father's request at a low wage, his work not being worth one half of a full journeyman's wage.

That after leaving Messrs Lambertons' employment he worked at his trade in Glasgow but never stayed more than a few months in any situation. That he then left his work as a patternmaker and became a traveller for his father; that he subsequently returned to his trade but has never been for any length of time continuously a self-supporting man. That he did not get on well with his family, and has always been a burden and a vexation to his father. That his spare time has always been devoted to silly philandering with girls, walking out with them and boasting of his conquests, yet that he was so effeminate and frivolous that even their parents seemed to regard him as too weak and silly to be harmful or to be treated seriously as a suitor.

That although he has received a good education his conversation was boyish, silly and conceited, and he was given to needless lying in order to magnify himself or his prospects. That he was commonly regarded as weak, unstable and flighty and as deficient in judgement and common sense.

Mr Peter McLean's testimony was most important. He informed us that Laurie has been courting his daughter Annie and that when she discontinued the intimacy Laurie had insulted and annoyed the whole family, renewing such conduct after apologising and promising to desist from it. Mr McLean was led by Laurie's whole conduct to regard him as not sound in mind and he spoke of this to Laurie's father. His opinion was that Laurie 'might at any time become a lunatic' and in that state be dangerous to his daughter. He told us that the feeling that Laurie was 'not right' made him tolerate and put up with his conduct in a way he would not otherwise have done. We satisfied ourselves that this opinion had been formed by Mr McLean long before Rose's death and it has not been changed by the facts which have become public nor by the foul slanders which Laurie has cast upon his daughter.

On one occasion, subsequent to Rose's death, Laurie met Annie McLean and her mother at Rothesay, and said to the former 'Lady, I'll do for you!'. Fearing violence Mr McLean for some time after this employed a detective to escort his daughter daily between the railway station and the school in Glasgow where she was engaged as a pupil [student] teacher.

Dr Farquharson of Coatbridge informed us that Laurie consulted him about three years ago that he regarded him then as of unsound mind and that he entered in his notes on the occasion of one of his visits, 'Poor Laurie more insane than ever'. These notes were destroyed two years ago. Dr Farquharson further informed us that Laurie was at that time suffering from the effects of masturbation, and that Laurie stated to us that he had long been addicted to that practice and had consulted Dr Farquharson on the subject.

The family history of the prisoner, prepared by the Rev Somers from sources we deem quite trustworthy, has been laid before us, and from it we learn that his:

Mother's uncle was eccentric.
Mother's aunt had five deaf and dumb children.
Mother's cousin is insane and in an asylum.
Mother's sister was insane.
Mother's brother was epileptic.
Own sister is insane.

We have satisfied ourselves by the testimony of others that this family history is correct.

Throughout our interview with Laurie his demeanour was such as became his position. He is a man of slight physique and of highly nervous temperament. He answered questions intelligently, in well-chosen words and without any sign of reservation or insincerity. He spoke without hesitation of what had occurred when Rose met his death and all he said was consistent with the statement he has made since the trial to the Secretary of State for Scotland.

He said that he had adhered to the statement made in his letters to the newspapers because he felt sure that he could not be convicted; and that he had misled his Counsel, being convinced that he was thus taking the best course to secure acquittal. When asked why, if his last statement were true, he had acted as he did with Rose's body? He was silent for a little and then said 'it was just madness'.

When asked why he wrote the letters to the newspapers, he said, after a pause, that it was chiefly to spite Cowan, his rival with Annie McLean. Asked why he took Rose's effects he said it was in order that it might be supposed they had left the island together.

When asked why he wore Rose's clothes, when he had better of his own, he could not give any explanation except that he thought no one would recognise them as belonging to Rose. When asked why he came back to Coatbridge where he was so well-known, he said it was to see Grace Chalmers, the girl to whom he has been writing from prison.

The death of Rose on the mountain, however it was caused, would in our opinion certainly and greatly agitate Laurie and would render a man of his mental constitution less capable even than usual of wise and right action. His behaviour then, on any theory of the death, was senseless and most compromising. His subsequent behaviour was consistent with the opinion we have formed of his character and mental state. His letters to the newspapers reveal his inordinate love of notoriety and his petty spitefulness. His extreme conceit appeared in his deeming himself wiser than his Law Advisers and his untruthfulness in his deliberately deceiving them.

His wearing of Rose's clothes in the place where they had been seen together showed a recklessness inconceivable in any reasonable man. And his return to Coatbridge where his arrest was certain is equally reckless and inexplicable. Three times on the occasion of this charge, and once before on the occasion of a charge of theft, Laurie has informed us that he had attempted to commit suicide. In such a man suicidal attempts are characteristic and so is their failure. Selfish cowardice both prompts the act and prevents its completion.

Founding upon all the facts herein detailed we have arrived at a definite opinion as to Laurie's mental condition. Although not deficient in intellect and education, he does not, and from his nature and organisation we think he can not, apply his intelligence to the regulation of his life and conduct. His actions are not guided by reason and a regard to consequences, or by a sense of duty, but are determined by impulse, selfishness, or vanity, and are distinguished by entire heedlessness of consequences.

His condition is not mere wickedness which knows the right and chooses the wrong. He appears to us to lack the faculty which characterises some men, of guiding his conduct by his knowledge.

On that respect and to that degree we deem John Watson Laurie a person of unsound mind.

Signed
Arthur Mitchell
WT Gairdner
D Yellowlees

It is worth taking a closer look at this medical report as its content was literally a matter of life and death: if it gave sound grounds for insanity then Laurie would probably live, if not he would certainly die. If we sum up the evidence presented in the report with respect to Laurie's insanity, we have: someone who can't settle down to a job, who could become obsessive in relationships, had a history of mental illness in his family, and was impulsive, selfish and vain. We all know people with some or many of these characteristics and would generally regard them as ordinary individuals with some problems, much like the rest of us.

It was masturbation that helped save Laurie's life. To the Medical Commission his addiction to this onanistic vice was the key piece of evidence that provided irrefutable proof of Laurie's 'insanity'. For over 250 years masturbation pre-occupied the medical profession, with one prominent psychiatrist describing it as 'the most commonly diagnosed and most enthusiastically treated mental disease in the history of medicine'. 'The heinous act of self-pollution, as it was known, was widely regarded as the cause of blindness, epilepsy, gonorrhoea and insanity, and almost any other condition they could not otherwise explain. With no evidence and little explanation, a causal connection was established between masturbation and serious mental illness. To the medical establishment this antisocial, profligate and seminally extravagant practice, with its reprehensible lack of self-control, represented all that was a threat to the Victorian ideals of family values and societal cohesion.

If those who met Laurie were impressed by his calmness under sentence of death, his cool demeanour would soon have evaporated had he known what he might experience in a lunatic asylum. In these institutions a range of bizarre and grotesque treatments for masturbation had been developed, from benign dietary changes to radical surgical interventions. The latter included the deliberate scarring of the penis in order to provoke a chronic ulcer, the insertion of electrodes into the bladder or rectum, and puncturing the prostrate with a needle. Castration was not off the list of options.

There were also mechanical restraints that included metal cages preventing access to the genitals, as well as spiked rings placed at the base of the penis, 'a bear trap for the erection'. Another contraption was tethered to the pubic hair which it pulled painfully taut in the event of arousal. The genitals could also be encased in plaster of Paris or the penis bound to the leg with the likes of the Stephenson Spermatic Truss. As late as 1936 medical textbooks were still advocating some of these methods.

Dr Yellowlees, one of the doctors who examined John Laurie, was described as 'an acknowledged expert on masturbatory insanity'. In March 1877, while at Glasgow Royal Lunatic Asylum (Gartnavel), he devised what became a standard surgical procedure using wire to sew up the foreskin 'so to fix the prepuce that erection becomes painful and erotic impulses very unwelcome'. Yellowlees was commissioned to write an article on the link between masturbation and mental illness in the *Dictionary of Psychological Medicine* (1892) where he further condemned the practice and elaborated on the severity of the mental and physical damage which he claimed it was responsible for.

The results of the Medical Commission's report on Laurie were forwarded to the Scottish Office for Lord Lothian to take account of, along with the recently presented petition. The concept of the Royal Prerogative of Mercy had been exercised since 1837 by the Scottish Secretary on behalf of the monarch. With only days to the execution the tension started to mount. It was thought that the longer the Scottish Secretary mulled over the decision the better for Laurie. The general feeling was that he would be granted a reprieve. However his family did not share this optimistic outlook and had prepared themselves for the worst.

Two days after the completion of the Medical Commission's report it was made known that the Scottish Secretary was in consultation with Lord Kingsburgh, the judge at Laurie's trial, with regard to its findings. The next day, just two days before the execution, an official announcement was made: 'In consequence of the Medical Commission having reported that the convict Laurie is of unsound mind, the Secretary for Scotland has felt justified in recommending that he should be reprieved.'

Laurie received the news with some equanimity. He was pleased but not overcome with emotion as he claimed to have been convinced of this outcome all along. His coolness under such harrowing circumstances was an eye-opener to all who dealt with him. Although Laurie has on occasion been described as of nervous temperament, notably by himself and the Medical Commission, at times of great stress, for example at his trial and in prison under sentence of death, he appeared to display exceptionally low levels of anxiety. The *Coatbridge Express* added its tuppence worth: 'He showed no symptoms of positive insanity, but his indifference to his position and to his fate, his strange remarks, and his mental attitude in relation to the various rumours upon which he was questioned indicated a form of mind that is almost phenomenal.' The *Evening Times* had the last word, 'Perhaps it is well for society that the daring criminal who had nerves of iron had also a brain of putty.'

Although Laurie now knew he was not to be executed, he was still in doubt as to his exact fate. No one was sure whether Laurie had been respited during Her Majesty's pleasure, a legal term for an indeterminate period of incarceration, or whether the sentence had been commuted to one of penal servitude, a finite term of imprisonment. Some thought Laurie's reprieve might just be temporary. On Friday both the Provost of Greenock and William Napier, the prison governor, received official notification from Lord Lothian: 'I am to signify to you the Queen's command and beg that the execution of the sentence of death passed on John Watson Laurie, presently in Her Majesty's prison of Greenock be respited until further signification of Her Majesty's pleasure.' Technically this meant the sentence of death was delayed while under review.

The death sentence was eventually commuted to life imprisonment but clarification of this would reach Laurie in a bureaucratically convoluted manner. From near his home at Newbattle, outside Edinburgh, Lord Lothian telegrammed Robert Cochran-Patrick, the Under-Secretary at the Scottish Office in London, asking him to give this news to the Prison Commissioners who in turn should inform, 'as soon as possible', the governor at Greenock Prison. The telegram from the Commissioners arrived at the prison at 11.50am on the Saturday, 'pardoning John Watson Laurie of the crime of murder and of the sentence of death passed upon him for the same; upon condition of his being kept in penal servitude for the term of his natural life'. The governor informed Laurie and then began the process for the prisoner's removal to Perth Prison. The same day as Laurie's reprieve, the following letter appeared in the 7pm edition of the *Glasgow Evening News*:

> Dear Sir,
> I am glad to hear that Laurie has been reprieved, as he is entirely innocent of this crime with which he is charged. I was within a short distance of both Rose and Laurie at the time the accident happened. I saw poor Rose slip and fall accidentally over the cliff, and then Laurie robbed him and hid him under the boulder.
> I daresay you will doubt the truth of my story but my reason for keeping quiet till now is because I feared it might get me into trouble if I revealed my secret,
> I am etc
> A Witness of Rose's death
> PS I will make no further communication.

Although capital punishment was not ended until the 1960s, efforts to have it abolished had been going on since the late 1700s. By 1889 it was a highly controversial topic with Scotland having a strong abolitionist lobby. A feature of this story, and one of the reasons Laurie was able to remain at large for so long, was a wide-spread abhorrence of the death penalty. There appears to have been a dramatic, and rapid, change in public opinion as it was not long since public executions like Dr Edward Pritchard, at Glasgow in 1864, attracted huge crowds of raucous and unruly spectators.

There had been much disquiet in Greenock that the town had the stigma, and expense, of holding the execution, especially since it had not the slightest connection with the crime. Only four executions had ever taken place in the town since it became a burgh in 1675. It had been widely presumed that the sentence would be carried out in Edinburgh. The barricades at the prison were quickly removed and the scaffold returned to Duke Street Prison in Glasgow, 'The Magistrates appear anxious to get rid of all associations in connection with the disagreeable affair which was thrust upon them.' At a later meeting of the Council it was proposed that in future the Prison Commissioners should foot the bill.

But this was far from the end of the matter. The medical report regarding Laurie's mental health was never published. There was growing unrest that the grounds on which Laurie was declared 'of unsound mind' were never made public. (In fact, the reasons for reprieving or not reprieving individuals were classified as Official Secrets.) There was no reference to insanity during the trial. There was even a question in Parliament as to what grounds Laurie's capital sentence was commuted. Again, there was no satisfactory answer. The *Saturday Review* of 30 November had a leading article, 'The Respite of Laurie'. It asked:

What was the view taken by the Scottish Office as to Rose's death, and in what precise way did Laurie's alleged insanity operate to bring about his reprieve? Has it, that is to say, been treated as exculpatory or merely as explanatory? Is it the official theory that he killed Mr Rose, but that, being of unsound mind, he is not criminally responsible? Or does the theory start with the assumption that Mr Rose's death was, as Laurie protested in his defence, accidental, and that the latter's insanity only comes in to explain his flight and concealment after the accident took place?

Now that Laurie was no longer a condemned man, he had the status of convict. There is a distinction between a convict and a prisoner. A convict was someone who was convicted of aggravated crimes and sentenced to at least five years penal servitude prior to 1891, three years thereafter. Due to his new status Laurie would be removed from the condemned cell, put into prison clothes and have his hair cropped close and maintained in this style by being cut every fortnight. Contemporary convict attire was as caricatured in cartoons, moleskin stamped all over with large broad arrows.

The next day Laurie was moved to Perth General Prison. Wrapped in a blanket and escorted by two warders, he was taken by cab to Greenock's Inverkip Street Station to catch the train for Glasgow. They were met at the Central Station by Superintendent John Orr who had been in charge of the case. They then went by cab to catch the Perth train at Buchanan Street Station where a crowd had gathered to catch a glimpse of the notorious 'Arran murderer': 'He looked pale and haggard, and from all appearances could not weigh more than eight stones.' He was described as unshaved and dressed in, 'tight-fitting body dress, knickerbockers, thick stockings to the knee, and white skull-cap'.

On his arrival at Perth Prison John Watson Laurie became convict 12/970. At reception his height and weight were measured, and a photograph taken in his convict's uniform. Due to his suicide attempts he was, 'Under special observation in cell from admission until 10 January 1890. Convict was found not to be insane.'

Traditionally prisoners spent the first nine months of their sentence in 'separate confinement' with little association save the chaplain and, when required, the medical officer. The idea behind this was to force the prisoner to meditate on their crime and its consequences. In his first month at Perth, Laurie would get a further reminder as to why he was in jail. He received a letter from Frederick Rose asking the whereabouts of Edwin's watch which the family were keen to retrieve as a memento: 'This seems to us to be the very least you can do in way of reparation for the great wrong which we have suffered at your hands.' Laurie eventually replied but his answer would be of little assistance to the Rose family : 'I have already stated that I threw the watch among the heather below the boulders where the body was found. I was very excited at the time, in fact I hardly knew what I was doing, so I am not sure whether it was immediately below the boulder or not.'

In July 1890 the doctor at Perth Prison compiled a further report on Laurie's mental health; he was of the opinion that Laurie was sane, and had been since his arrival there: 'I have always found him calm and collected, and his conversation entirely free from incoherence or delusion. He is undoubtedly a man in whom the moral sense is low and defective, but intellectually all his faculties are apparently perfect and unimpaired.'

After his probationary period at Perth, Laurie would serve the rest of his sentence at the recently opened Peterhead Prison, thirty miles north of Aberdeen on the rocky Buchan coast. Most Scottish prisoners serving long sentences would now be housed there and Peterhead would go on to become Scotland's toughest and most infamous jail.

Chapter Ten

Her Majesty's Pleasure

John Laurie first entered the confines of Peterhead Prison on 16 September 1890 when he became Convict 275. For the duration of his stay he would be referred to by this number or, in written reports, as 'the convict named on the margin'. He would soon learn there were few opportunities to dress up or leave without paying, though he did try.

There has always been debate about the purpose of prisons and the balance between punishment and rehabilitation. Laurie's time in Perth and Peterhead would encompass two disparate regimes. Perth was a General Prison, as opposed to a convict prison, that held prisoners from all over Scotland serving nine months or more. For a long time it was regarded as Scotland's foremost jail and held on longest to the more traditional penal practices. Peterhead was one of the first 'Public Works' prisons in Scotland – more of which anon. To understand Laurie's experiences in the Scottish penal system we must briefly look at the English model as much of this had been adopted north of the border, though in a rather flexible and inconsistent manner.

In the first half of the nineteenth century few prison places were required as most offenders were either fined, hanged or transported. The emphasis was to get rid of wrong-doers, hence transportation to New South Wales, Tasmania (Van Damien's Land), Bermuda and Gibraltar. When these destinations had absorbed what they could there was a frantic search for new dumping grounds: Labrador, New Guinea and the Falklands were all tried unsuccessfully. With the Penal Servitude Acts of 1853 and 1857 the government attempted to end transportation in favour of confinement with hard labour. The Acts introduced the modern concept of prison as a place of punishment rather than a holding facility for those awaiting trial, execution or removal abroad. The term penal servitude referred to a sentence of imprisonment in lieu of transportation, comprising both incarceration and hard labour.

Initially there were not enough prison places to cope with

the change in policy. In Scotland this initiated a programme of centralisation where small local prisons were gradually closed and eventually replaced with large new establishments such as Glasgow's Barlinnie (1882), Peterhead (1888), Aberdeen (1890) and Inverness (1901). Convict prisons were distinct in that they were administered by central government not, as previously, by local authorities.

Through the nineteenth century much of the British penal system evolved on a trial and error basis. Originally the 'separate system' was dominant, with prisoners isolated at almost all times and a great emphasis placed on not being allowed to speak to each other. At chapel there were screened booths, and in the exercise yard masks were worn so they could not see or communicate with other inmates (the masks were only briefly experimented with in Scotland). The rationale, as with Laurie at Perth Prison, was to force the prisoner to focus on their crime and, on a more practical level, to separate first offenders from the influence of hardened criminals. Although there was a strong focus on religion and moral improvement, separation and silence were at odds with reforming convicts through secular and religious education.

It was eventually realised that the separate system did not work. It was impossible to enforce, and it was also realised that conditions were sometimes better the porr experienced outside. Consequently, unproductive labour and military-style discipline were introduced to act as a deterrent to paupers. The answer was the silent system: 'hard labour, hard fare, hard board', which was adopted from the 1860s onwards. Prisoners worked in groups during the day with solitary confinement at night and silence at all times. Emphasis was placed on a military-style regime with long periods of hard labour, to both espouse a sense of discipline and break the convict's will. Some association was gradually permitted, initially at chapel and exercise. Silence was difficult to enforce as prisoners found ways to communicate using signs and signals.

Within penal servitude 'hard labour' did not always mean chained convicts breaking rocks. It had a more subtle definition, an often inhumane regime where prisoners worked on their own in silence on purposeless tasks such as the treadmill, which forced you to climb the equivalent of Goatfell four times a day, or the crank which had to be turned 14,400 times daily. There were also productive or semi-productive tasks likes tailoring or the mind-numbing oakum, untwisting and teasing out old ropes for use in caulking the seams of ships. These were all part of Oscar Wilde's contemporary experience in Reading Gaol. Perth Prison also had many of these elements and Laurie would have spent much of his time there teasing oakum.

In Scotland the penal system developed its own separate identity. Treadmills, for example, were never introduced. Policies were less uniform over the country with individual governors having a large say as to how their establishment was run. Many favoured productive labour as this contributed to the expense of keeping convicts in prison. When Laurie went to Peterhead he found that, as a Public Works establishment, almost all the hard labour was productive. Hard labour was only abolished in Scotland in 1950.

Prior to the construction of the likes of Peterhead there was little accommodation for long-term prisoners in Scotland. Convicts were initially housed at the General Prison at Perth, then sent on to one of the Public Works prisons in England like Portland, Chatham or Portsmouth. As the name suggests, prisoners at these establishments worked for the benefit of the public, usually in the construction of docks and sea defences. Built initially to hold 208 inmates, Peterhead's population would peak at 455 in 1910.

Once inside the prison Laurie's chains and handcuffs were removed, he was placed in a cell and given a hot dinner. After his meal he would have his hair cropped and then be taken for a bath while his ordinary prison clothes were returned to Perth. He would be asked by the head warder about his crime and sentence.

Laurie was then issued with the Peterhead prisoner's uniform: heavy flannel shirt, moleskin waistcoat and knee breeches, brown worsted jersey, woollen stockings and jacket. Convicts were also given a glengarry-type hat of thick brown wool, strong well-nailed boots, cell shoes, a pair of braces and a handkerchief. On the right arm of the jacket each man had a badge with his registered number and his sentence above it. Laurie would have an 'L' to signify he was a lifer. This information also appeared on the left side of the hat so a prisoner could be identified from any direction. In winter there were heavier woollen jackets, warmer underwear and gloves for those working outside.

Laurie also received a set of books: a bible, prayer book and hymnary, as well as the prison rule book and a library book. Once these items were issued he was taken to the hospital for examination by the prison doctor who would assess what type of work he was suitable for. This was divided into three categories: hard labour, light outside labour and light indoor labour (often referred to as hard, medium and light). The doctor would also make a note of Laurie's weight, height, eye and hair colour, any identifying marks and relevant medical history:

Complexion, pale.
Hair, brown.
Eyes, grey.
Height, 5ft 6in
Weight, 131lbs

Laurie was then taken to the governor's office where certain rules, not in the ordinary rule book, were read out. These included: 'Convicts confined in HM Prison Peterhead are hereby warned that they are liable to have swords, bayonets or rifles used against them if they attempt to escape either when inside or outside the prison or if they at any time, either singly or in combinations, attack or attempt to attack or forcibly resist a prison officer.' Laurie was also informed that no work was required on his first day, but on the next he would join a squad of around 25. He was then taken to one of the main halls and placed in the cell that would be his home for the remainder of his stay.

All the cells at Peterhead were identical, 7ft long, 5ft wide and 9ft high a third the size of Mrs Walker's small outhouse in Brodick. The only natural light was from an 18-inch (50cm) square window but the bars and twisted glass prevented much light entering the cell. There was a small ventilation hole in the window through which you could see out, but which let in cold draughts. The only furniture was a hammock slung on iron hooks, a small folding table hinged to the wall, and a stool. Laurie was also issued with a water jug, wash basin, towel, milk jug, horn spoon, salt dish, a slate and slate pencil, commode, soap, washing and dusting cloths, whitening and cleaning rags and a small brush.

The bedding comprised a mattress, two sheets, two blankets (three in winter) and a cover. Prisoners were not allowed to use their bed during the day unless the doctor gave special permission. There was a single candle for use at night. On the outside of the door there was a spy-hole, known as a 'Judas-hole', and above this a card indicating the prisoner's crime and sentence. A prisoner never knew when they were about to be observed as warders wore special slippers over their boots so they could not be heard approaching.

If Laurie wanted to attract the attention of a warder there was a wooden signal, painted red, which could be slid into a visible position. Prisoners then had to communicate with warders by writing on their slate. Some of these messages were not very complementary and could get you several days on bread and water, the normal punishment for minor misdemeanours.

Peterhead Prison was a cold place in winter as the heating was very ineffective, a water pipe along the cell wall and coal stoves in the main hall. The blankets were for use at night only and you were not allowed to wrap them around you at other times. In winter it was common to have to get up at night and exercise to keep warm. Mists, known as haars, frequently crept in from the North Sea, blocking out the sun. At these times the eerie atmosphere was enhanced by the lugubrious moan of the foghorn from the nearby lighthouse on Buchan Ness, nicknamed 'the Boddam coo' (cow).

On the outside world there was a great appetite for information on life in prison. The *People's Journal* printed an article by one recently released convict which described the unwavering daily routine and the military-style discipline prevalent at Peterhead. However, it was this rigid time-table that enabled many prisoners to handle their time inside. (Interviews with newly liberated prisoners were reworked by journalists which gave the impression that convicts were more articulate and educated than was the case):

All convicts got up at 5am in summer and 5.30 in winter, and 6.30 on Sundays all the year round. At 5.30 in summer and six o'clock in winter the officers come in, and each takes his place at his respective wards. The first class officer in charge then takes his place at the desk and gives the command, 'Signals all out' and rings a hand bell as a further instruction to those prisoners who may not hear his voice. Each prisoner then puts out a little signal painted red and made like a flag.

The officers count the various wards by marching up the corridors and back again. They then report in rotation to the officer in charge the number of signals out. They are written down and totalled up, and the numbers compared to see that every man in the prison is accounted for. This process is continued every time you come into your cells after being outside, or before meals are supplied, whether you have been outside or not.

The officers next give the signal, 'Unlock' when the officers proceed thus. The doors of the cells of the two orderlies in each ward are opened, who take their turn week about in acting a attendants on their fellow prisoners inside. Each cell door is opened in turn, and each prisoner empties his slops into a large urn carried by the orderlies.

They then show their bedclothes as follows: bed cover, three pair blankets, two canvas sheets, mattress of oakum down, and hammock, one of the most comfortable beds I ever lay upon. They then put out their stool, with their milk jugs on it, and shut their cell door for the present.

The orderlies then proceed to dispose of water urns, after which they fall in at the place where the food is kept, and each in turn lifts the basket or board containing the supplies for the various wards.

The porridge is in tin cans, and is placed on each man's stool according to the quantity he is entitled to. After this the orderly gets the milk can, and with the officer who opens the door of each cell, and the prisoner inside lifts up his stool, and the officer measures out his allowances of milk or tea, and he takes it inside and shuts his door. This goes on till every one is served, and all meals are done in a similar manner.

Conditions at Peterhead were generally an improvement on Perth. Prisoners would have their own cells and work in association; they were 'required to be industrious' but any conversation beyond what was absolutely necessary was still prohibited: 'A prisoner shall at all times maintain silence. He shall not speak nor attempt to speak to any other prisoner.' The silent system was enforced less rigorously when working outside at the quarries. However the new prison would introduce ankle irons, the lash and civil guards with rifles, all previously unknown in Scotland.

The origins of Peterhead Prison are related to the oil industry. Not the twentieth century with its oil rigs and roustabouts, but the earlier quest for whale oil.

Peterhead, known locally as the 'Blue Toon', had a population of around 11,000 and was one of Britain's major fishing ports. In 1890 there were around 3000 curers, coopers and gutters employed in the town, with most of the cured fish exported to Germany, Poland and Russia.

There had been many tragedies to sea-farers in the area and large breakwaters to create a Harbour of Refuge were long mooted to make the area safer, not just for its 500-strong fishing fleet but also civilian and Royal Navy craft. The government chose Peterhead because 'it is situated mid-way between the Firths of Forth and Cromarty. The coast on either side of it is of an exposed and dangerous character; it is the centre of the great fishing industry on the east coast; it is so formed by nature as to afford all the physical advantages of ample space, depth of water and anchorage of the best description; and it is in the vicinity of extensive granite quarries from which inexhaustible supplies of material can be obtained for the construction of the works.'

But who would pay for its costly construction? The inventive solution was to build a prison nearby as a repository for dangerous characters from Glasgow's criminal underworld, and use this convict labour to quarry and prepare the stone required for the breakwater. The premise for Peterhead Prison was therefore not prisoner rehabilitation, but maritime safety. The south breakwater, started in 1889, was 2850ft (865m) long, 56ft (17m) wide, and completed in 1914. The north breakwater was not completed till 1956. Although it took seventy years to finish the Harbour of Refuge, when completed the breakwater was said to be the largest in the world.

When the prison was still in the planning process, some pressed for it to be located near the granite quarries at Stirling Hill, three of miles south of Peterhead; but it was eventually built at the original proposal, on the peninsular of Salthouse Head, the southern arm of Peterhead Bay. Savings were made on the initial design by reducing the height of the perimeter wall, replacing water closets with dry closets, and changing the proposed stone chapel to a corrugated building. The first cell block was constructed by contract labour.

The arrival of the first batch of twenty chained convicts, in August 1888, created great excitement in the town when crowds packed the railway station to catch sight of the 'connies' as they became known locally. The early arrivals worked on the remaining prison buildings which were fully completed by 1891, the only male penal establishment in Scotland. There were eventually two massive granite barracks: A Hall which housed 320 in separate cells, and B Hall which had 114 lodgers. During Laurie's time at Peterhead numbers did not build up as quickly as expected and were sometimes in decline: there were 330 inmates in 1893, 374 in 1896, 269 in 1905. For much of this period B Hall was closed as the accommodation there was not required.

The governor of Peterhead Prison from its inception was S A (Simon) Dodd. Like most prison governors, he was an ex-military man, formerly an army major. The appointment of Dodd was controversial. Some newspapers pointed out that he was brother-in-law of the chairman of the Prison Commission, Andrew Beatson Bell, and they were critical that longer serving and more experienced candidates had been passed over in the selection process.

As well as the governor, the staff included a medical officer, two head warders, a school master, a resident chaplain and two visiting chaplains. At Laurie's time there were twelve armed guards and around fifty warders with cutlasses on shoulder belts. The regulations for the former included: 'The prison guard will at all times exhibit a smart and soldier-like bearing whether on or off duty', and 'must not for an instant allow their vigilance to relax'. Prisoners were not allowed to talk to a warder without permission and could not come closer than 'an arm's length plus that of the cutlass'. This regulation was in force till 1923. The cutlasses were in use till 1939, the rifles till 1959.

The armed guards were deployed outside the prison walls: at the quarries and around the Admiralty Yard. The latter was the centre of construction operations, a large compound located between the prison and the start of the south breakwater. Convicts did not work on the breakwater itself where local labour was used, but were employed within the compound to prepare the material for its construction: concrete blocks finished with dressed granite. In the yard there were stores for sand, cement and coal; facilities for mixing concrete and casting building blocks, as well as workshops for carpentry, smithing and stone dressing. Laurie was initially employed as a joiner in the carpentry workshop.

Around the main prison buildings and the yard was a 20-30ft granite wall with an unchallenging 6-foot high metal fence on the outer perimeter. Barbed wire was a much later addition. These defences were constantly scoured for weaknesses and occupied the thoughts and dreams of many inmates; some would succeed in surmounting them, but usually not for long. The record for escaping from Peterhead Prison is held by Johnny Ramensky who absconded five times between 1934 and 1958. The longest he was at large for was nine days though the furthest he managed from the jail was the outskirts of Aberdeen.

On top of the wall around the Admiralty Yard were several wooden guard boxes manned by armed guards. The guards communicated with each other using a semaphore signal with either their arms or flags, for example, 'stop work', 'take shelter', 'all right'. In the event of an escape a whistle was blown to sound the alarm. In Laurie's time the guards carried Snider carbines which fired cartridges of buckshot. This was later changed to service rifles which were more accurate, had a greater range and had five shots instead of one. This increase in security was a reaction to a perceived threat that the prison might come under attack from outside, especially by Sinn Feiners. The regulations for the use of firearms included: 'It must be distinctly understood that it may be necessary for a sentry to fire upon a prisoner before blowing his whistle or hoisting the alarm signal on his semaphore. The main object is to frustrate the attempt at escape and in certain cases any delay might defeat that object.'

After breakfast was over, prisoners were marched off from the cells to line up with their party in the prison yard, before dispersing to their respective work in the quarries, Admiralty Yard or the prison workshops. This often presented a bizarre sight as men of all ages, shapes and sizes, and in all manner of physical condition, quick marched to the best of their ability. The writer in the *People's Journal*, quoted previously, went on to outline the morning routine:

> The officers then proceed to get their own meals and return again at 7.15 when the cell doors are all opened and your empty food dishes collected. You sweep out any dust in your cells. Doors are left open, and you stand to attention two paces back from the door. The command having been given to bring out each ward the men are brought two paces to the front in rotation, right and left turn as the case may be, and they march off in single file to the parade ground, where you fall in with your respective parties altogether, and their duties are varied.
>
> The officer in charge of each party calls the men to attention and tells them to cover off. The roll is called and names answered. You then extend with outstretched arms, palm upwards, and dress up for inspection by loosening all buttons, holding up your arms, cap off, the object of this being to show that no one has anything about him that he is not entitled to have, and if so he has to give an account of it, or if he cannot, take the consequences. This is also repeated every time you go out and in from, or to, labour. Each prisoner is also searched in his cell once a week according to prison regulations.

This latter search was a particular bone of contention, especially in mid-winter, as prisoners were stripped and left to stand naked in the cold for some time. During the working day each hour was heralded by a 'hooter' or steam whistle. The working hours compared favourably to similar jobs outside prison. Laurie was in his cell around 11.30am for dinner, back to work for 1pm, to return at 5.30pm for supper. Prisoners were locked up at 7pm; there was a bell at 7.45pm for lights out and bed. No prisoner could go to bed before this under penalty of punishment.

There were 13 work parties at Peterhead which included cooks, laundry staff, joiners and blacksmiths; gardeners and house cleaners; tailors, shoemakers and bookbinders. The tradesmen, such as bookbinders and joiners, were regarded as 'medium labour' whereas those involved in patching, knitting and oakum teasing were seen as 'light indoor labour' and were incorporated into the tailors' party. There were eight other groups who worked outside the walls of the prison, all classified as 'hard labour'.

In the joiners' workshop John Laurie shared a workbench with three other cons he had become friendly with: William Goodfellow, 'Scotch Jamie' and a man called Sutherland. Laurie would reflect on this as his happiest, or least unhappy, period in Peterhead. The work was interesting: making wheelbarrows, hammer shafts and other implements needed at the quarry and breakwater.

When they were able to talk there would be some great stories. Goodfellow and 'Scotch Jamie' were two of Scotland's most notorious burglars who spent much of their lives in prison, early criminal celebrities whose names were well-known to the public. 'Scotch Jamie' (sometimes 'Scotch Jimmy') alias Peter Smith, real name James Muirhead, 'Scotland's greatest burglar' was a specialist house-breaker and safe-blower. Originally from Fife, he trained as a joiner in Edinburgh. His nickname came from a time in Dartmoor Prison where he learnt much of his trade as safe-breaker and con man. Muirhead's partner-in-crime and loyal look-out, Thomas Rice Reid, was another regular in Peterhead whom Laurie befriended. Reid's modus operandi was stealing explosives from one of Scotland's many mines, then breaking into the company offices to blow up the safe containing the weekly payroll.

Muirhead was pictured by one detective as 'a delightful old vagabond with the mind of a burglar and the heart of a child'. A colourful character, he was also portrayed as 'well-waxed moustache, fashionable clothes, and gold-rimmed eye glasses'; he claimed to only work at weekends when he dressed as a businessman to inspect possible targets. Scotch Jamie spent thirty years in jail between 1878 and 1914; four of his six sentences involved what he described as 'serving his country' at

Peterhead Prison which he referred to as the 'The Hydropathic' or the 'Salthousehead Sanatorium'. For a while he went straight and exchanged the jemmy for the greasepaint as he toured the country as a successful music hall act, 'lecturing' on prison life and performing humorous sketches like 'Jamie's Dilemna'.

Muirhead was soon back in Peterhead. Not the prison but heading the bill at the town's Rescue Hall where he drew a roaring trade. (The Beatles also performed there but to a smaller crowd). The *Dundee Weekly News* wrote the following review: 'Scotch Jamie is now on a successful visit to Peterhead at the Rescue Hall, and it is a curious fact that he, for the first time in his career, has had to pay his own fare, the government on all previous occasions having done so.' The appreciative audience would doubtless include some of his former warders attracted by the posters pasted around town:

A SEARCHLIGHT ON CONVICT PRISON LIFE: UNIQUE, SENSATIONAL AND REALISTIC

See him in Life, and hear him relate the thrilling experiences of his past life. This is not a film, but the One and Only Scotch Jamie, who will appear in person, in his new and original speciality: '28 Years behind Prison Locks, Bolts and Bars'. It absolutely bristles with excitement and amazing life pictures of intense interest, and beats anything yet depicted on the screen. No such pictures of Convict Prison Life have ever before been placed to the public view. Don't miss this rare opportunity of seeing and hearing the man of whom you have all read so much.

The evening's star turn was introduced by the chairman: 'To Entertain! not to burgle, The Notorious King of Cracksman! now reformed, The World-Renowned Scotch Jamie!!' On his tours around the country Muirhead would appear in Laurie's home town, doubtless relating anecdotes of Coatbridge's most infamous son. The reviewer in the *Coatbridge Leader* said this: 'Scotch Jamie is responsible for the sustained interest shown here in his appearance, which is received with great applause.' In 1918, aged 70, Muirhead returned to Peterhead for a longer run. Twelve years in fact, after attempting to blow open a pawnbroker's safe in Glasgow's Bath Street. After pleading with the authorities not to let him die in prison, he passed away in Glasgow's Stobhill Hospital in 1922.

The food, clothing and bedding at Peterhead were better than many other prisons. However this was not on compassionate grounds but to maintain what was essentially a crucial workforce in good physical shape. The clothing issued reflected that the men would often be labouring outside in harsh conditions. Although they did not work in heavy rain they had to contend with the raw cold and bitter winds of winter.

Prisoners ate on their own in their cells. There were three categories of diet depending on the type of work performed, whether light, medium or hard labour. The diets only really differed in the size of the portions. The menu was unwavering in routine: oatmeal porridge, potatoes, barley broth with boiled beef chopped among it, and bread which was made by the prisoners under the guidance of a special warder, usually a time-served baker. The prison offered some welcome variety in the portions if not the ingredients. On Fridays there was fresh fish and suet pudding. The latter was for many cons, if not all, the highlight of the week. The exact food portions were listed in prison regulations: 'Breakfast: 8oz porridge and three-quarters of a pint of milk. Dinner: 2pts barley broth made from ox heads, hough and suet, three-quarters of a pound of wheaten bread. Supper: 2lbs potatoes, half a pint of milk or porridge.'

However, this was the official version. One former inmate provided a prisoner's perspective: 'However good, bad or indifferent, appetising or otherwise, these latter dietaries may strike the reader, it must be understood that the respective menus are only what a prisoner is supposed to get by some process known only to the initiated; the poor prisoners portion is always minus at least one-third of its proper quantity, and is served up for delivery fully an hour or two before it is taken to the cells where it arrives always in a semi-frozen state.'

Records of life at Peterhead in its early days are hard to find. This was largely because many of the convicts were illiterate, and if not, any writing materials, even a pencil stub, were 'prohibited articles'. There was a prison teacher who held classes in the evening, compulsory if you were unable to reach a certain standard of reading and writing. When convicts were released from prison it was common for newspapers to approach them and offer a fee for an account of their experiences inside. These were inevitably sanitised versions, as any ex-inmate who was overtly critical of the prison or its staff knew what to expect if they were unfortunate enough to return. As well as *The People's Journal*, there was also a big demand for this type of story from D C Thomson's *Weekly News*.

William Goodfellow was one Peterhead con who agreed to participate. He first became friendly with Laurie when they were members of the prison choir. Goodfellow, a cabinet-maker by trade, was known as the 'Gentleman Burglar' and regarded by old lags as 'the cleverest cracksman of his time'. He arrived at Peterhead the same year as Laurie, 1890, serving 12 years for a series of burglaries that included two in the ubiquitous Cambridge Street. He lived in Glasgow's up-market Kelvinside district, next door to the Procurator Fiscal, where he had his own horse and carriage. He also had a villa in Dunoon where he used his yacht to commit burglaries in neighbouring resorts. His last sentence was for house-breaking in 1919 when he was nearly blind. He died in Barnhill Poorhouse in 1929, aged 68. One journalist recalled him: 'In his early days he was a bit of a beau, and well fitted the description of swell cracksman. A tall hat, dress coat, and monocle were his sartorial fancies at that period, and to those he added a distinguished appearance and manners which disarmed suspicion.' In one of his articles in the *Weekly News* Goodfellow noted:

In regard to the actual murder of Rose, Laurie solemnly assured me that he was innocent. Rose, according to his story, had fallen a victim to his botanical zeal in attempting to procure a specimen of a rare, particular plant growing on a dangerous part of the rock. Falling from a great height he had been accidentally killed, and Laurie getting frightened and losing his head, determined to conceal the body. Being hard up he was tempted to take Rose's valuables, and so, from one blunder he went on to another, until he found himself incriminated to such an extent that he felt his case hopeless, and got into a state of despair. It was merely a case of robbery and concealment of the body of Rose. But one false step had led to another in the whole mad business, culminating in the frenzied attempt at suicide.

The Prison Commission for Scotland was established under the Prisons (Scotland) Act of 1877 which also changed the funding of prisons from local taxation to central government. It was the forerunner of the Scottish Prison Service and was responsible for administering and inspecting prisons. A representative of the Board visited Peterhead every month. Prisoners could write to the Prison Commissioners to make complaints or requests.

The Board of Commissioners consisted of two salaried members and two ex-officio members. The latter rarely visited the prisons, and prison management was to all intents and purposes in the hands of the other two. Dr James Devon later became a Prison Commissioner, but in an earlier post as medical officer at Barlinnie Prison he was critical of their role: 'If, by any chance, one of these should be an incompetent person, the power of the other, administratively, would be supreme; and the bureaucracy would become an autocracy. There is no independent inspection of the work of the Board; the Commissioners report on their own work.'

James Muirhead was in broad agreement with Devon regarding the efficacy of the Commissioners. On one of his short spells outside, Muirhead wrote a chapbook, *The Horrors of Convict Life in Peterhead; Startling Disclosures*. Despite the dramatic title this was a courageous polemic, considering the repercussions should he return to the prison, that argued articulately for a less brutal and more compassionate penal system. Regarding the Prison Commissioners, he had this to say:

Of course there are officials to whom it is supposed that the prisoner may appeal when he is of the opinion that he is being treated otherwise than is warranted; but a 'lag' may as well appeal to a stone wall for redress, as appeal to these officials who visit the prison once every month for the supposed purpose of remedying any grievance. These officials are, like their rules, held to be infallible, and all complaints, however justifiable, receive but scant attention, and the applicant is treated with a contempt that is indescribable by an authority who may be truthfully portrayed as a nonentity pitch-forked into a sinecure. This official is, I believe, chosen simply on account of his obvious ignorance of common sense.

Between 1885 and 1889 responsibility for prisons in Scotland was transferred to the newly-revived post of Secretary for Scotland (now Secretary of State for Scotland) whom prisoners could petition for clemency, release etc. John Laurie would regularly communicate with both the Commissioners and the Scottish Secretary. With personal correspondence tightly controlled and vetted, these regular appeals became an important outlet for expressing grievances and letting off steam. As Laurie's family ties loosened they became for him a crucial link with the outside world, as well as his sole hope of rejoining it.

Chapter Eleven

The Soul of the Transgressor

We hear little about Convict 275 during his first two years in jail. There are few reports against him and by all accounts Laurie is an exemplary prisoner trying to keep his head down and stay out of trouble. When he makes his first petition to the Secretary for Scotland, on 7 December 1892, we find out why: Laurie expected to be released after two years. Most lifers served 10, 12 or 15 years; 20 years in exceptional circumstances. When his expected liberation did not materialise Laurie felt hard done by. However he is also contrite and remorseful for what he has done; he wants to go abroad 'where I may lose my identity and be forgotten': 'I need not dwell on the hardships of convict life but I supplicate your Lordship to rescue me from another winter in Peterhead. To those who are strong and hopeful years of imprisonment are preferable to death, but had I only my own feelings to consult I should certainly prefer to die. If the executive of my country cannot comply with my request then it will be a mercy if the mortification I experience puts an end to my miserable existence.

Peterhead Prison used the stages system, introduced by the 1857 Penal Servitude Act, where marks were gained through diligent work and good conduct, and deducted for breaking the rules. Through this process prisoners were able to receive remission on their sentence, potentially three months off for every year served, known as release on licence or 'ticket of leave'. They could also earn a gratuity, payable on discharge. After their liberation individuals had to report to a police station every month for the duration of their licence.

In the system there were four stages, each lasting a minimum of a year: probation, third, second, first; each identified by a different coloured stripe on the prisoner's collar. Prisoners were required to achieve a certain amount of marks in order to reach the next stage. Progression through the stages brought benefits such as a lighter job and increased frequency of letters and visits. For example, Class 3 prisoners were entitled to a visit and a letter ever six months, Class 2 every four months and Class 1 every three months. Progression through the stages also brought more exercise on a Sunday. Laurie gained Class 1 but soon lost it.

The maximum number of marks you could earn in a day were 8 for a steady, hard day's labour; 7 marks for a less industrious day and 6 for a moderate day's work. The system was very bureaucratic with prisoners assessed every day and tallied up every three months. On the table in his cell Laurie would have a card showing the number of marks earned during preceding quarters. As well as being deducted marks, misdemeanours could result in other punishments such as less food, and isolation from other prisoners at exercise or chapel. For more serious offences there was hard labour or confinement in the even more uncomfortable 'separate cells' which prisoners called the 'chokey'. These punishment cells had a guard bed, one without a mattress. There were two 'menus': 'chokey diet' which was plain bread and water, and 'skilly diet' which included an additional pint of gruel.

Prisoners were not the only ones breaking the rules. Warders were frequently suspended for drunkenness or falling asleep on night duty. James Muirhead had much to say in his book about the regime at Peterhead which he summed up as 'unnatural silence', 'semi-starvation', and 'dog-like obedience':

It is hardly possible to convey to the outside public the one-sided nature of prison discipline. No matter how many prisoners witnessed a case of ill-treatment, on no account would their word be taken as evidence against a warder. Knowing this fact, there are certain warders who, in their narrow-minded tyranny and cruelty, almost do as they like to persons whom they take a dislike against. These men by their ingenious system of persecution, continually wearying and harassing their prey with every petty torment that their cunning and ignorance can devise, inflict, in their ill-will towards their victim, wounds more bitter than tongue or pen can describe.

Muirhead goes on to outline what, psychologically, was the toughest punishment inmates faced, the pitch-black cell known as the 'darkie':

The prisoner lies day and night on a wooden guard bed, not

knowing whether it is day or night, deprived of God's blessed light. Consider for a moment the indescribable agony of thick darkness, thick enough almost to be palpable and suffocating with its desert like solitude and desolation, shut in by double doors for a lengthened time. This is enough to make the strongest man shake in the balance on the verge of madness and sanity; the slow leaden moments pass so that seconds appear as minutes, minutes as hours, and hours seem weeks, and no wonder that many an unhappy prisoner in this position has prayed for death to come to the rescue.

For serious offences there was also corporal punishment and 'restraint of the limbs' for up to three days. The latter involved the use of leg irons or a straight-jacket. But the most feared was being tied down to a triangular frame, the 'three-legged Betty', and flailed with the cat-o'-nine-tails or birch rods (some jails charged for this service). The cat, as it was known, was made up of nine knotted thongs designed to lacerate the skin and cause intense pain. At the end of the flogging most victims were semi-conscious and had to be carried back to their cells.

Although Laurie's behaviour was generally good at the start of his sentence, it soon deteriorated, as outlined in his disciplinary record for the first four years:

1890 (28 April) Disobedience of orders. Seven days separate exercise.

(21 June) Talking through the partition in wall to the prisoner in the adjoining cell. Fourteen days separate exercise.

1891 (11 May) Irreverent behaviour during Divine Service. 240 marks [deducted]

(12 Oct) Disobedience of orders. 240 marks

(23 Nov) Having improper matter written on his slate. Admonished

(9 Dec) Conversing with other convicts. 240 marks

1893 (12 June) Having prohibited articles (pen and written communication) concealed in his cell. 240 marks

24 July 1. Attempting to escape from custody.

2. Having a prohibited article (map of Scotland) in his possession. Thirty strokes of birch rod. Parti-coloured dress

and leg irons for six months.

On Monday 24 July 1893, Laurie was part of a carpentry squad working on a new accommodation block for warders being built just to the north of the prison. The site was surrounded by a wall about eight feet high. That morning there was a thick haar covering the coast and one of the civil guards, who usually accompanied the men when outside the main walls, had not turned up. Laurie decided the time was right. He used a scaffolding plank to scale the wall and then made a run for it. The guards blew their whistles to raise the alarm. One guard attempted to shoot him but later claimed the rifle misfired.

By this time Laurie had crossed the main Peterhead road and sprinted towards Bellevue Cottage to the north of the Reform Tower. Several warders and guards set off in pursuit and soon gained on Laurie as his stamina failed him. In a curious parallel to his initial arrest near Larkhall, he ran through some fields then jumped a fence to hide in a small plantation near the cottage. He was soon discovered, shackled and escorted back to the prison. Laurie later revealed the crucial mistake he made. Due to nervous excitement he had sprinted off far too rapidly and due to his unfitness had quickly run out of steam. He was soon apprehended by the guards to whom he quietly surrendered, 'Yet I was handcuffed, knocked down, kicked, jumped upon, then pitched over a wall.'

It was headlined in newspapers as, 'Exciting Incident at Peterhead Prison, the Escape and Capture of Laurie: Laurie characterised his captors in language wholly inconsistent with the ecclesiastical office which he fills, that of precentor in the convict prison chapel.' That evening the governor wrote up the day in his official journal: 'Convicts out working as usual. Infirmary, 8; Separate Cells, 8; Total 326. Three reports and eleven interviews. This morning at about 7.40am Reg. 275 J W Laurie, under a life sentence, attempted to escape custody. He was one of the joiners' party employed at New Quarters. After commencing work he sprang over a low wall and made off. He was pursued and captured. Guard Graham who was on his post close by stated that he loaded and pulled trigger but that the cartridge misfired. The head warder recovered the cartridge soon after and saw no indentation on cap. Cartridge exploded at once when fired again. Guard Graham suspended from duty pending enquiry.'

Edwin Rose's brother Frederick wrote to the press complaining about Laurie's lack of supervision and the ease of his escape. A newspaper report of the incident stated: 'It is understood that the punishment for an attempt to escape is that the prisoner has a belt of iron riveted around his waist, similar bands put round his ankles, and these are bound together by heavy chains. He has to wear these ornaments night and day.' Laurie would have the leg irons for six months. The shackles did not just restrict movement, they jangled constantly and made uncomfortable bedfellows.

About two weeks after the escape attempt the governor made another journal entry: 'Corporal punishment awarded to Reg. 275 J Watson Laurie at nine this morning in presence of Governor and medical officer. Thirty strokes of birch rod were inflicted.' The parti-coloured uniform that escapees were forced to wear was known by prisoners as the 'canary suit', a jester-style outfit that was half yellow, half black: one leg yellow, one leg black etc. This humiliation would weigh particularly heavy on Laurie who as we know was very fastidious about his appearance; the prison chaplain went so far as to describe him as 'inordinately vain'.

With his bid for freedom Laurie brought on himself the opprobrium of the penal establishment and scuppered any chance of an early release he may have had. The recriminations were calamitous for him and would last for years. He had made the prison security look ineffectual and, probably worse, was held responsible for these failings being broadcast in the press. Due to this, and his increasingly poor conduct, Laurie was forced to work in the quarry or at the yard: breaking rocks or mixing cement. For over a decade his constant carping would revolve around a desire to return to his former job, the less harsh conditions of the joiners' workshop. He ended one letter to the Commissioners with: 'If you are not yet satisfied that my punishment has been proportionate to my offence, then gentlemen, I have nothing more to say, I have nothing more to hope.'

The unsuccessful jailbreak was a pivotal event in Laurie's prison life. Once regarded as a model prisoner, his behaviour went quickly downhill. His misdemeanours, previously minor infringements of the rules, become more violent. A fellow inmate, Daniel Donoghue, a pickpocket from Dundee, recalled how after the escape attempt the once cheerful Laurie became sullen and antisocial. William Goodfellow confirmed this in in one of his articles:

Laurie appeared to me at first to be of a very cheerful disposition, and, judging from his general appearance, no one would have suspected that he carried such a load of care on his shoulders as a life sentence.

After his attempted escape, however, I observed a gradual change came over him. He became morose and reserved in his manner, and seemed to have a notion that everyone was down on him. He told me so himself. For one thing, he didn't seem to get on very well with his fellow-prisoners or they didn't get on with him. At any rate, he was frequently in trouble for quarrelling, and for some time after his attempted escape his life was anything but a bed of roses. On various occasions I had observed him either in irons for some offence or on his way to the 'chokey', and it was most disheartening no doubt to be under such a cloud.

I remember once his telling me, years after the event, that when he failed in his attempt to escape he didn't care much what happened. Life had become nothing but a monotonous drag, and, as the years went by and his health began to fail, he didn't even seem to care whether he ever got his liberty again or not. I was certainly astonished at the difference in his whole outlook.

Five months after his escape attempt, Laurie again petitioned the Secretary for Scotland for clemency, this time using some wry humour: 'My Lord, a year has passed since I begged to be released. Since then I regret to say I tried to dispense with a regular discharge, in consequence of which I am still enduring punishment.' He takes the opportunity to complain that he didn't have a fair trial, and that he is being picked upon, mistreated and bullied by other prisoners. In a later communication Laurie confirmed what William Goodfellow had said about him in his article: 'My object is to get out of this at once and I become less and less indifferent whether it be alive or dead.'

In the few years after Laurie tried to abscond there were several similar incidents though none got the same amount of publicity. One of the most persistent in trying to hightail it from Peterhead Prison was an Aberdeen burglar named Watson. He made several attempts, including one in April 1894 when he did not get far from the prison. This was not surprising as he was chained at the legs and arms at the time. Two years later another escapee was captured within minutes. A more humorous incident occurred when a convict was mistakenly left behind at the quarries. A heavily armed posse of guards met him walking meekly back to the prison along the railway line.

This specially built railway, operational by the end of 1889, was used to transport convicts the two and a half miles from the jail to the granite quarries at Stirling Hill. Work parties boarded the train about 30m from the prison's South West gate and reached the quarry in about ten minutes, transported in four specially constructed carriages with no windows, each holding 30-35 convicts. Today this has significance to railway enthusiasts as the first state-owned, passenger-carrying service in Britain.

The atmosphere in the quarries was strange. You could see movement, people swinging hammers, and hear the clanging of crowbars and the loud crack and crash of rocks breaking, but rarely the sound of a human voice. Occasionally a sympathetic guard would allow a little conversation, warning convicts on the approach of a stricter colleague. All blasting operations were carried out by contracted labour directed by a quarry master. Convicts were supervised by armed guards with loaded rifles who commanded the heights above the quarries. In July 1931 24-year-old George Kynoch was shot dead while attempting to escape.

Meanwhile, the south breakwater was making steady progress seaward. Granite was transported from the quarries by railway engines with names which Laurie, a confirmed monarchist, would have approved: *Victoria, Alexandra, Prince of Wales, Duke of York*. Using a steam barge the granite boulders were formed into a rubble mound, the foundation for the huge concrete blocks from which the breakwater was constructed. These blocks, of 60 or 200 tons, were made at the yard by crushing the granite and mixing it with cement. They were then placed in position on the breakwater using a steam powered 'Titan' crane.

For the next few years John Laurie, now free of his iron shackles, was occupied mixing the cement. In one week he reckons to have turned over 100 tons six times. He also has to break up the granite with a 28lb hammer. He still desperately wants to be transferred back to the less back-breaking joiners' shop where the work was lighter and more interesting. Laurie petitions the Secretary for Scotland on 20 March 1895 when he explains how, since the start of his sentence, he has tried to avoid 'being the cause of any unpleasantness and I have quietly submitted to all the degradation heaped upon me'. He continues that he has come to a point where he is no longer prepared to put up with this and hints at ending it all: 'If the promise of release is not made good, then there is an end to the matter, there is an end at once to my sorrows and my capacity of endurance.'

For some time the head warder had been complaining about how difficult it was to get Laurie to do his share of the work. On 22 August 1895 Convict 275 was yet again reported for idleness, after repeated cautions, and given one day's bread and water 'on the understanding that he was going to improve'. He doesn't. Laurie's frequent transgressions mean he is constantly punished in a similar manner. His most common misdemeanours are conversing with others, indolence, quarrelling with another prisoner, assaulting another prisoner, insolence to an officer, refusing to work, disobedience of orders. The violence with other convicts reflects the fact he feels he is being bullied and insulted, 'being kicked about by all and sundry', including on one occasion having a stone thrown in his face. The weapon of choice for inmates was a stone concealed in a large linen handkerchief, the prototype of the pool ball in a sock.

In prison the ability to stand up to violence and assault showed you 'were able to handle yourself' a requisite quality in gaining the much sought-after accolade of 'respect'. An ability to successfully negotiate this stage of prison life ensured that the rest of your stay would have fewer problems.

Since his escape attempt Laurie's frustrations are reflected in an escalating charge sheet of rule-breaking as he attempts to fight the system and cares little about the consequences. His number of punishments peak in 1897 but tail off to a rare trouble-free year in 1901. For the rest of his time at Peterhead, save for a spike in 1903, his behaviour generally improves, with only two or three recorded instances of misconduct per annum. As mentioned, entitlement to visits varied with the prisoner's Class. However, even the most favoured, Class 1, could only expect a twenty minute visit every three months. But visitors could not just turn up unannounced: 'When a prisoner is entitled to receive a visit, the Governor will send notice to such friends of the prisoner as he (the prisoner) may desire to visit him.' For the visitor it could be a very lengthy journey for such a short time, a constant source of complaint. For Laurie's family it meant a return trip of nearly 350 miles. The frequency of visits, and of letters, was later changed to one a month. (During the riot and rooftop hostage siege at the prison in 1987, one of the prisoners' banners read: 'To [sic] Far For Visits.')

Letters could be no longer than four pages of notepaper. People got round this by writing the letter conventionally, before turning the page 90 degrees and writing across what they had already put down. The result was perfectly legible and doubled the amount that could be written. All letters in and out of the prison were read by the authorities who could withhold them if they thought it right to do so. The main grounds for these suppressed letters, as they were known, were if they were not easy to read, if they contained 'indecorous or improper manner' or 'anything beyond domestic and personal matters'. Due to the mundane content of the infrequent correspondence and the restrictions on reading material, prisoners were virtually starved of any news of the world outside. If a scrap of newspaper was left over from some packaging or was blown into the yard, convicts would go to extraordinary lengths to try and retrieve it.

To read the many accounts of Laurie's character in official reports one could be forgiven for assuming him to be a slow-witted and somewhat naive person, possibly with mild learning difficulties, what was known at the time as 'feeble-minded'. There is a saying that we really do not know someone until we read what they have written. This appears particularly true of Laurie. In his personal correspondence, verbose language aside, he comes across as a well-educated, intelligent and articulate individual. On 23 October 1895 he wrote the following to his father but the letter was suppressed (the reason was most likely Laurie's complaints about the working conditions):

My dear Father, the month of June and three months more are of the past and I have seen you not. Had you indeed come to this place you would have shown the greatest benevolences to one who pretends to have no claim whatever on your kindness; such a visit, in any case, would have done more harm to you than good to me. I dare say that you may have heard from some source or another how bad a time of it I have had, you cannot but be aware that it is a dog's life at the best. Cowper has it that 'tis liberty alone that gives the flower / Of fleeting time its lustre and perfume; and we are weeds without it.' It would be idle to deny that some of us have been as rank weeds when brighter things could have been expected, and the poet makes the distinction, but I hold that no man has a title to be called good who does not wish the good of others…

I scarcely know how to proceed with a letter in which I have nothing very pleasing to say and would not willingly be thought to want due respect and consideration even for those who have barely permitted me to escape 'with the skin of my teeth'. Ingratitude is certainly a base thing, but is there much reason to be grateful? The past is without remedy and shall be without resentment, for I have never been one to hold out in stubborn malignity. The customary happiness has been released a little, but that only indicates the calm before the storm, or rather, the lull during the storm. You may imagine how unpleasing the reflection is that the wretches whom it seems necessary to conciliate are the most deplorable that I can conceive: liars and criminals by profession.

The state of my constitution is by no means consolatory. I am subject to the most miserable dejection of spirits and this condition was not improved when in early summer the plague of influenza laid hold on me. Leaving dysentery and colds out of the question, my other casualties have been an eruption of the skin and excessive trembling, the result I was told of hard work in hot weather. I am often a cripple and my lungs cannot but have suffered from the 'devil's dust' amongst which my lot has been cast. I was told that at the end of last winter my appearance was that of an old man and I never was so 'flesh fallen' as I have been this summer. I don't believe that a collier with a five ton output to his credit has worked harder than I have and if coal dust is penetrating, pulverised chalk and sand is equally so whist added to this must be the distress occasioned by the lime.

It is, however, useless to complain, you cannot help it and after all I am not much worse than I was, for although I have forfeited (to use the expression of the Chronicle) the high privilege of being a joiner, these were circumstances that I have since become more and more indifferent to, till I have arrived at the stage of thinking contemptuously of what only deserves to be thought of in that manner.

We have had a taste of cold weather already; last night when lying awake, which a difficult digestion generally contrives to make me do, a furious hail storm struck the prison roof and hail and sleet showers have continued intermittently today. I am thinner in the skin than most people, so that cold is a terrible reality to me. Write to me and let me know how you are. I suffer much anxiety for you, for should I never see you again, I would simply be inconsolable as long as I lived. I shall write you again if I can at the New Year,

I am, my dear Father,
Your affectionate son
John W Laurie.'

When, three years later, Laurie receives a letter informing him of his father's death, he has, as procedure, to obtain permission to reply. In the meantime he continues with the hard graft involved in the construction of the breakwater, 'The Governor still sends me to the hardest and most health-destroying labour in the works.' He feels he has so often been exposed to the cold, and had to live on bread and water, that the laborious manual work is destroying his health. He asks for a week's rest. After examining Laurie the prison doctor concludes: 'I see no reason to recommend his withdrawal from hard labour. He is sane.'

Convicts were entitled to a change of clothing if they got wet, but many complained that this was often refused, or torn and threadbare underwear provided as a replacement. (Until drugs became a problem in the twentieth century, underwear and tobacco were the two main sources of prison disputes, some escalating into full-scale riots.) When Laurie wrote his brother Gavin, in January 1899, he again grouses about the work he is made to do:

> It has been no uncommon thing for me to turn over three times, 20 tonnes of concrete; or working in a mucus membrane tormenting, vocal cord singeing, air vessel stuffing atmosphere of burnt lime dust, to shovel up 18 tonnes of Portland cement. You would never suspect pure air to be a desideratum on the Aberdeen coast; but as it was Solomon who decreed that the soul of the transgressor should eat violence, you don't look for any to minister to a mind diseased, a person mutilated, worn down by hard circumstances, by illness and fatigue. Aye, it was a flattering tale that hope told.
>
> Trusting that the sombre aspect of my condition may be your only affliction, and that Agnes and all the others are well, I am,
> Your loving brother,
> John W Laurie

On Saturdays, after washing out their cell, inmates were given a change of underwear, were shaved and had their hair cropped. One of the designated barbers was Archibald Robertson, 'the Keppochill murderer', a distillery worker originally from Port Charlotte on Islay, jailed for killing his cousin by cutting her throat. Most people would be unnerved by the likes of Robertson standing behind them with an open razor, but such was prison life it passed with little comment. On Saturdays there was also a longed-for bath, one of the few pleasures in prison, though the time allowed to soak was limited, as one ex-inmate ruefully reflected, 'An electric eel can hardly beat the speed that a prisoner takes his bath in Peterhead.'

On a Sunday there was no work but it was compulsory to attend chapel where one of the warders played the harmonium. With few of the prisoners being religious, attendance at Sunday chapel could be seen as yet another case of enforced conformity, another tedious and compulsory chore. This was far from the case. It was one of the few, if not only, occasions when prisoners would hear someone addressing them in a humane manner. It was also the only part of the prison that bore any resemblance to the outside world.

Much of the convicts' lives consisted of prolonged sensory deprivation: not allowed to talk much, and not able to see or hear much due to cells and high walls; an almost sterile atmosphere where smells and taste, especially regarding food, took on exaggerated significance. One of the few times convicts were permitted to use their voices, the hymn singing at chapel was particularly moving, performed with rousing and heartfelt enthusiasm and warmth. Many visitors commented on how affected the congregation of hardened criminals became.

With his fine tenor voice, John Laurie was the precentor, the person who leads the congregation in singing, as was mischievously pointed out by the press after his escape attempt. There was an hour's choir practice on a Saturday afternoon when the hymns for the Sunday service were rehearsed. Prison humour meant the 24th Psalm was sung with particular gusto: 'Lift up your heads, you gates; be lifted up, you ancient doors.' On the outside world a popular song of the time was sung to the tune of a Salvation Army hymn:

I do believe, I will believe,
That Laurie killed poor Rose
And on Goatfell he shed his blood
And stole away his clothes

Despite sessions of exercise and optional Bible class, Sunday could be a long day especially for those unable to read. With normal routine disrupted they were left to ruminate on the vicissitudes of life. Some prisoners developed interests to pass the time. Richard Tobin was from Laurie's neck of the woods, an Irish miner recruited to work in the Lanarkshire village of Cleland. Serving a life sentence for the murder of his wife, he had half-a-dozen pet mice in his cell which he taught to do various tricks. Inmates often befriended the pigeons that frequented the prison buildings. Scotch Jamie took to writing and got permission to compile a book which included over a thousand patriotic and love songs, as well as some sonnets.

Laurie's most popular reading material was either related to music or to shorthand which he studied diligently for several years. Prisoners were issued with a library book every week, delivered to their cell by the schoolteacher while they were out at work. For those able to read, books were one of the few pleasures in prison. But having no choice in their reading material was yet another source of contention among inmates. Laurie's love of grandiloquent language was reflected in his persistent quest for the authoritative *Chambers Dictionary*; not issued as a library book as was the norm, but for his own personal use in his cell. When, after many years of badgering, the authorities eventually acquiesce, this large and expensive volume was used as a weapon in the war for control and compliance, being withdrawn and returned depending on Laurie's behaviour.

In the prison there were three denominations: Roman Catholic, Presbyterian and Episcopalian. Laurie occasionally requested to change congregation and join another choir, but permission was required to do this. When he left the Church of Scotland for the Episcopalian Church, he regretted the move and eventually returned. However his reasons for changing were often less to do with religion than his frequent fall-outs with the respective chaplains who were often delegated educational matters, for example, whether a prisoner should be permitted a certain book they had requested.

Laurie did not hit it off with the Presbyterian chaplain, the Reverend David Sutherland, formerly minister at Beauly. The chaplain, in turn, didn't care much for Laurie describing him as 'a little man with sharp, ferrety eyes, meticulously neat in his person, and given to affected precision of speech'. The Reverend Sutherland also commented: 'In the case of Laurie there is an astonishing degree of cunning exhibited.'

Part of Laurie's gripe with Presbyterianism was that he saw it as a Highland religion. Many of the Glasgow policemen he had given the run-around for so long were Highland Presbyterians. Laurie had presumed that the judge at his trial was also a Highlander of this denomination, but he wasn't – Lord Kingsburgh was a member of the Catholic Apostolic Church which, confusingly, was not Catholic. In Laurie's paranoid thinking they all held a grudge against him; he was a victim of 'a base conspiracy' which also explained why he was having such a hard time in prison. The chaplain noted how Laurie often construed parts of the sermons to be specifically directed at him. (His sister Agnes had also done this with her minister in Coatbridge.)

By the end of the century Laurie would have completed 10 years in prison. In November 1899, Governor Dodd wrote to the Prison Commissioners in Edinburgh, relating how his progress had not been good: during this period Laurie had incurred 58 breaches of prison discipline that included insolence to officers, fighting with fellow prisoners, and disobedience of orders. However the most serious blotting of his copybook was his escape attempt in 1893. Attached to the governor's report was an update by the medical officer, W J H Sinclair: 'This prisoner is in good health. There is no indication that his mind has been prejudicially affected by imprisonment.' If this was true it would not be for long. The first two years of the new century were dominated, in Laurie's case, by a deterioration in both his physical and mental health..

Chapter Twelve

The Term of his Natural Life

At the start of the new century Laurie's spirits were lifted by British victories in the Boer War, whereas many of his fellow inmates, often of Irish descent, wanted to see the Empire crushed. Laurie's politics were always those espoused by the Conservative and Unionist Party and prison life had not dulled his admiration of the monarchy. There is now a new strand in Laurie's correspondence as he argues that his loyalty to Queen and country, under such hostile circumstances, should be favourably recognised with regard to an early release.

Laurie writes his brother Gavin, now a partner in the Airdrie Coal Company, asking after his children, James and Mary. He also writes his aunt Bella in Moffat to whom he is more downbeat: 'There has been alleviation and amelioration but I am if possible, more worn; and I feel more sad. I am very, very weary of it all, but will not distress you with further complaint.'

In July 1900 Laurie suffered an attack of appendicitis and was admitted to the prison infirmary where he would remain over the summer. The accommodation in the hospital was in individual cells which included a padded cell and an isolation unit for infectious diseases. Unlike the ordinary prison cells they had large windows of plain glass that provided views of Peterhead harbour and the coming and going of the herring fleet. The hospital building was a quieter environment at the north-east corner of the prison overlooking the sea, and to the convicts was a highly sought-after location that induced much feigned injury and illness. One particular attraction was that the medical officer had the power to order whatever diet he felt beneficial in each particular case. Convicts could find themselves enjoying long dreamt-of luxuries like brandy, Guinness, chicken, custard and other delights.

In the infirmary Laurie would be entitled to more reading material. There was also a garden which was used for convalescence. During his stay he continued to petition the Secretary for Scotland but is now less coherent, his normally neat and steady handwriting more shaky, his introduction even more obsequious: 'Indeed I am far from wishing that any respectable person would squander a single moment in alluding to the complaints of the very scum of the scum.'

Most of the beds in the infirmary were occupied by convicts injured while working in the quarries, most often fingers, shins and toes crushed or lacerated by falling granite blocks. To initially break up the rocks, holes were drilled and filled with explosive. Two men struck a heavy boring rod with a sledge hammer while two more were needed to give the rod a half turn between each blow. It could take several days to bore a hole by hand. There was a warning horn three minutes before a shot. In February 1891 an explosion at Stirling Hill seriously injuring one of the convicts after a nitro-glycerine cartridge failed to ignite, lying unexploded among the debris until struck by the convict's pick.

There were also fatalities due to falling rocks. Like the explosion, these were not unique to Stirling Hill but relatively common occurrences in quarries throughout the country. In one incident, in October 1893, blasting left a 12-ton rock perched precariously. Henry Hanly, a 25-year-old Glaswegian, and another convict named Murray were ordered to move it. Hanly was lowered at the end of a rope in an attempt to free the rock, but the rope slipped leaving him dangling over a 50ft (15m) drop. Exposed to falling rocks, he was fatally injured after his breast bone was broken in three places, three ribs were shattered and his left leg broken. At the fatal accident enquiry there was much debate over the type of knot used.

The quarry was the scene of other incidents. On 20 January 1898 Warder Ross was violently assaulted when a convict attacked him with a shovel, striking him several times, including once on the head after he had stumbled and fallen. The warder managed to defend himself with his cutlass and eventually disarmed his attacker, breaking the convict's arm.

The stresses of prison life meant the threat of suicide or self-harm was never far away. On 3 June 1891 the governor reported: 'Robert Kean was remanded to the Commissioners for wilfully injuring his hand by placing it under wagon wheel.' Some prisons, like Chatham, became notorious for this type of extreme self-harm: placing limbs on the tracks between the wheels of moving railway trucks. When similar incidents escalated at the Kent prison, with amputations being performed every couple of weeks, an official investigation concluded that 'self-infliction of injury is merely a form of malingering'.

In 1893 one inmate at Peterhead was so desperate to end it all he drank a tin of red lead paint left lying in the prison yard. He had swallowed around two pints before warders spotted him and managed to snatch the tin. The convict was taken to the prison hospital in a 'weak but not dangerous condition' as he had vomited up most of the paint.

Suicidal prisoners were able to create a noose from the straps which attached their hammock to the wall, and then use it to hang themselves from the ventilation slot in the cell window. The following prisoners were some who chose this method to take their own life: David Forrester in November 1893, only three weeks into his sentence; James Wiggins in January 1900, and 29-year-old John Stevenson, serving four years for theft, in 1907. There was also a long casualty list of those who died suddenly or too early from illness; were crippled or killed by work, or went insane and were sent to the likes of the Criminal Lunatic Department at Perth Prison.

After illness or injury prisoners were usually given sedentary labour until they had fully recovered. This would be in the likes of the tailors' shop working on patching, oakum or knitting stockings . In Laurie's case he was granted this lighter work over the winter until the start of the warmer weather when he would be expected to return to the construction of the breakwater.

For some of this time Laurie was back working with oakum. Although regarded as light indoor work, done repetitively this was an exasperating and very frustrating activity. Prisoners were given quantities of old hemp rope which had to be untwisted and broken down into smaller sections, usually by rolling them on their laps till they became loose. This became successively difficult as strands were unravelled into yarn, and yarn into hemp fibres. After a couple of hours the fingers started to bleed. The end product, oakum, was sold to ship builders (hence the term, 'money for old rope') where it was mixed with grease or tar for use as caulking to fill gaps between the wooden planks of ships and make them watertight.

One prisoner who also spent some time teasing oakum was Peterhead's most distinguished inmate, Dr James Colquhoun, the ex-Treasurer of the City of Glasgow who was jailed in 1899 for fraud and embezzlement. His trial created something of a sensation. Colquhoun was very overweight and spent much of his early time at Peterhead in the infirmary on account of his diabetes; there were accusations of favouritism due to who he was. After his recovery he was put to work on oakum alongside Laurie who by all accounts did not take to him.

While Laurie was in hospital with appendicitis, the governor made the following note: 'The above convict's conduct in prison has been indifferent, but latterly it has improved. He has incurred no report since last October.' For the rest of the year and throughout the next (1901), Laurie is more compliant and less demonstrative. This was doubtless related to his poor health and corresponding breaks from hard manual labour. But there was another more significant factor. Laurie was in sight of completing 12 years, a milestone which offered a realistic chance of release. There is a corresponding improvement in his behaviour. There is a well-documented phenomenon within prisons where lifers start off as very disruptive and belligerent characters with a reputation for aggression towards staff and fellow inmates. After a few years their behaviour mellows with less violence, a more co-operative attitude, tidier cells, and even a born-again religious outlook. It often works.

In his petition of 12 February 1901 Laurie claims that he has been an invalid since his attack of appendicitis the previous July. His complaints include severe rheumatism in his shoulder and problems with his bowels; he wants to be discharged without delay on grounds of ill-health: 'That I am broken down, and so completely as to preclude all hope of anything beyond partial recovery there is now no room to doubt.' Dr Sinclair responded, 'He is probably malingering.'

Laurie's fortieth birthday was on 15 March 1901, a significant occasion in anyone's life. However, it is highly unlikely there were any candles in Laurie's porridge as no one at Peterhead Prison was aware of the anniversary. Laurie often gave his date of birth as 15 March 1864 and this is what was recorded on his prison records (it was eventually changed). During the day there was a sudden deterioration in his mental condition and he was transferred to the prison hospital where he was placed under observation. The hospital notes reveal that Laurie became increasingly anxious that some people, especially his stepmother, were spreading rumours about the sexual peccadilloes of his youth, 'hateful lies extremely prejudicial to my character'. His medical notes go on to record that he denied ever visiting a lady in Coatbridge at midnight by climbing up to her bedroom through the window. Nor were any charges of bestiality true.

Despite his downturn in health, Laurie continued to petition the Secretary for Scotland for clemency. There is a change of tack as his letters adopt a more confessional tone with regard to Edwin Rose's death. Whether this is related to Laurie's increasing paranoia is unclear. Thoughts of release are rarely far from any prisoner's mind, as are thoughts of how they can make more headway in this direction. Whatever the reason, Laurie attempts to remedy any accusations that he lacked remorse or had failed to take responsibility for his crime. The first of these statements was on 1 April 1901:

My Lord, All that remains for me to unfold is that it was I who pushed Mr Rose into the water-course on the side of Glen Sannox. I finished the insane action and the life of my companion by throwing several stones at his head. The rest is known how I conveyed him over the rocks and concealed him. What I can say for myself but that it was the work of a distracted fool.

Your lordship stands in no need of being informed that many young men have gone far astray and in the end displayed the highest qualities. All that I can plead is that I have now reached a time of life when the faults of youth can no longer be accounted either temptation or excuse, so that there is the probability that I shall so conduct myself during the days which may remain to me as one who has read the best lesson from the varied experience he has undergone.'

Two weeks later Laurie wrote to the Prison Commissioners:

Gentleman, Had I committed a thousand crimes I could have

no sense of personal dishonour in recounting them all, for I am assured that nothing can surpass in baseness much that has come to my knowledge here. It is likely enough that my step-mother has given expression to hateful lies about me, but only the vilest b*****d would expect me to support what she may have said. Let it suffice gentlemen, I shall do nothing of the kind.

There is a zigzag lane in Glasgow nearly opposite Bothwell St, and passing along this one evening on my way to meet a friend, a Miss Joannie Dickson, who was an assistant in the warehouse of Mr Lorimer, stationer, which is adjacent to the Renfield Street end of the lane. As I turned the sharp angle of the lane I surprised three work-worn girls who were, in the words of Mr Colin Brown, to whom I related the occurrence, 'giving relief to their pent up feelings'. I don't know what complexion this simple incident may have been given to wear. It happened nearly twenty years ago and I really have spoken much nonsense in that time. But believe me, gentlemen, I never perpetuated any violence on a prostitute unless unintentionally overturning a drunken one, who linked her arm in mine on the street, can be called violence.

Kindly order a retreat, gentlemen, for all the powers of hell may not induce me to discuss anything outside my case, or oblige me to admit what I have emphatically denied.

I am, gentlemen,
Your obedient servant
John W Laurie

From Laurie's paranoid perspective the situation was this: his stepmother, as well as a Mr Dunlop, and 'a prisoner who is not in favour of the government' had all made disparaging statements that cast aspersions about his earlier life. Because of this the authorities had assumed that he is guilty of other, as yet undisclosed, matters which they feel he should own up to. The Mr Dunlop mentioned was an acquaintance of Laurie with whom he had a long-running dispute, the origin of which is not clear. This quarrel was the object of some enquiry from Sir Arthur Mitchell during Laurie's psychiatric evaluation at Greenock Prison. Laurie later revealed that he thought one of the cited incidents would be construed as rape. However the medical officer's report concluded that there was really no substance to the allegations: 'The prisoner has from time to time lately made statements similar to those in his petition to the Prison Commissioners. He says that he has been led to suspect that persons who are not friendly to him are spreading reports that he has been guilty of unnatural crimes. The stories he accounts are all built upon a substratum of fact, trivial occurrences in his life which are capable of being misrepresented by designing persons. I think it is probable that this prisoner has always been to a slight extent the subject of perverted sexual instinct, and that there is a tendency to further perversion in this direction'.

Although these accusations were by and large exaggerated, Laurie insisted, and would continue to do so for the rest of his days, that nothing would make him admit to further failings or to betray those loyal to him. (Who the latter party are is never made clear.) From now on he maintains this uncompromising stance in almost all of his written communication, which are invariably concluded with a characteristically verbose flourish. The following is a typical example of this idiosyncratic trait: 'I am neither to be intimidated nor cajoled into admissions and acknowledgements defamatory to my own character, and involving a betrayal of the integrity of those to whom I am under the most sacred obligations.'

On 15 May 1901, still at sedentary labour, Laurie once again petitioned the Secretary for Scotland, this time adding some detail to the brief confession he made six weeks earlier: 'My Lord, Before Rose and I set out to ascend Goatfell we had all been drinking together in the hotel at Brodick, and Rose presented one of the young men with a bottle of whisky in token of the trouble he had undertaken of purchasing a pair of gaiters similar to those he wore, and transmitting them to Mr Rose... On the summit of Goatfell Rose produced his brandy flask, so that we left for Glen Sannox in rather high spirits and quoting about the scenery of the glen, from the *Ivanhoe* time card, he observed that it was 'savagely grand'. As he wore a glazed waterproof, though it was a fine evening, I remarked that he presented a 'savagely grand' aspect himself, and to my surprise he retorted by striking at me with his walking stick. I repelled the attack with a blow which caused him to roll down a declivity and pitch into a water-course at the bottom, and I must admit that I also threw a stone at his head. I afterwards dragged him out and over the rocks to a place of concealment. I had a quarrel too about this time with a Mr Dunlop at Rothesay. He knocked me down with his fist, which I resented by dealing him a stroke on the shoulder with my umbrella. I regret these occurrences very much, they have been the occasion of great sorrow and no one has suffered more than myself.'

In the above petition Laurie was also at pains to point out that he has matured from the frivolous behaviour of his youth, and asks to be moved somewhere 'more favourable to convalescence'. When this request is rejected it is a bitter pill to swallow: 'Nothing can exceed the misery of my condition, and I think nothing can surpass the atrocious vindictiveness of those who seem determined that I shall suffer.'

In 1901 a new theme emerges in Laurie's correspondence: he claims his food is being drugged for the purpose of making him 'utter self-accusatory remarks'. He makes a connection between his meals being tampered with and his recent 'confessional' statements. For the rest of his time in prison Laurie maintains that the authorities are poisoning his food in an attempt to make him admit to the wrongdoing he is accused of by his stepmother and others.

Another early inmate claimed a similar thing. John Mclean was a Glasgow teacher and political activist who was jailed twice for contravention of the Defence of the Realm Act due to his public opposition to the First World War. Mclean described Peterhead as 'an intractable hell through the drugging of the food'. He thought the prison doctors were doing this to break his physical and mental health in order to negate his political threat. Mclean refused to take the prison food and was consequently force-fed. At Perth Prison, prior to Mclean's transfer to Peterhead, Dr James Devon, now one of the Prison Commissioners, informed the Scottish Office that 'we are dealing with a man who is insane but not certified'. At his trial in 1918 Mclean declared: 'I have stated in public since that I would rather be immediately put to death than condemned to a life sentence in Peterhead.' He went on to describe the prison as 'that Scottish abode of scientific torture'.

John Mclean was undoubtedly a serious political threat to the establishment, the Union Jack waving John Laurie certainly was not. However Laurie continued to complain of a nasty taste in his mouth due to the drugs he insisted were being added to his food, to make him provide further confessions. When Dr Sinclair updated his medical report on Laurie he concluded that there was an overall improvement in his mental state and behaviour: 'His conduct is good and his demeanour is not such as to attract the notice of his fellow prisoners, and he has not obtruded himself on the notice of officials in such a way as to raise the question of his sanity at any time since last report.'

By the autumn of 1901 Laurie has completed 12 years, his long hoped-for chance of liberation. A petition at this time betrays his sense of optimism: 'I again solicit my release without further delay.' He claims that his crime was no worse than other prisoners who had been released earlier. Laurie also rehashes, with the help of his dictionary, some familiar themes: he makes great play of being a loyal subject and supporter of the government; he continues to claim his food is being tampered with, and that his stepmother, and others, are continuing to spread derogatory stories besmirching his good name:

It cannot be that I am the most flagitious individual in all Scotland, though from the appearance matters have been made to assume, one might almost fancy that such is actually the case. That I have been shamefully traduced, there is only too much reason to fear, but surely your Lordship does not require that I shall appease my own character and thus give colour to the spiteful accusations of persons, for the most part ill-disposed to the government and consequently no friends of mine.

This particular petition, described as 'given in a halting and somewhat disconnected way', appears to have been given serious consideration, prompting another medical report from Dr Sinclair. The medical officer had by now read so many of Laurie's letters that his own writing style is beginning to ape that of his prolix patient. Dr Sinclair writes the following in his report:

These statements by his traducers [one of Laurie's favourite words] he fancies may cause the authorities to think that there are other matters which although undiscovered are unsatisfactory, and that the authorities would like him to make a clean breast of all before considering his liberation.

The ornate and pedantic style of the prisoner's petition is characteristic, and is another manifestation of the love of show which induced the prisoner to commit murder in order to possess himself of the money, clothing and appurtenances of his victim so that he might prolong his holiday and make a better show. His crime indicates defective mental processes, defective reasoning, under circumstances in which a properly balanced mind would have at once realised the disproportion between the possession of a few fine things and the awfulness of his means of obtaining them - murder.

There is little doubt that the prisoner is mentally defective. His crime indicates defective mental processes and defective reasoning. He has always been, although not to the extent of rendering him irresponsible. There is reason to believe that his mental defects have tended to increase during his imprisonment; and the probability is that, under the stresses of continued penal servitude, further increase will ensue. The prisoner gives no evidence of sorrow or remorse for his crime. He is not in any way depressed. He appears to have little, if any, family affection. He is quiet and well-behaved. He is fond of talking of the most indecent matters relating to the sexual and does so without any semblance of shame.

His heart and lungs and kidneys are healthy. His appetite and digestive functions are good and he is well nourished, weighing 146lbs, 15lbs more than on reception.'

Laurie's hopes are shattered when his petition is once again refused. He insists it should be reconsidered. He also wants to retract his statement that Rose met his death at his hands which he claims he only made because he thought he was about to be freed: 'It is perfectly true that Mr Rose did fall into a ravine or water-course, but I now beg to retract having said that he met his death at my hands; and had I understood that your Lordship acquiesced in the treatment I have received I never would have made the statement.'

When Laurie argues that other prisoners who had committed worse or similar crimes were being released from Peterhead before him, he does have a point. Throughout his time in jail he would hear of prisoners being liberated while his own incarceration continued. Joseph Calabrese, an Ayrshire ice cream vendor who murdered his wife and four children with an axe, was freed on licence after 10 years in Peterhead. Unlike Laurie, Calabrese was not certified insane. However there are some cases which have more similarities to that of Laurie's.

Archibald Robertson, the afore-mentioned prison barber, was originally sentenced to death commuted to penal servitude for life, after murdering his cousin. His reprieve followed a similar path to that of Laurie's with a medical committee, including Sir Arthur Mitchell and Dr David Yellowlees who had both examined Laurie, reporting on his state of mind. The result was that Robertson was 'respited by Her Majesty pending further signification of her pleasure'. This eventually became a reprieve, presumably, like Laurie, on the grounds of insanity. He was eventually discharged on licence from Peterhead after 20 years.

Perhaps the nearest example to Laurie's circumstances was Hector Mackenzie, a farm labourer convicted of the murder of Isabella Lamont at Fort George near Nairn, who was released in 1904 after 15 years. Like Laurie, his death sentence was commuted as several reports claimed him to be of unsound mind. His liberation was initially delayed as there was no one willing to take responsibility for him, after his home parish of Applecross refused. He was eventually handed over to the Inspector of the Poor in Inverness. This may also have been part of Laurie's problem – that his family had wiped their hands of him. With the release of Mackenzie, Laurie became Peterhead's longest-serving inmate.

Those who were discharged from Peterhead were given little preparation or guidance for life outside. The only change in routine, prior to liberation, was that inmates were allowed to let their hair grow. On the day of release their own clothes, taken from them at the start of their sentence, were returned to them. After years on a prison diet these could prove an ill-fitting outfit, and the longer the sentence the more unfashionable the garments.

It could add up to a tragicomic sight. Beyond Peterhead's gates the first steps of freedom were often accompanied by a profound sense of unreality, compounded by acute anxiety at having to face a long-forgotten and much-changed world. They were escorted to Peterhead Station where a train ticket was purchased for them and they were given some bread and cheese for the journey home. The warder would see them to a carriage, shake their hand and wish them good luck. They would need it.

Behind the scenes there was much discussion as to what to do with Laurie. Some felt he should be transferred to Perth, some not. But how clear was the law and the guidelines in dealing with a prisoner, certified insane *after* his trial, who had now served a long sentence and who had been assessed as sane by different doctors on several occasions?

During the mid-nineteenth century there was a series of legislation that tackled the complex issue of criminal insanity. By the Lunacy (Scotland) Act 1862 insane prisoners, on the expiry of their sentence, might be detained in the lunatic department of the General Prison at Perth, or in a local prison or asylum until liberated in due course of law. The Criminal and Dangerous Lunatics (Scotland) Act 1871 empowered the Secretary of State to liberate persons detained during the royal pleasure on certain conditions, although they could be recalled if any of these were broken.

The indeterminate 'royal pleasure' was largely used in connection with those who were found insane at the time of committing the offence, or who were found 'insane in bar of trial'. The latter was a plea where the accused's state of mind, at the time of trial, was such that the person could not understand the proceedings against them, or adequately instruct their legal representatives. Laurie's problem was that he been found insane *after* his trial and had his death sentence commuted 'upon condition of his being kept in penal servitude *for the term of his natural life*'. The nub of the matter was whether prisoners in Laurie's category could be released on licence. As mentioned, Hector Mackenzie and Archibald Robertson had been.

Many prisoners were at the mercy of what was on file about them in official reports, compiled primarily by prison governors and medical officers. The nature of closed, insular institutions like Peterhead Prison was that subjective opinion, petty grudges even, could filter into official reports on which important decisions regarding a prisoner's future were based. If there was any prevarication over what action to take, the default procedure, certainly in Laurie's case, was to ask for yet another medical report. In terms of psychiatric evaluation these were, in today's terms, rudimentary to say the least.

It is often dangerous to make psychological assumptions without specialised medical knowledge. However, even to the layman it would appear evident that Laurie ticked many of the boxes on the psychopathic checklist: lack of empathy and remorse, exploiting others for their own benefit, pathological lying, manipulation, sexual promiscuity, unwillingness to take responsibility. The narcissistic element is present in Laurie's self-absorption and dressing up to elicit admiration from others; there was also a fragile ego and the concomitant inability to take criticism, which often led to disproportionate anger or rage. These latter factors may well have contributed to what happened on Goatfell. The word psychopath was in use in Laurie's day, but as a general term for mental disorders. It was only later in the twentieth century that it became associated with criminal and anti-social behaviour.

On 4 April 1902, James C Dunbar reported to the Prison Commissioners with regard to Laurie. After examining him on several occasions, he concluded that he was insane and was a suitable case for transfer to the Lunatic Department at Perth Prison. Dunbar's opinion was based on the fact that the convict 'has erotic sexual instincts, has delusions of suspicion, and has during the last two years shown other symptoms of progressing mental enfeeblement'. When this report arrived at the Commissioners in Edinburgh, an unsigned note was appended: 'Approve of above but report from Dr Sinclair should first be obtained.'

Sinclair duly completed yet another medical report on Laurie, his fourth within a year, which reached the Prison Commissioners on 14 April 1902. This time the Peterhead medical officer's assessment of Laurie was much more encouraging: Convict 275 was working quietly and steadily and obeying the rules of the prison. He was spending his spare time reading, and learning shorthand in which he had made much progress. Dr Sinclair concluded his account with, 'No sign of confusion, good physically, appetite good, sleeping well.'

A further cryptic note was added to the end of this medical report: 'We must act wisely in respect of this man.' The person who appeared to have the final say as to Laurie's future was Thomas Fraser, professor of medicine at Edinburgh University. As medical adviser to the Scottish Prison Commission, Fraser visited Peterhead every three months. James Dunbar wrote the following letter to Professor Fraser:

You will note in the MO's report that this convict has delusions of suspicions and other signs of abnormal brain action, viz impaired memory and want of natural emotions, also that MO does not consider that his mental condition has deteriorated during the last six months.

The gist of the case appears to me to be this: the convict was years ago certified to be insane and on the grounds of insanity his death sentence was commuted to penal servitude for life; in prison his mental condition has deteriorated, he will in all probability never be fit to trust with liberty. He will probably become so insane as to require his removal to Perth at some future date, hence the question of when is the right time for his removal, should that be after further deterioration or should that further deterioration be anticipated and perhaps avoided. It may be well to ask a further report from MO six months hence and reconsider it then.

Professor Fraser responded, 'In view of the further information and especially of the full report of Dr Sinclair, I do not think Lawrie (sic) should be transferred to the Lunatic Department of Perth Prison.' This single sentence sealed Laurie's fate. Laurie appealed to Lord Balfour of Burleigh, the Conservative Scottish Secretary (1895-1903), to review the decision not to release him, this time affecting his oft-tried tactic of patriotism tinged with some grudging remorse: 'If your lordship can be prevailed upon to reconsider my petition of the 4 October [1901] I trust that it may be borne in mind, that though I may have done one or two things in my time I ought not to have done, no one can deny that

I have the interests of the nation and the empire very much at heart, and this is perhaps more than can be said of some who seem to enjoy your Lordship's confidence.'

There was still no joy, though Balfour (unbeknown to Laurie) thought his case should be seriously considered when he had completed 15 years. Laurie's letters now briefly focus on more mundane topics, especially in correspondence with his aunt Bella in Moffat, his father's sister; one of few family members he was still close to, and who was keen to assist her nephew in any way she could: 'The swallows were about a month behind time, a couple of swifts, indeed, put in an appearance on the 6 June, but they were too swift by far and must have regretted their long wings for once. We have barely had two or three fragments of warm days altogether, but we must not complain too loudly on this score.' Laurie's Christian faith is still strong and he ends the letter with a quote from the Bible accompanied by a final patriotic flourish, 'Though He slay me, yet will I trust in him. Long live the King.'

Chapter Thirteen

The Vituperation of my Traducers

Laurie continued to be obsessed with his food being drugged despite the Chaplain warning him that references to poisoning would only prolong his stay. The authorities now recorded Laurie's conduct as 'indifferent' and saw no great change in his mental condition though it was noted that he is occasionally 'experiencing delusions'. This observation is backed up in one petition where Laurie protests how his unwavering loyalty to the Crown had still not gained him his freedom, pointing out that the recent Diamond Jubilee, the Coronation or the King's visit to Scotland would all have been fitting occasions for his release. Laurie is soon put under medical observation.

In October 1903 Lord Balfour was replaced as Scottish Secretary by Andrew Graham Murray. For Laurie it took some time for the penny to drop that the new incumbent was the same person who led much of the prosecution against him at his trial back in 1889. Ironically, Murray was now the Conservative MP for Buteshire which covered the islands of Arran and Bute, the principal locales of Laurie's downfall. Since their last meeting Murray had got tongues wagging through his close relationship with Queen Marie of Romania, grand-daughter of Queen Victoria.

By September 1904 Laurie is again reported as suffering delusions. A feature of prison life is that the torpid confinement and insular environment make it hard to let go of any injustices or perceived wrongs. It is easy to become obsessed by particular topics and Laurie is no exception as his habitual fixations continue to gnaw away at him. The poisoning of his food and the alleged attacks upon his character dominate his correspondence with the Scottish Secretary through the first decade of the new century.

November 1904 was 15 years since Laurie's trial and conviction. With good conduct a prisoner under a life sentence could reasonably expect to be released after this period. However 'good conduct' is the crucial phrase with regard to Laurie's continued incarceration, as Governor Dodd summed up in a brief note: 'During that time his conduct has been unsatisfactory. At present he is employed on the public works, and during the last three months he has, however, worked quietly and well. He is recognised as being unstable mentally.'

During 1904 Laurie is reported for three offences including, 'Insubordinate conduct in workshop (shouting to Governor when making his visit).' Laurie does himself no favours by continually denigrating those who have a powerful say with regard to his release. In a petition to the Scottish Secretary he describes the Peterhead governor as, 'a perfect monster of iniquity'. He starts one letter to the Commissioners with, 'The Governor, whose diabolical practices are by no means unbeknown to you'. Scotch Jamie was doubtless thinking of his friend John Laurie when he wrote the following:' One of the greatest hardships of the prison discipline is that in the case of 'lifers' whose conduct may have been insubordinate, though they may have spent fifteen years within prison walls, no amelioration of their condition is allowed. They have earned a bad name, and the utmost severity is meted out to them without any regard to individual temperament'.

During 1905 we hear little of Laurie. In the press there are rumours that his mental state is causing concern. There is only one piece of correspondence for the year, a letter to 'Lord Graham Murray': 'My Lord, I have fallen into the hands of a parcel of miscreants and exposed to a perpetual menace of death, am debarred from apprizing my friends of my extraordinary plight.'

By 1906 Laurie seems to have finally conceded that he has exhausted all possible avenues for securing his release: the number of years he has completed, his ailing health; what he has had to put up with in prison, confession and remorse. Even his unfailing loyalty to the crown, under trying circumstances, has made no difference. He seems resigned to his fate and appears to fade into the fabric of the prison. From now on his petitions become lifeless clones of each other, each more forlorn and despondent than the last. Laurie seems to have finally run out of ideas, ending his regular tirade to the Secretary for Scotland with, 'I have been systematically poisoned for sixteen years, am at present employed in a granite quarry, and having said so, I can not see that anything further remains for me to say.'

The mind-numbing routine and petty vindictiveness of convict life goes on: 'As if it were not enough to torture me with poison, the night patrol keep up an incessant disturbance outside my cell so as to deprive me of sleep. They had a long spell of it last night, from eight o'clock until seven am this morning.' John Maclean also experienced the negative side of the warders:

Of course, anything can be made a crime, and by nagging and threatening to bring men before the Governor the warders are able to make their charges lives unbearable. The purpose is to break up the men's nervous system, and veritable wrecks are made of many. It is the systematic nagging that causes periodic outbursts of the men against one another and against the warders. It must be borne in mind that the warders just carry out the instructions that come from the head warder and finally from the doctor, and that they are watched to see that they carry out their instructions.

Descriptions like this demonstrate how difficult it could be, despite the best intentions, to stay on the straight and narrow and just do the time. Here are Laurie's misdemeanours for 1907:

28 February: Disobedience and insolence to a warder
13 May: Disobedience and destroying prison property (milk jug)
30 September: Having prohibited articles (written communication, pencil and piece of steel) and refusing to work.

In May 1908 the governor, Major Dodd, retired and there was a relaxation from his iron rule. He was replaced by Major Playfair for a few months before James Stewart took over as governor until 1929. There was now the occasional concert and prisoners were allowed some news of the outside world with selected items from newspapers read out. Through Laurie's incarceration prison conditions gradually improved. The Prison Act of 1898 incorporated many of the recommendations of the Gladstone

Report of three years earlier. This was one of the first attempts to reform and rehabilitate as well as punish. Diet was improved and there were more visits, letters, books, and less confinement in cells. A little recreation in association was also encouraged. Some punishments were abolished including the darkened cell, while conversation was permitted at authorised times.

However, improved conditions did not mean convicts were keen to prolong their stay. September 1909 was the twentieth anniversary of Laurie's capture near Hamilton. Twenty years was normally the maximum time for lifers and Laurie would be confident of imminent release under licence. There were rumours going around that he had already been freed: 'A report reached the *Daily Record and Mail* last night that John Watson Laurie had been liberated from Peterhead convict prison.' (17 May 1909) It was claimed he had applied for a job at an ironworks. Some acquaintances of Laurie were convinced they had seen him in Greenock.

John Cowan, his rival for Annie McLean, was now headmaster of Bank Public School in New Cumnock in Ayrshire. Cowan wrote to the Secretary for Scotland requesting protection from 'molestation by Laurie', as he reckoned he still held a long-standing grudge and, if released, would be a dangerous threat to himself and his family. Cowan also asked for assistance to obtain a new post in one of the larger cities, 'where a man may work as a unit in a crowd and be at peace'. In the desultory letter Laurie wrote to the *Glasgow Herald* from the Northern Bar in Aberdeen, on 27 August 1889, he tells of an encounter with Cowan's brother James in Glasgow: 'I met him one morning in Shamrock Street, not Cambridge Street, and I caught hold of his arm, when he asked a boy to call a policeman. There was no striking on either side, but if there had been, I leave these who know us to judge who would have come off second best.'

The Scottish Office response was that Cowan's fears were exaggerated, but they also suspected he may have an ulterior motive, presumably to prolong Laurie's incarceration. Nevertheless they took John Cowan's concerns seriously, yet another obstacle in Laurie's hopes of freedom. They also decided to investigate what type of character Cowan was. The report came back: 'Cowan is of an abnormally nervous temperament which might lead him to be unduly apprehensive.' The press also picked up on the rumours of imminent release, with the *Weekly News* writing to Laurie on 6 September 1909:

> Dear Sir,
> In view of your impending liberation it has occurred to me that you might be disposed to consider an offer for the publication of your experiences. If so I shall be glad to arrange for one of our representatives meeting you on your release provided you inform us as to the date, or arrange a meeting either in Glasgow, Dundee, Edinburgh or Aberdeen. I shall be glad to hear from you.

It was now realised by the authorities that Laurie was the only prisoner at Peterhead who had been there more than 15 years. Behind the scenes, between November 1909 and January 1910, there was again much activity as to what should be done with him. The Prison Commissioners met on 15 November to discuss the case of 'The Arran murderer'. They felt that the contents of Laurie's most recent medical report suggested that his release would be neither beneficial to himself nor the community at large, 'There seems little ground for suggesting Laurie's release.' Here is an extract from the Medical Report (9 November 1909) referred to above: 'This prisoner in my opinion is mentally defective; his whole history exhibiting an entire lack of the moral sense; careful scrutiny reveals the degenerate, physically, intellectually and morally. Suspicious in a very high degree, every effort of the staff is misrepresented. The Chaplain preaches at him, drugs his food, the staff generally are in collusion to ruin his health etc, etc. These and such statements as these he has given expression to for years.'

A month later the Secretary for Scotland wrote that he was strongly against the release of Laurie. He had discussed it with the commissioners who were of the same opinion. Although he had taken into consideration protests against his release, the prime factors in coming to this conclusion were Laurie's 'doubtful sanity' and how the case was considered at Laurie's trial in 1889, especially by Lord Lothian who had intimated that Laurie's case should not be reviewed with a view to release after 20 years.

The upshot of these considerations was that the authorities felt they were left with three possible options: to move Laurie to the Lunatic Department of Perth Prison, but there was currently no room there; 'to treat with other weak-minded convicts as soon as we have provision for them', or lastly, leave him where he was. It was felt, especially by the Peterhead governor, that the latter course might discourage other prisoners on long sentences, but it was pointed out that they all regarded him as 'feeble-minded' and considered this the reason he had not been released.

On 12 March 1910 Laurie introduced himself to the new Scottish Secretary (there wasn't one) in his characteristically grandiose style:

> My Lord, I did not hear 'who' is the new Secretary for Scotland, but as it has been usual for me to address all the Scottish Secretaries, I believe that were I to accoutreate the last memorial I addressed to your predecessor by repeating it, I should fairly meet the exigencies of the situation.
>
> I have been more than twenty years in prison and have not yet been told anything definite about my release. It cannot be that my personal character is such as to raise any difficulty about the matter, or to justify the treatment I have received.

On Thursday 27 April 1910 there is a picture in the *Daily Record and Mail* of five convicts, all heavily manacled, at Aberdeen Station. In the centre is John Laurie who is now on his way from Peterhead to Perth Prison. The picture's caption read: 'The Arran murderer, however, has aged considerably. His hair, cropped in close accordance with prison rules, is quite grey, and his face is wan and haggard. He walks with a stoop, and his whole appearance points to his being in the latest stages of senile decay.' The latter part of this is journalistic hyperbole as in reality Laurie does not look frail and has his head bowed solely to avoid the camera.

After several months in the General Prison at Perth, John Laurie was admitted to the Criminal Lunatic Department on 24 August 1910. He was officially certified as suffering from progressive dementia. The governor of Perth Prison noted in his official journal: 'Convict 470/10 John Watson Laurie, Life Sentence, and Prisoner 203/10, Robert Duff, sentence 9 months. Certified insane and duly reported today.' After twenty years in an extremely tough regime, many thought the move to the less harsh environment of Perth was because of his age and time served. John Thomson, an Airdrie burglar, knew Laurie in Peterhead: 'No I don't think he had gone off his head to be sent there. It was only after twenty years in Peterhead when he might have been released. No one could be got to look after him. He was a peculiar man in many ways, and, contrary to the usual practice, would not talk about his crime.'

Perth Prison was one of Scotland's oldest dating back to the Napoleonic Wars. The building that became the Criminal Lunatic Department was originally used to house French prisoners who spent much of their time there making the likes of dominoes and straw dolls for sale at the local market.

Prior to 1839, there was no separate provision in Scotland for people with mental health problems who had committed serious crimes. These 'lunatic prisoners' were detained in local prisons along with other inmates unless a burgh maintained a separate asylum. It was realised that the mixing of the criminally insane with other prisoners was not a good fit. There was little medical provision in ordinary jails. Those deemed insane had different needs, and could present complex challenging behaviour towards both staff and other inmates. On the other hand they were often subject to taunts and worse, and were exposed to others being released while their internment continued indefinitely.

The Prisons (Scotland) Act 1839 addressed criminal insanity for the first time. In 1846 part of the General Prison at Perth, a two-storey building with wings at either end, was adapted to house insane prisoners. Downstairs there were day rooms as well as cells with 1 to 4 beds. Upstairs were single rooms with iron bedsteads and straw mattresses. Apart from a small library there was little effort to occupy the inmates. The emphasis was still on security rather than treatment, with restraints (iron shackles) still in use. In 1856 one report recorded three patients under restraint: 'One had an iron chain placed round his waist, to which one hand was fastened; another had a hand fastened in a similar way, and his legs were hobbled by rings placed round the ankles, and connected together by an iron chain.'

In 1855, Dr David Skae of Royal Edinburgh Hospital called for one single institution in Scotland, an early example of concentrating specialist services. In 1865 this was realised with the opening of the Criminal Lunatic Department within the General Prison at Perth. In 1877 it held 57 patients: 41 male, 16 female. Places were always at a premium and this lack of accommodation was one factor in the prevarication regarding Laurie's future.

From 1878, when a medical superintendent was appointed, Perth Lunatic Department begun to develop along the lines of a psychiatric hospital, the forerunner of Carstairs State Hospital. Like the contemporary Broadmoor Hospital in Berkshire, Perth appeared to have an enlightened regime which elicited excellent reports from the Prison Commissioners, and many inmates were successfully transferred to ordinary asylums. However there was as yet few effective treatments for mental illness and emphasis was placed on the well-being and happiness of the patients, still referred to as 'lunatics'. In 1904 a report recommended the word 'lunatic' should be discontinued, and 'hospital' substituted for 'asylum', but it was many years before this was implemented.

Laurie found conditions at Perth much more amenable than Peterhead: he was free to talk and wander about. Even better, there was no sign of cement, quarries or breakwater, just a garden to tend or sit in as the mood took him. At the time of Laurie's move there was accommodation for 87 patients, each with their own room. There were frequent visitors, concerts and, eventually, trips outside. There was a gramophone and a wireless where he could finally hear the football results.

Despite the more lenient and relaxed regime, the move to Perth was still a profound shock. Laurie had completed what he termed the 'extreme penal limit' of twenty years and expected to be a free man. His diatribes continued. On 25 February 1911 he wrote the Secretary for Scotland, now the Liberal John Sinclair, complaining of his unexpected move to the Perth Lunatic Department. Sinclair was memorably described by Prime Minister H H Asquith as 'brain of a rabbit, and temper of a pig'; not the best attributes for dealing with Laurie's rigid and seemingly immutable mindset: 'I only wish to state that nothing has happened nor can happen to induce me to say anything that would in the smallest degree reflect on my personal character, and never shall I be so lost to all sense of honour as expose to the vituperation of my traducers anyone who may have befriended me.'

During 1912 Laurie's brother, Gavin, came to see him and presented him with a violin, the instrument he had played as a young man. A journalist who visited Laurie wrote: 'He plays the violin and he plays it well. In his room I saw a violin and case, and no doubt when nights are long John will be one of the star artistes in the common room where there is a piano.' Another newspaper reporter interviewed him in prison around this time:

The criminal department of the Penitentiary is a rather 'free and easy' establishment. Men seem to work or idle as they please, and when I came across Laurie in a quiet part of the garden he was standing near a bing of stones with hammer in hand, and using the hammer was apparently as much of a recreation as a task. He turned round as I approached. Could this be Laurie, the man who had served a life sentence in Peterhead, and who during his incarceration was spoken of as a rather difficult fellow to deal with?

Was this the man who had made several attempts to break the iron bonds of Peterhead, and who had been shot at by pursuing guards? Truth in this instance was strange indeed. If the Prison Commissioners were called upon to rebut a charge that convict life is ruinous to physical health they could not produce more convincing evidence than Laurie, on whom the weight of fifty-one years sits very lightly.

Let me describe him. He is of middle-height and slimly built. His cheeks have the warm glow of health and vigour, and he pierces you with bright blue eyes. His hair, though short, is strong. Here and there silver streaks are strongly marked. Laurie wears a slight, fair moustache, and, neatly dressed in a tweed suit, he looks for all the world a man of forty-one years of age. In conversation he is a pleasant fellow whose speech has the liquid quality of the 'west'.

Laurie, so far at least as my brief acquaintanceship with him revealed, was perfectly normal. He spoke intelligently, quietly, and even kindly, but I learned that his mental weakness displays itself in a hallucination that the warders are putting poison in his food.

As mentioned, a major obstacle to Laurie's release was that, back in 1889, his sentence was commuted on condition that he was 'kept in penal servitude for the term of his natural life' rather than the more flexible, 'reprieved during Her Majesty's pleasure'. At Perth he was technically no longer 'in penal servitude' but had entered an asylum for the criminally insane where your legal status was more equivocal. Inmates charged with murder at Perth Criminal Lunatic Department fell into three categories: insane in bar of trial, found insane when committing offence, and Laurie's category, committed murderers transferred from Peterhead. By 1912 over forty criminal lunatic murder cases in the first two categories were either liberated on licence or transferred to a district asylum. Records also show that between 1907-12 two prisoners in Laurie's category appear to have been conditionally discharged. By December 1912 Laurie's future was once again being assessed. On 2 December Dr John Macpherson, Commissioner in Lunacy, filed a short report: 'He is in good health, clean and tidy in his appearance, inoffensive in his demeanour, a good worker, and free from any obvious faults or vices. He is weak-minded, somewhat vain, and suffers from delusions of poisoning and slight delusions of persecution. He is a suitable case for transference to an asylum.'

Two weeks later the medical adviser for Perth responded that Laurie could be looked after in an ordinary asylum just as well as in a secure one, but the problem was that he was still under sentence and this could well interfere with his transfer: 'I am not prepared to advise his discharge from sentence as I consider it of importance that his future detention in some place of safe custody should be secured.'

The Secretary of the Prison Commissioners, D Crombie, had been studying the legal situation with regard to Laurie's position. He found that the Secretary for Scotland informed the Crown in 1889 that 'convicts certified to be insane cannot be regarded as eligible for such licences and should therefore be detained in prison till expiration of sentence'. Since then this had become the official line and it was consequently unlikely that the Secretary for

Scotland would make an exception in Laurie's case. The other possibility was to grant Laurie remission of the remainder of his sentence but this also appears to have been given short shrift.

The only case Crombie could find with similar circumstances to Laurie was the afore-mentioned Hector Mackenzie who was also certified insane after his offence was committed. Mackenzie was very ill when released from prison, and died of stomach cancer six months later, so there may well have been compassionate grounds in his case. With regard to Laurie Combie felt that, unless there was a change in the policy of the Scottish Office, no remission of sentence nor licence would be granted. He thought that Laurie was likely to remain in the Criminal Lunatic Department for the rest of his days unless his mental health recovered or he was moved to a district asylum at the government's cost.

This intransigent position towards Laurie throws up many questions. Crombie makes the proviso 'unless his mental health recovered', yet there are medical reports throughout his time in prison which conclude that Laurie is sane. Many of his psychological symptoms appear to be a product of prolonged incarceration. At the time of Laurie's reprieve in 1889 there was a great deal of surprise that his sentence was commuted to one of penal servitude for life. Surely, if he was then regarded as of unsound mind, he should have been treated as what was termed a 'lunatic prisoner' and not a convict? Should he not have been sent to Perth Lunatic Department then? Was there some agenda to keep him in prison, perhaps due to his escape attempt, his denigration of the governor or constant pestering of the Prison Commissioners and Scottish Secretary?

Laurie's continued detention after the First World War (for a total of 30 years by 1919) is equally curious. The war and the effects of shell-shock produced radical new ideas and therapies, and a more compassionate view of mental health. This also manifested itself in a more liberal attitude to imprisonment: the broad arrows were removed from clothing, flogging was abandoned, as was the cropping of prisoners' hair; religious services were no longer compulsory. Separation and silence had contributed to high rates of insanity and were abolished in 1922.

Visitors to Perth Prison who encountered Laurie remember a healthy-looking man of pleasant disposition who looked younger than his years, not someone who had recently endured over twenty years of hard labour within a brutal regime. A prison photograph, taken in May 1919, vouches for this. With the growing realisation that he may never be released, Laurie's bitterness and anger gradually subside and he ultimately appears to accept his fate: this is going to be home for the rest of his life.

On 15 April 1915 Laurie wrote to the Reverend Robert Somers, now a minister in Moffat, who had made a statement after the trial with regard to Laurie's sanity. Somers' testimony helped save Laurie from the gallows but ironically now seemed part of the problem preventing his release. To Laurie's habitual rants regarding his food and his unrecognised patriotism, he adds another bone of contention, the medical profession within the penal system. He goes on to say that his experience of doctors during 25 years in the prison system has convinced him that they are as capable of 'as profound a depth of cowardly meanness' as anyone, 'I would a thousand times be dead than be an inmate of a madhouse.'

Laurie's never-ending incarceration was making him something of a celebrity. There was another article featuring him in the *Weekly Record*, 'My Prison Talks with Laurie, by a released prisoner'. It stated how just about everyone in the prison, or who had some connection with it, believed that Laurie would end his days there:

Why this should be so, and why Laurie should be treated as an insane criminal, are mysteries that puzzle his companions in misfortune at Perth. For there is no gainsaying the fact that Laurie is as sane in thought, speech and action as the average man or women who walks the street.

If you chanced to meet Laurie on the street, and were told that he had spent more than three decades in durance vile, you would not believe the statement. It would sound absurd to associate such a fresh-complexioned, healthy-looking man as Laurie with such a terrible fate. No tinge of prison pallor marks his face. His cheeks are red with the glow of health and a life spent largely in the open air. His eyes are bright, and his fine teeth would be the envy of a man half his age. He holds himself erect, walks smartly, and certainly does not look his age.

Without a doubt, he is the neatest man in the prison. He is very particular about his clothes and his cleanliness. John is both clean in speech and in person. And nothing pleases him better than to be furnished by a warder with some wax with which to point the ends of his moustache. The warders like him and it is seldom he runs short of this little luxury.

Laurie owes his splendid health to the circumstance that those confined in the lunatic wards at Perth spend most of their time in the six-acre vegetable and flower garden attached to the prison. He loves flowers and he likes to raise good vegetables.

There was also a programme of regular lectures and concerts. Choir practice was held on Friday evenings. Laurie was still a fine singer and participated in concerts organised with the help of the Perth Prison Aid Society. One of the volunteers was Lucy Meldrum, an attractive young woman in her early twenties who entertained the inmates both as a choir member and solo singer. Laurie was permitted to sing duets with Lucy who described him as a polite, well-spoken man who was good company and always appeared immaculately groomed. It is a real testament to Laurie that after decades of often inhumane treatment, he could appear to have the same positive characteristics he had as a young man. There's more. On the sheet music for one of their duets he wrote a love letter to Lucy which was disguised to look like song lyrics. During a concert he slipped this among her music so she would take it away with her. All the brutality that decades of the prison system could muster had failed to knock the romantic out of John Watson Laurie.

In 14 January 1925 one newspaper began a campaign for Laurie's release, 'The mind reels at the thought of forty years in jail. There have been cases like this in Siberia, though no one would quote Siberia as an example to a civilised nation.' On 1 May 1926 there was the following headline in the *Perthshire Advertiser*, 'Tragic Episode in Perth Prison, Notorious Criminal Becomes Paralysed, Convict who played the Fiddle and Wrote Songs'. That April Laurie suffered a stroke which resulted in the paralysis of his left arm and leg, 'He never regained his usual strength and vigour again, but was able to be in the airing yard every day.' The article about Laurie was accompanied by his official prison photograph. This had been obtained illegitimately by the newspaper and precipitated an internal investigation within the prison to discover and discipline who was responsible.

It was now two years since Laurie had heard from his brother Gavin, whom he had not seen since he gifted him the violin in 1912. He asked the prison authorities for help in contacting him. On 26 August 1929 Laurie made a further request on official prison notepaper. (The first item to be filled in on the form was, 'Lunatic's Name and Registration No.') Laurie went on to write:

Sir, Come the third of next month I will be a prisoner for forty years, and as I was born on the 15th of March 1861 am therefore 68 years old. Through the kindness of the authorities I have been allowed to go down town now and again since 1921. On two occasions this year I have inspected St John's Church, have climbed Kinnoull Hill, and on the 25th of the past month I had a trip to Dunkeld.

We were fortunate in having extremely fine weather on both days and I never enjoyed myself better all my life. It was my first experience riding in a motor omnibus and it was 'altogether splendid'. Then there is the Sandeman Public Library and the Natural History Museum. Both of which I have visited only once. What I would like to do now, if you will kindly grant the reasonable request, is to allow me to go in and out at my own free will, which I have proved by years of good conduct I am perfectly entitled to do. If you will grant me this I promise that I will so conduct myself that not the strictest official could exceed it.

Three days later the Medical Superintendent responded:

Secretary, The inmate named overleaf has always been well-behaved and exemplary in his conduct. The various outings he has had have been much appreciated by him and I should like those to continue as often as possible provided he is accompanied by a warder. He expressed no desire for conditional liberation and as long as he remains an inmate of the Department he cannot possibly be allowed to go about alone. He is expansive and talkative and would soon fall into company and probably discuss the Department and the affairs of other inmates.

Some time ago an article regarding his condition appeared in the local papers, and I have no doubt that this would occur again if he were granted liberty to go about alone.[66]

In March 1930 Laurie suffered a second stroke during the night which resulted in 'transient mental confusion' and a speech impediment. These soon passed but both his sides were now paralysed and he was practically confined to bed, although his appetite remained good. By August he was unable to feed himself and most things had to be done for him. His brother Gavin came to visit along with his nephew James.

Laurie died on 4 October; he was 69 years old.

Even in death you could not throw off your prison identity. The governor, L Mackie, wrote the Scottish Secretary: 'I beg to report that the insane convict named on the margin died at 3.55am today'. He had spent 41 years in prison, the longest anyone in Scotland had been incarcerated for. His nephew James took care of the funeral arrangements. The ashes of John Watson Laurie, 'The Goatfell murderer', were interred on 7 October 1930 in the Western Crematorium Glasgow. Several newspapers picked up on the sad event. The *Glasgow Herald* noted that it 'recalled one of the most remarkable dramas of crime and retribution in the judicial annals of Scotland'

SOURCES

The following is a list of the main sources consulted during the preparation of *The Goatfell Murder*. The most useful were William Roughhead's *Trial of John Watson Laurie* (which he attended as a young lawyer), the archives of the Isle of Arran Heritage Museum, and the following items from the National Records of Scotland: *Precognitions against John Watson Laurie* (AD/14/89/176), *Prisoner's Record* (HH/15/1), *Trial Papers* (JC/26/1889/203).

Books and Articles

Andrews, Jonathan, and Smith, Ian (eds), *Let there be Light Again* (1993).
Baddeley, MJB, *The Highlands of Scotland* (London, 1881).
Bremner, David, *The Industries of Scotland* (Edinburgh, 1869).
Campbell, Robin, N., 'The Arran Murder of 1889', *Scottish Mountaineering Club Journal*, 2001.
Drummond, Peter & Smith, James, *Coatbridge Three Centuries of Change*, (2014).
Goggs, FS, 'Arran', *Scottish Mountaineering Club Journal*, 8 (1904).
House, Jack, *Murder Not Proven* (Glasgow, 1984).
Jeffrey, Robert, *Peterhead* (Edinburgh, 2013).
McCrone, Ian, *Clyde Pleasure Steamers* (1986).
Hugh Macdonald, *Days at the Coast* (Glasgow, 1878).
Macdonald, JHA, *Life Jottings of an Edinburgh Citizen* (1915).
Macdonald, JHA, *A Practical Treatise on the Criminal law of Scotland* (Edinburgh, 1867).
Miller, Thomas, *The Monkland Tradition* (1950).
Milner, G, *Studies of Nature on the Coast of Arran* (London, 1894).
Murray's Handbook to Scotland (London, 1894).
Oliver and Boyd's Scottish Tourist (Edinburgh, 1860).
Paterson, Alan JS, *The Golden Years of the Clyde Steamers (1889-1914)*, (Newton Abbot, 1969).
Peden, Alan, *The Monklands, An Illustrated Architectural Guide* (Edinburgh, 1992).
Ramsay, AC, *The Geology of the Island of Arran from Original Survey* (Glasgow, 1841).
Ritchie, James Ewing, *Christopher Crayon in Scotland*, (London, 1883).
Roughead, William, *Trial of John Watson Laurie* (Edinburgh and

London, 1932), (Notable British Trials series).

William Roughead, *Twelve Scots Trials* (Edinburgh, 1995).

Muirhead, James (Scotch Jimmy), *The Horrors of Convict Life in Peterhead* (1906).

Stevenson, Alexander, *Guide to the Romantic Castle of Tillietudlem* (Hamilton, n.d.).

Williamson, Captain James, *The Clyde Passenger Steamer* (1904).

Peters, Tom, *Salthousehead Remembered* (1998).

Newspapers

Aberdeen Weekly Journal (August 1889).

Airdrie Advertiser (August 1889, August 1917).

Airdrie and Coatbridge Advertiser (August 1889).

Ardrossan and Saltcoats Herald (May 1889, August 1889).

Coatbridge Express (October 1889- December 1889).

Dundee Evening Telegraph (November 1889).

Glasgow Herald (November 1889).

Leicester Chronicle and Leicestershire Mercury (September 1889).

The People's Journal (June 1904, May 1933).

Laurie's Letter to the *North British Daily Mail*, 10th Aug 1889

Dear Editor,

I feel that I should write a long detailed letter to your paper, but I am in no mood to do so.

I rather smile when I read that my arrest is hourly expected. If things go as I have designed them, I will soon have arrived at the country whose bourne no traveller returns, and since there has been so much said about me, it is only right that the public should know what are the real circumstances which has brought me to this.

Three years ago I became very much attached to Miss Annie McLean, teacher, Garnethill Public School, and residing at Rosehall, Coatbridge. My affection for this girl was at first returned, so much so indeed that she very soon became my mistress and continued to be for more than a year until I discovered that she was encouraging the attentions of another man, namely John Cowan junior, teacher Old Cumnock, who took every opportunity to depreciate me in her estimation.

Since then I have been perfectly careless about what I did, and my one thought was how to punish her enough for the cruel wrong she had done me; and it was to watch her audacious behaviour that I went to Rothesay this and last year. I may say that I became acquainted with another young lady, whose good qualities I sincerely wish that I had learned to appreciate sooner, as if I had I would have been in a very different position today.

As regards Mr Rose, poor fellow, no one who knows me will believe for one moment that I had any complicity in his death. The morning I left for Arran I was in the company of two friends on Rothesay pier when Mr Rose came to me and said that he was going to spend a few days with me at Arran.

I was very much surprised at this, as my friends could vouch, for I had not invited him. We went to the top of Goatfell, where I left him in the company of two men who had come from Loch Ranza, and were going to Brodick.

I went down to Corrie and met some friends, and we afterwards visited the hotel, where we met several of the gentlemen who were camping out, and I left for Brodick about ten.

I can easily prove what I say is true, but I decline to bring the names of my friends into this disgraceful affair, so will content myself by wishing them a last adieu.

Yours truly,
John W Laurie.

APPENDIX TWO

Laurie's Letter to the *Glasgow Herald*, 24th August 1889

Sir,

I expected the letter which I so foolishly addressed to the *Mail* would have been my last, but I read so many absurd and mad things in the daily papers that I feel it my duty to correct some of them and the first of these is the assertion that I am kept out of the way by friends. I have not come across a friend since I left Glasgow, nor have I been in communication with anyone. I don't deny the fact that I would like to meet some of my friends again, but I am more careful than allow myself to be lured like the moth to the flame.

Although I am entirely guiltless of the crime I am so much wanted for, yet I can recognise that I am a ruined man in any case, so it is far from my intention to give myself up.

I first went to Glasgow in the spring of 1882, but being among strangers I became homesick, so was glad of the offer held out to me of something to do at Uddingston. Messrs John Gray & Co. were at the time making a winding engine, also several steam cranes, for the underground railway, and during the months of June, July and August I assisted Mr John Swan to make the patterns. I remember Mr Swan as being a very nice gentleman, but I have no recollection of a man the name of Alexander.

I was not at Hamilton eight weeks ago, and I certainly did not smile at Alexander on the way there. If I had travelled on a train where I was known, don't you think it likely I would have left at the first stoppage? The stories about me being seen are all imagination. I have not been seen by anyone who knows me, and I have been travelling all the time in England and Ireland, and as I can see that this is no land for me I shall be off again.

It is true that I did take a room for a week at 10 Greek Street, Liverpool, which I paid in advance. I only stayed three days. I did not board with the lady of the house, and after destroying my papers, I left my box, with no intention of ever calling for it again, as it was an encumbrance to me. The *Mail* takes credit to itself in this case, which does not belong to it at all, for it was a friend of mine who felt it his duty to inform the authorities that Mr Rose left Rothesay with me, and when I saw from an evening paper that Mr Rose had not returned to his lodgings, I began at once to arrange for my departure, for I had told so many about him.

Seemingly there was a motive to do away with poor Rose; it was not to secure his valuables. Mr Rose was to all appearances worse off than myself, indeed he assured me that he had spent so much on his tour, that he had barely sufficient to last till he got home.

He wore an old Geneva watch with no gold albert attached, and I am sure no one saw him wear a ring on his tour, and no one saw me wear one, and well knew that he was speaking a lie when he said he saw me wear a ring in Rothesay. A nice picture this fellow made of me, purely out of ill-will, because I had fooled his precious brother. He says that when he saw me I was wearing a ring and had one of my hands gloved; this is a preposterous falsehood; indeed his whole story from beginning to end is a lie.

I met him one morning in Shamrock Street, not Cambridge Street, and I caught hold of his arm, when he asked a boy to call a policeman. There was no striking on either side, but if there had been, I leave these who know us to judge who would have come off second best.

However these are trivial matters uninteresting to all but those immediately concerned, and as I am not inclined to say any more. I hope this will be the last the public will hear of me.

Yours truly,
John W Laurie.

APPENDIX THREE

List of Witnesses at Trial of John Watson Laurie, 8th November 1889

(Those not called to give evidence named in italic)

Witnesses for the Prosecution

1-3. (1) Mary Currie, wife, (2) Flora Currie, daughter, and (3) *John Currie*, son, all of John Currie, Iona Place, Port Bannatyne, Buteshire.

4. *Margaret Thomson*, wife of Matthew Thomson, Iona Place, aforesaid.

5. Francis Ord Mickel, Frairsbrae Villa, Linlithgow.

6. William Thom, commercial traveller, Linlithgow.

7. Andrew Francis Craig Gilmour, student of medicine, High Street, Linlithgow.

8. Rev. Robert Hind, The Manse, St. James Street, Paisley.

9. Rev. Robert Ritson, Avon Street, Motherwell.

10. John McCabe, Cramlington Cottage, Leechlea, Hamilton.

11. Alexander Morrison, 14 Carfin Street, Govanhill, Glasgow.

12. Thomas Purdon, 38 Marlow Street, Kinning Park, Glasgow.

13. *William Horton Smith*, 2 Granby Terrace, Hilhead, Glasgow.

14. Esther Walker, wife of William Walker, Invercloy, Brodick, Arran.

15. Said *William Walker*.

16. *Flora Shaw*, widow, Invercloy aforesaid.

17. Isabella Wooley, wife of Alexander Wooley, baker, Brodick, Arran.

18. Benjamin James Rose, 89 Sarsfeld Road, Balham Park Road, London, SW.

19. William Munro, police sergeant, Lamlash, Arran.

20. William Munro, police constable, Brodick, Arran.

21. Alexander Stewart, police constable, Kilchattan Bay, Buteshire.

22. Francis Logan, fisherman, Corrie, Arran.

23. David McKenzie, shepherd, South High Corrie, Arran.

24. Alexander Kerr, jun., shepherd, Sannox, Arran.

25-26. (25) *Evelyn Hay Christian Norrie*, and (26) *Henry Augustus Christian Norrie*, Coltbridge Hall, Edinburgh.

27. Archibald Young, fisherman, Corrie, Arran.

28. Angus Logan, quarryman, South High Quarry aforesaid.

29. Duncan Coll, police constable, Shiskine, Arran.

30. John Mackay, chief constable of Buteshire, Rothesay.

31. Ellen King, widow, 106 North Frederick Street, Glasgow.

32. *Finlay Kerr*, police sergeant, Port Bannatyne, Buteshire.

33. James Gordon, police constable, Rosebank, Dalserf Parish, Lanarkshire.

34. Rev. Gustavus James Goodman, The Manse, Walker-on-Tyne, England.

35. *John Borland*, missionary, 6 Antigua Street, Greenock.

36. Neil Fullarton, physician and surgeon, Lamlash, Arran.

37. Andrew Gilmour, physician and surgeon, Linlithgow.

38-39. (38) Frederick William Francis and (39) Edward John Francis, 262 Brockley Road, Brockley, London, SE.

40. James Wilson, 2 Shaw Place, Greenock.

41. *John William Macalister*, 14 Hamilton Drive, Hillhead, near Glasgow.

42. *James Archibald Anderson*, 80 Finnart Street, Greenock.

43. Archibald Kerr Bruce, 23 Kelly Street, Greenock.

44. *John Barr Cumming Newton*, Chesterfield Terrace, Royal Street, Gourock.

45. Margaret Livingstone, barmaid, Corrie Hotel, Corrie, Arran.

46. Mary Robertson, 5 Hill Street, Kilmarnock.

47. Jane McLellan, residing with Ronald Currie, MD, Skelmorlie, Ayrshire.

48. Matthew Eaglesome, letter sorter, 106 North Frederick Street, Glasgow.

49. *John Eaglesome*, 9 Harbour Street, Girvan.

50. James Gillon Aitken, 3 Landsdowne Place, Shawlands, Glasgow.

51-52. (51) *Andrew Gilchrist Allan* and (52) *William Gilchrist Allan*, 15 Melton Terrace, Langside, Glasgow.

53. *Margaret Nicolson*, laundress, 84 Dundas Street, City, Glasgow.

54. John Alexander Porter Napier, 518 Springburn Road, Glasgow.

55. George McMaster, 294 Springburn Road, Glasgow.

56-57. (56) *William Elliott*, sub-inspector, and (57) *John Neil*, criminal officer, Central District, Glasgow Police.

58. Jane Vannan, 3 Commercial Road, South Side, Glasgow.

59. William Johnstone, clerk, 26 Sunnyside Road, Coatbridge.

60. Peter McLean, grocer, 150 Whifflet Street, Coatbridge.

61. *Grace Chalmers*, clerk, Caledonian Buildings, Coatbridge.

62. *James Reid*, station master, Ferniegair Railway Station, Lanarkshire.

63. Michael Crown, miner, Buchanan's Buildings, Greenfield, Hamilton.

64. *Alexander Kirkwood*, miner, Merryton Rows, Lanark Road End, near Hamilton.

65. *David Paton*, Claremont Place, Larkhall, Lanarkshire.

66-68. (66) Mary Rebecca Alice Rose, (67) Louise Rose, and (68) *Frederick Louis Rose*, Wisset Lodge, aforesaid.

69. *Richard McElwain Head*, 1 Oxford Villas, Wandle Road, Upper Tooting, London.

70. Sydney Alfred Newman, 379 Brixton Road, SW, London.

71-72. (71) John Silverman and (72) *John Frederick Chick*, Olive House, High Road, Balham, London, SW.

73-74. (73) James Baldwin and (74) *Reuben George Baldwin*, 2 Spring Terrace, Beechcroft Road, Upper Tooting, London, SW.

75. James Goodman, builder, 1 Mostyn Road, Brixton, London.

76. *Alexander McKillop*, joiner, South Sannox, Arran.

77. Alice Barnes, 96 South Lambeth, Road, London, SW.

78. Elizabeth Ennitt, 10 Greek Street, Liverpool.

79. John Pyper, criminal officer, Western District, Glasgow Police.

80. *James Ferguson*, detective sergeant, City Constabulary, Liverpool.

81. *Annie McLean*, residing with the said Peter McLean.

82. *Henry Dougall*, 78 Grove Street, Cowcaddens, Glasgow.

83. *John Boyd*, chief constable, Glasgow.

84. *William Wharton*, station master, St. Pancras Passenger station, London.

85. Alexander Macdonald, Douglas Hotel, Brodick Arran.

86. Henry Duncan Littlejohn, MD, Royal Circus, Edinburgh.

Witnesses for the Panel (Defence)

1. Ann McEachern, domestic servant to the Rev. Andrew Brown, Kirkintilloch.

2. Peterina McDonald, domestic servant, 3 Rillbank Terrace, Edinburgh.

3. *Robert Strathern*, CE, Wellington Street, Glasgow.

4. *Robert Simpson*, CE, Glasgow.

5. *George Garrett*, Dunbeth House, Coatbridge.

6. Patrick Heron Watson, MD, Edinburgh.

7. C W Macgillivray, MD, 11 Rutland Street, Edinburgh.

8. H A Thomson, MD, 6a Bruntsfield Place, Edinburgh.

9. *Gavin Laurie*, store manager at Gartsherrie.
10. Miss Jeanie Park, residing at Kelburn, Baillieston.
11. Miss Minnie Park, residing at Kelburn, Baillieston
12. Cosimo Latona, guide and residing at Corrie.
13. *All the witnesses in the Crown list of witnesses.*
14. *Duncan Hay*, residing at 14 Norfolk Street., Glasgow.

INDEX

Adela, SS 8

Annandale, John 22, 32–33, 39–42, 45–48, 59–63, 75–79, 104

Arran 3, 6–8, 16, 21–22, 24–25, 30, 32–42, 44–45, 47–49, 51, 53, 58–63, 66–67, 69, 71–80, 82–84, 87–88, 94–96, 99, 102, 104–105, 107, 125–126, 128–129, 140, 191, 195–196, 206, 208, 212–214

Baddeley, M J B 50, 52, 73, 124, 126, 206

Balfour, Lord 101, 104, 107–108, 188–189, 191

Rose, Benjamin 61–62, 70–72

Black's Guide to Scotland 65

Brodick 6, 32–44, 47, 49, 50–57, 59–64, 66–67, 69, 71–74, 78, 80, 83, 101, 103, 107, 109, 122, 124, 128–130, 146, 181, 208, 212, 214

Caledonian Railway 7, 20, 21, 64–65

Cir Mhor 73–75, 105, 126

Clyde, River 7

Coatbridge 8–16, 18, 38–39, 57–59, 66–67, 76–80, 84, 88–90, 92, 94, 98, 104, 112, 114, 119, 127, 131, 133–134, 137, 154, 173, 179, 206–208, 213–214, 216

Coatbridge Express 18, 84, 104, 119, 137, 207

Columba SS 24–25

Corrie 32, 34–35, 42–45, 47, 50–52, 54–56, 68–69, 70–75, 77–78, 80, 94, 105, 108, 122, 124–125, 129–130, 208, 212–213, 215

Dundee Weekly News 154

Evening Citizen 63, 103, 124

Falls of Clyde 65–66

Francis, Frederick 52–54

Gartsherrie Academy 9, 12

Gilmour, Andrew 43–45, 47, 55–56, 68–72, 99, 105, 120, 212–213

Glasgow 6, 8–11, 1–18, 20–22, 24–26, 28, 30–37, 40, 41, 44, 46, 51, 53, 55–56, 58–67, 76–81, 92–94, 96, 98–99, 101–103, 105, 111–112, 11–120, 123, 127, 129–130, 13–133, 136, 138–140, 144, 149, 155–156, 172, 178, 180, 182, 194–195, 205–207, 210, 212, 213–215

Glasgow Citizen 53

Glasgow Evening News 138

Glasgow Fair 21, 25–26, 29–30, 35, 40–41, 46, 55–56, 59

Glasgow Herald 56, 74, 76, 82, 89, 92, 97–98, 102, 111, 119–120, 194, 205, 207, 210

Glasgow Waxworks 118

Glenburn Hotel 28–29, 33, 39–42, 46, 57–59, 61

Glen Rosa 34–36, 4–47, 49, 51–52, 62, 67, 69, 72, 74–75, 103, 105, 124,

RYMOUR BOOKS

poetry · history · debate

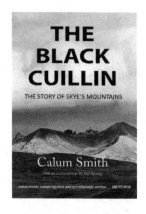

also available from Rymour Books

Calum Smith

THE BLACK CUILLIN

' …exhaustively knowledgeable and scintillatingly written… ' JIM PERRIN

A major work of research and history—not only of climbing but also of social developments and the significant personalities involved in events surrounding Skye and the Highlands over the last two centuries. A must read for anyone with an interest in the history of the island and Scotland. DENNIS GRAY

also available from Rymour Books

Simpson Grears

THE FOOT OF THE WALK MURDERS

EDINBURGH—Scotland's capital city.
HAMISH McDAVITT—ex-archivist and local historian, sometimes known as the 'wee dram detective' for his ability to solve conundrums over a glass of his favourite whisky.
SIXTEEN—original classical detective stories set in the heart of the old city.